BON

ENCYCLOPAEDIA

JOVI

BON JOVI Encyclopaedia
by Neil Daniels

A CHROME DREAMS PUBLICATION
First Edition 2009

Published by Chrome Dreams
PO BOX 230, New Malden, Surrey,
KT3 6YY, UK
books@chromedreams.co.uk
WWW.CHROMEDREAMS.CO.UK

ISBN 9781842404645

Edited by   Richard Ruck
Cover Design   Sylwia Grzeszczuk
Layout Design   Marek Niedziewicz

A catalogue record for this book is available from the British Library.

Printed in the UK by CPI William Clowes Beccles NR34 7TL

BON
ENCYCLOPAEDIA
JOVI

BY NEIL DANIELS

INTRODUCTION

PHASE ONE ('84-'88)

100,000,000 Bon Jovi fans can't be wrong; at least that's what the record sales indicate...

Sure, Bon Jovi may not be the darlings of the music critics but in the author's opinion their first four albums ('84s *Bon Jovi*, '85s *7800° Fahrenheit*, '86s *Slippery When Wet* and '88s *New Jersey*) represent some of the best mainstream American melodic rock of all time. Hands up how many of you sing along to 'Livin' On A Prayer' when it blasts out of the speakers down at your local?

When you divide Jovi's career into four broad phases, skipping over the tours and solo work and just concentrating on the actual studio albums, it becomes apparent that their most creative and, well, exciting period is emphatically 1984-1988.

The band grew better and better with each album until they reached a creative climax with the chart-topping *New Jersey*. Personally, for me their best album is a toss up between *Slippery When Wet* and the aforementioned *New Jersey*. It's well-known that the band hate *7800° Fahrenheit,* but it is not a bad album at all and they have certainly made worse. Admittedly, even for the period, they look daft on the back of the cover, but the record is an underrated gem despite receiving famously scathing reviews in *Kerrang!* and other journals – it certainly deserves reinvestigating if you haven't played it in years.

PHASE TWO ('92-'95)

In 1992 they returned after a brief sabbatical with the U2-inspired *Keep*

The Faith; evidently their focus was less on rock and more on pop, but with "mature" lyrics and a polished production. They also released a decent, if predictable, greatest hits collection called *Cross Road* in '94. But despite glimpses of hope, 1995's *These Days* is an album filled with too many ballads and chart hopefuls.

PHASE THREE ('00-'05)

They took another break in the second half of the 1990s and then returned with the half-decent *Crush* in 2000; but its follow-up, *Bounce,* is a superior album. However, *This Left Feels Right* was pointless and is not much fun to listen to. *Have A Nice Day* (2005) is a much, much better *rock* album and a close return to the glory days of the eighties. Sadly, their "rock rebirth" didn't last long...

PHASE FOUR (2007)

In this period they produced what is surely their worst album: *Lost Highway.* It's a dull mid-paced country-pop effort; and despite the odd sporadic moment of entertainment and a couple of good melodies, it's just boring and uneventful. At best, *Lost Highway* is a failed experiment.

Putting those thoughts into perspective it is easier to lose sight of the fact that they started out as a rock band. Don't forget that Bon Jovi rose to fame during an era in which their contemporaries were bands like Twisted Sister, Dokken, Warrant, Ratt, Mötley Crüe and LA Guns. Jon was never really comfortable with these comparisons, having been inspired by serious artists like Bruce Springsteen, Southside Johnny and U2. When the nineties arrived it was time for a change in

You can't really argue with that kind of success!

What this book attempts to do is give the entire story of Bon Jovi in the form of an encyclopedia, by covering relevant and associated subjects from A through to Z. Certainly a book about Bon Jovi is as much a book about Jon as it is about all the band members, but hopefully you'll still get a good idea of the musical accomplishments of Messrs Richie Sambora, Tico Torres and David Bryan as well as the band's 'non-official' bassist Hugh McDonald and his predecessor, the original Bon Jovi bass player, Alec John Such. Of course, Jon has had a semi-successful film career too and has released a couple of solo albums, as have Richie Sambora and David Bryan; details of all these are also included in the main part of the book.

The purpose of this book is to give the reader and a rounded, factual view of the people Bon Jovi have collaborated with over the years, the music they have made and records they have released, tours and concerts they have played and numerous other associated subjects. There are numerous contributions from various musicians and performers who have worked with Bon Jovi or members thereof, and when you read the mini-biographies, interviews and quotes you should get an idea of what it is like to play with one of the world's biggest-selling acts. Not only that, but there are contributions from many revered rock scribes, songwriters, producers and even fashion designers, just to spice things up.

It is certainly the case that some entries require more detail than others, depending on the importance of the subject to the band's history or how much has been

sound and image, and that's exactly what happened. Jon has changed his image so much over the years that it's become pretty obvious, even from a hack psychologist point of view, that he keeps trying to re-invent himself to keep up with the times. Richie Sambora has pretty much stayed the same, as have the other guys in the band, but *not* Jon. He wants to be taken seriously and dressing up like a rock star is not part of the plan. Why? It works for Lemmy, Steve Tyler and Keith Richards; they dress like rock stars and they're taken seriously. Nevertheless, Jon is one of the world's most recognised entertainers and certainly does his bit for charity so you can't really knock him for that.

That's the music – what about the awards? Bon Jovi are undoubtedly one of the most successful bands in the business and the awards speak for themselves. For starters, just take a look at these facts:

- 19 singles in the American *Billboard*
- Hot 100.

- *New Jersey* spawned
- five *Billboard*
- Hot 100 singles.

- They have sold over 120 million albums worldwide over their career to date.

- They were the first rock band to have a Number 1 hit single in the *Billboard* Hot Country Chart.

- In 2006, they played three sold out gigs at New Jersey's Giants Stadium.

- From October to November 2007, they played 10 consecutive sold out gigs at Newark's Prudential Center. 150,000 fans attended those shows.

published previously on the connection. We all know about Bruce Springsteen and it would be fruitless to spend pages telling his story. But what about Southside Johnny and The Asbury Dukes? What about Bruce Foster from Shark Frenzy? By stringing these stories and entries together we achieve a complete history of Bon Jovi different to any previously published.

It's also interesting as a reader and fan of Bon Jovi to learn about or be reminded of some of the more important and memorable gigs the band has played over the years. Who remembers their first trip to the UK supporting KISS in 1984, the opening night being at the Brighton Centre on September 30? Or their first headlining gig at the Dominion Theatre in London on May 23, 1985? For some, this book will be a trip down memory lane; for others it should fill in a few gaps in your knowledge of the band; newcomers to the Bon Jovi camp will hopefully see it as a nifty learning tool.

Books like this are not meant to be read from cover to cover; instead you can dip in and out of it at your leisure and chose to read the bits that interest you the most. More importantly, encyclopedias of this nature can act as reference tools to check facts, figures, and specific dates relating to the subject. The word 'encyclopedia' is quite rigid so the author has tried to make each entry as friendly and conversational as possible, whilst also providing the necessary information on the themes, subjects and music of BON JOVI.

Keep the faith,

Neil Daniels
October 2008
neildaniels.com

ACKNOWLEDGEMENTS

I'd like to thank the following people for their help with interviews, research, and for their thoughts and opinions...

THE MUSICIANS

Frankie Banali, Steve Blaze, Mick Coll, Roy Davis, Don Dokken, Bruce Foster, Tony Franklin, Sid Glover, Richard Hofherr, Pete Jupp, Holly Knight, Bruce Kulick, Tommy Mandel, Tony Mills, Jason McMaster, Herman Rarebell, Johnny Rocker, Robert Säll, Stuart Smith, Billy Squier, Marc Storace, Kasim Sulton, Mike Tramp, Joe Lynn Turner, Jonathan Valen, Greg Wells, Ron Wikso and Lenny Wolf.

THE PRODUCERS & SONGWRITERS

Andreas Carlsson, Tommy Marolda, Tim Palmer, Kevin Shirley and Michael Wagener.

THE ROCK SCRIBES & PHOTOGRAPHERS

Bailey Brothers, Shari Black, Dante Bonutto, Ron Boudreau, Kieran Dargan, Malcolm Dome, Ross Halfin, Michael Heatley, Dave Ling, Mónica Castedo-López, Joe Matera, Joel McIver, Bruce Mee, Derek Oliver, Jason Ritchie, John Tucker, Mark Weiss and Jeb Wright.

THE PR PEOPLE & MANAGERS

Mick Brown, Sharon Chevin, Kas Mercer, Lisa Walker and Marko Wolf.

EVERYBODY ELSE

Rock fashion designer Ray Brown. Derek Shulman of DRT Entertainment, Bon Jovi fan Julia Braun, Rob Johnstone at Chrome Dreams, my partner, Emma, and my family and friends. Apologies if I have missed any names.

ABOUT THE AUTHOR

BOOKS BY NEIL DANIELS

Neil Daniels has written about classic rock and heavy metal for a wide range of magazines and fanzines. He currently writes for *Fireworks, Powerplay* and *Get Ready To Rock.com*, and occasionally contributes to *Rock Sound* and *Record Collector.* His reviews and articles have also appeared in *The Guardian, Big Cheese, Drowned In Sound.com, Carling.com, Unbarred.co.uk* and *Planet Sound* on *CH4 Teletext.* Neil has contributed articles and reviews on cinema to the academic publication *MediaMagazine* and the popular arts ezine *musicOMH.* More information is obtainable at *neildaniels. com.* His favourite Bon Jovi album is *Slippery When Wet.*

Defenders Of The Faith: The Story Of Judas Priest (Omnibus Press, 2007)

Robert Plant: Led Zeppelin, Jimmy Page & The Solo Years (Independent Music Press, 2008)

Dawn Of The Metal Gods: My Life In Judas Priest & Heavy Metal With Al Atkins (Iron Pages, 2008)

SOURCES

The following publications and websites have been invaluable in terms of research and for confirming various facts, dates and details.

MUSIC BOOKS
Friend, Lonn
Life On Planet Rock
(Portrait, 2006)
Jackson, Laura
**Jon Bon Jovi:
The Biography**
(Portrait, 2003)
Wall, Mick
**Star Trippin': The Best
Of Mick Wall 1985-91**
(M&G, 2006)

REFERENCE BOOKS
Betts, Graham
**Complete UK Hit Singles
1952-2005**
(Collins, 2005)
Roberts, David (Managing Editor)
**Guinness World Records:
British Hit Singles & Albums
19th Edition**
(Guinness, 2006)

MUSIC MAGAZINES
**Classic Rock
Fireworks
Hard Roxx
Kerrang!
Metal Attack
Metal Edge
Metal Forces
Metal Hammer
Powerplay
RAW**

WEBSITES
amazon.co.uk
billboard.com
bostonmagazine.com
getreadytorock.com
manchestereveningnews.co.uk
perezhilton.com
prucenter.com
sleazeroxx.com
sunmedia.ca
time.com
timesonline.co.uk
wikipedia.com

BON JOVI RELATED
WEBSITES
bonjovi.com
backstagejbj.com
Tico-Torres.com
hueymcdonald.com
davidbryan.com

A&M STUDIOS

While staying at a rented mansion in the glamorous Hollywood Hills (which he dubbed 'Disgracedland') Jon Bon Jovi recorded his first solo album *Blaze Of Glory* (with co-producer Danny Kortchmar) at A&M Studios in Los Angeles during the Spring of 1990. At that time the A&M Studios was owned by PolyGram, but when the label was sold to Universal in 1998 the studio was disposed of, and is now owned by Jim Henson Productions.

AARON, LEE

Canadian singer Lee Aaron supported Bon Jovi on their debut UK headlining tour in 1985, playing sold out shows in Manchester, Birmingham, London, Newcastle and Edinburgh. The band were on the road to promote their first two albums and had picked up a considerable fan base in Britain.

Now a jazz singer, her 1980s output includes hit singles 'Whatcha Do To My Body' and 'Sex With Love' and albums *Metal Queen* and *Bodyrock,* which attest to her musical foundations in Canadian metal and glam rock.

Visit *leeaaron.com*

Lee Aaron

ACADEMY AWARDS

Also known as The Oscars, the Academy Awards is the highest profile annual awards event. The Academy Of Motion Picture Arts And Sciences honours those who work in the film industry with the highest form of media recognition and the famous gold statuette.

In 1991, Jon Bon Jovi's song 'Blaze Of Glory' (from *Young Guns II*) was nominated in the category of 'Best Music: Original Song.'

ACCESS ALL AREAS: A ROCK & ROLL ODYSSEY

Running for 90 minutes and re-leased in 1990, *Access All Areas* is an entertaining behind the scenes documentary following Bon Jovi on their lengthy *New Jersey Syndicate* tour from 1988 to 1990. The documentary was released as a standard VHS but was also included as part of the double VHS version of *New Jersey: The Videos.*

ACER ARENA

A concert venue in Sydney, Australia. Bon Jovi played here on January 21, 2008 and tickets for the show sold out within record time.

They were on the road to promote their greatest hits package and the *Lost Highway* opus.

ADVENTURES OF FORD FAIRLANE, THE

A 1990 comedy directed by Renny Harlin and starring Andrew Dice Clay and Wayne Newton. Richie Sambora contributed his version of Jimi Hendrix's 'The Wind Cries Mary' to the soundtrack. The song was also a B-side to his solo single 'Ballad Of Youth.'

AIR CANADA CENTRE

Bon Jovi are the only band to have played five sold out concerts at Toronto's Air Canada Centre, breaking their own record of three nights. Daughtry supported for all the shows, which were performed on:

December 6, 2007
December 7, 2007
March 10, 2008
March 12, 2008
March 13, 2008

ALL ABOUT LOVIN' YOU

The third single release from the 2002 album *Bounce*. It was issued in the UK on May 24, 2003 and peaked at Number 9 and spent six weeks in the singles chart.

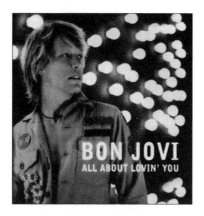

Track Listing:
(CD)
1. 'All About Lovin' You'
2. 'All About Lovin' You' *(Acoustic)*
3. 'Postcards From The Wasteland' *(Demo)*
4. 'All About Lovin' You' *(CD-ROM video)*
(DVD)
1. 'All About Lovin' You' *(Music video)*
2. 'Alive' *(Demo)*
3. 'Everyday' *(Demo)*
4. 'All About Lovin' You' *(Making of the video)*

ALL-AMERICAN REJECTS, THE

Hailing from Oklahoma, The All-American Rejects are: Tyson Ritter (vocals, bass guitar and piano,) Nick Wheeler (guitar, vocals and keyboards,) Mike Kennerty (guitar and vocals) and Chris Gaylor (drums and percussion.) They formed in 2001 and achieved major success with their second album *Move Along*, released in 2005.

Tyson and Nick guested for a version of 'It's My Life' during Bon Jovi's *MTV Unplugged* performance on June 22, 2007. The All-American Rejects supported Bon Jovi on November 9 and 10, 2007 at The Prudential Center in Newark, New Jersey.

Nick Wheeler told the Prudential Center website (*prucenter.com:*)

"It will be an honour to share the stage with a band that is responsible for me doing what I do for a living. And in their home state, too!"

They supported Bon Jovi again for the American leg of their 2008 *Lost Highway* tour. Those dates were:

July 7 – Palace of Auburn Hills, Michigan
July 9 – TD Banknorth Garden,

Boston
July 10 – TD Banknorth Garden, Boston
July 14 – Madison Square Garden, New York City
July 15 – Madison Square Gardens, New York City

Visit *allamericanrejects.com*

ALL-STAR CONCERT IN CENTRAL PARK

On Saturday, July 12, 2008, Bon Jovi played a free concert on the Great

Lawn in New York's Central Park, dubbed 'All-Star Concert In Central Park.' Over 60,000 fans attended.

The concert was in association with Major League Baseball and was introduced by New York Mayor Michael Bloomberg; guests included senior figures from Major League Basketball and Bank of America. Quoted on *billboard.com*, Jon said: *"I've travelled the world again, and New York is still the greatest city in the world...This will be our major stadium production"*

ALL STAR REVIEW, THE

The name of the session band that worked with Jon Bon Jovi on the recording of his four track demo 'Runaway,' which was produced by Billy Squier at Power Station Studios in June, 1982. The band was drummer Frankie La Roca, guitarist Tim Pierce, bassist Hugh McDonald and E Street Band pianist Roy Bittan. They were integral in helping Jon make the demo that kick started his career and got him a deal with PolyGram in 1983.

ALLY MCBEAL

A successful American TV show that ran from 1997 to 2002. The series centred on a young lawyer named Ally McBeal (played by Calista Flockhart) who worked at a Boston law firm alongside some ec-

centric fellow lawyers. The show was created by David E. Kelley.

Throughout 2002, Jon Bon Jovi starred as the character Victor Morrison in a total of 10 episodes during the final series of the show. His scenes were filmed in Los Angeles.

The episodes in which he appeared were:

1. 'Blowin' In The Wind'
2. 'One Hundred Tears'
3. 'A Kick In The Head'
4. 'The New Day'
5. 'Woman'
6. 'Homecoming' *(He performed 'Some Enchanted Evening' in this episode)*
7. 'Heart And Soul'
8. 'Love Is All Around: Part 1'
9. 'Love Is All Around: Part 2'
10. 'Another One Bites The Dust'

ALWAYS

Written by Jon Bon Jovi and taken from the 1994 collection *Cross Road: The Best Of Bon Jovi*, 'Always' is a popular power ballad that was recorded at Emerald Studios in Nashville with producer Peter Collins on July 5, '94. It was recorded by Kevin Shirley and mixed by Bob Clearmountain.

'Always' was actually a re-recording of their own song which was originally intended to feature on the soundtrack to the '93 film *Romeo Is Bleeding*; but the band allegedly disliked the film and chose not to become involved.

'Always' was issued as a single in the UK on September 24, 1994 and hit Number 2 in the Top 40, spending 18 weeks in the charts. It did equally well in the States and reached at Number 4. It became the band's biggest selling single, shifting 1.5 million in the States and 4 million globally.

(UK) Track Listing:
1. 'Always' *(Edit)*
2. 'Always'
3. 'Edge Of A Broken Heart'
4. 'Prayer 94'

AMATO, DAVE

An American singer and guitarist who has worked with Black Oak Arkansas, David Lee Roth, Rick Springfield, Ted Nugent and Mötley Crüe as well as several others. He joined Richie Sambora's solo band for a short tour of the US in support of *Stranger In This Town*.

Visit *daveamato.com*

AMERICA: A TRIBUTE TO HEROES

Jon and Richie Sambora took part in this universally televised event on September 21, 2001. The concert, a fundraiser for the victims of 9/11, raised over $150 million for the United Way Relief Fund. They performed an acoustic version of 'Livin' On A Prayer.' Other musicians to take part included U2, Sting, Billy Joel, Paul Simon and Neil Young.

AMERICA THE BEAUTIFUL

A TV special in memory of the victims and their families of the 9/11 terrorist attacks on the United States. Aired on September 23, 2001, Bon Jovi was amongst the performers.

The show took its name from the famous patriotic song. Jon Bon Jovi and Richie Sambora re-recorded a version of the song in October '01 as an exclusive Mp3 download file on

their official website *bonjovi.com*. Jon introduced the track himself:

"Hi, this is Jon Bon Jovi. In light of the tragic events of September 11, we've all tried to do something, anything, to help the recovery efforts that have affected so many families here in our area. We gave blood, made sandwiches, donated clothes and money, and we sang. We sang for our country, to our country, as our way of saying we're one, united. I recorded this with the help of some friends and I hope that you'll enjoy it. Download it, keep it, save it, play it, be proud of it, and I'll ask you to do so with your hearts as well as your wallet because I'm asking you to download it and send a donation, anything you can. Just send it to libertyunites.org. *Thank you."*

AMERICAN DREAMS

An American TV series that ran from 2002 until 2005. The series was set in Philadelphia in the sixties and early seventies, and follows one family through the massive cul-

tural changes that occurred at that time. Richie Sambora starred in one episode ('The Long Goodbye') as his guitar hero Eric Clapton (during his time in The Yardbirds) singing 'For Your Love.'

AMERICAN IDOL

A television reality show, in which members of the public audition in the hope of becoming an *American Pop Idol*. The original UK version of the show, *Pop Idol*, was created by pop music mogul Simon Fuller, and Simon Cowell is a judge on both versions.

On May 1, 2007, during the promotional run for *Lost Highway*, Bon Jovi took part in an hour-long episode of *American Idol*, in which each contestant sang a Bon Jovi song after some mentoring from Jon.

The contestants:

Phil Stacey – 'Blaze Of Glory'
LaKisha Jones – 'This Ain't
A Love Song'

Blake Lewis – 'You've Give Love
A Bad Name'
Chris Richardson – 'Wanted Dead
Or Alive'
Jordin Sparks – 'Livin' On
A Prayer'
Melinda Doolittle – 'Have
A Nice Day'

AMERICAN MUSIC AWARDS

An awards ceremony that recognises the best in American popular
music, although non-American artists (such as Eric Clapton) have won
awards. It has been held annually
since 1973 when it was organised by
Dick Clark.

In 1987, Bon Jovi won the award
for 'Favorite Pop/Rock Band, Duo
Or Group' and in 2004 they won the
prestigious 'Award Of Merit' and
performed 'Have A Nice Day' at the
glitzy ceremony. As a solo artist Jon
Bon Jovi won the 'Favorite Pop/Rock
Single' award for his song 'Blaze Of
Glory.'

AMERICAN SOCIETY OF COMPOSERS, AUTHORS AND PUBLISHERS (ASCAP)

An American organisation that pro-
tects its members against such crimes
as copyright infringements and
royalty fraud. A non-profit making

company, it holds an annual awards
ceremony. In 1991, Jon Bon Jovi
won an ASCAP Award for the song
'Blaze Of Glory' in the category of
'Most Performed Songs From Motion
Pictures.'

ANCOL STADIUM

Ancol Stadium is situated in
Jakarta, the capitol of Indonesia.
On May 6, 1995, in an echo of Led
Zeppelin's July 5th. 1971 Milan concert, a riot broke out when hundreds
of police officers tried to prevent
frustrated, ticketless Bon Jovi fans
from breaking into the stadium; such
scenes are not common at Bon Jovi
gigs but this was an exception.

ANIMALS, THE

A Sixties pop group that was part
of the hyped-up British Invasion of
America, along with The Beatles,
The Stones, The Who, The Kinks
et al. Their most famous song is a
cover of the traditional 'House Of
The Rising Sun.' As a teenage music fan in the seventies, Jon Bon Jovi
first learned this song when he began
taking guitar lessons. Bon Jovi can be
seen singing two Animals songs ('We
Gotta Get Out Of This Place' and 'It's
My Life') on the deleted 1993 VHS
release *Keep The Faith: An Evening
With Bon Jovi.*

Visit *members.aol.com/ TheAnimalsSite*

AOR

AOR is an abbreviation of the term *album-oriented rock*. AOR is a commercial style of rock music that is produced for the radio and mass consumption and was especially popular during the eighties. These days AOR is less popular but still retains a dedicated fan base around the world. Famous AOR bands include Journey, Toto, Boston and Heart. AOR was especially prevalent on the West Coast of America. These days it's rarely claimed that Bon Jovi have ever been an AOR band, nevertheless, their music during the eighties was certainly developed with an eye for American FM radio and thus mainstream/commercial success.

Robert Säll of the Swedish AOR band Work Of Art says,

"I remember when Slippery When Wet *came out. I was in fourth grade and was a KISS fan. Back then, you were either a KISS or a Bon Jovi fan so I tried my very best NOT to like* Slippery When Wet. *However, it didn't take long before I had to surrender because this record is simply brilliant. It also marked the beginning of a life long love affair with AOR music. Also, I learned that you actually can love BOTH bands..."*

APPLEBY, SHIRI

An American TV actress who had a significant role in the cancelled sc-fi TV series *Roswell*. Appleby has also appeared in *Thirtysomething*, *Knots Landing*, *ER*, *Baywatch* and *Xena: Warrior Princess*.

She appeared in the Bon Jovi music video 'It's My Life.'

ARENA ROCK

In the eighties Bon Jovi were undoubtedly kings of arena rock. Since then, of course, they have progressed to stadium rock. Arena rock is anthemic rock music that is written and performed by melodic rock bands. It was especially successful in the 1980s when traits of the genre in-

Robert Säll

cluded huge stage productions with lasers, dry ice, smoke machines, video screens and stage pyrotechnics as well as a big drum riser and massive amps. Since stringent health and safety procedures came into force many of these visual spectaculars have been toned down. Fans would often hold up their cigarette lighters during a power ballad, but these days mobile phones have replaced the lighter. Fellow arena rock bands of the eighties include Aerosmith, Mötley Crüe and AC/DC.

ARMAGEDDON

Directed by Michael Bay and released in 1998, *Armageddon* is a big-budget science-fiction film about an asteroid that is on a collision course with Earth. The film stars Bruce Willis, Billy Bob Thornton, Liv Tyler and Ben Affleck. The soundtrack features a host of big names, including Aerosmith, Journey and ZZ Top. Bon Jovi contributed the song 'Mister Big Time,' which was mixed by the revered Kevin Shirley at Avatar Studios in New York City.

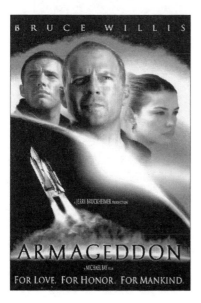

ASBURY JUKES, THE

Backing band for the New Jersey singer-songwriter Southside Johnny. When Jon was a teenager he dreamt of being in The Asbury Jukes; they were local heroes and a fine example of some home-grown success. The line-up of the band has changed many times over the years. Some of the musicians have ended up in The Max Weinberg 7, a backing band on the US TV talk show *Late Night with Conan O' Brien*. Jon's previous band The Wild Ones supported Southside Johnny and The Asbury Jukes in the early eighties.

Visit *southsidejohnny.com*

ASBURY PARK

A city on the Jersey Shore that has provided inspiration to many New Jersey singer-songwriters such as Bon Jovi and Bruce Springsteen. Jon and other members of the band would spend summers at the coastal resort, although during the seventies it was run down and outdated. Since 2002, Asbury Park has had a major facelift and as such there has been a revival of interest and tourist figures have shot up.

ASTORIA THEATRE

A dark and dingy but likeable concert venue in central London; its exact

address is 157 Charing Cross Road. Despite having a capacity of just 2,000 people some big name bands have played there in the past decade, including The Rolling Stones, Pearl Jam, Oasis, a reunited Black Sabbath and U2. It has a smaller sister venue next door called the Astoria 2 (previously known as The Mean Fiddler.) In 2008, it was announced that The Astoria would be knocked down to make way for transport development in the area.

A band like Bon Jovi, who have been a stadium act for around 20 years, wouldn't normally play at such a small venue but on November 4, 1992 they performed a "secret" gig there to promote *Keep The Faith*.

Black Velvet editor and Bon Jovi fan Shari Black was in attendance. She remembers:

"I'd heard the band were going to be doing a 'secret show' and decided to take the day off work and go down to London on the off-chance. Jon and Richie were doing an interview in the morning at Radio One – and announced that the show would be at the Astoria live on air. The only way you could get tickets was by going to the Astoria in person. I rushed there and got a ticket – and then decided I might as well stay there and queue

up for the show. I was first in line and ended up being front row for the show. I remember that Jon stage dived twice, which is something he doesn't usually do – but because the venue was so tiny and packed, he amazed us all and dived into the crowd, not once but twice."

ATLANTIC CITY EXPRESSWAY

Jon Bon Jovi put this 10 piece R&B covers outfit together in the late seventies. One member was a certain David Bryan Rashbaum who was more than efficient on the piano and keys. They were moderately successful in the NJ area, playing to a couple of hundred people in bars and clubs such as The Stone Pony and Fastlane. With 10 members in the outfit, it was hard trying to make a living, although they picked up some fans in local heroes Southside Johnny and a certain singer/songwriter by the name of Bruce Springsteen, who saw first the band perform at the famous Fastlane club. Allegedly Springsteen

joined them onstage on several occasions, churning out old R&B numbers and even some of his own songs. Jon stayed with the band for about a year before he moved to NYC and worked at Power Station Studios, and formed The Wild Ones with guitarist Dave Sabo.

ATLANTIC RECORDS

Formed in 1947 by Ahmet Ertegün and Herb Abramson, Atlantic is one of America's most revered record labels, having signed such esteemed artists as Led Zeppelin, Ray Charles, Crosby, Stills and Nash and Cream, amongst many others.

Atlantic was one of two major record labels that were eager to sign Jon after hearing 'Runaway.' Ultimately, he went for PolyGram after forming a rapport with Derek Shulman, one of the company's senior executives.

Atlantic's parent company is the Warner Music Group.

AUGUST 7, 4:15

The penultimate track on Jon's 1997 solo opus *Destination Anywhere*. It was written as a personal tribute to Katherine Korzilius, who was tragically murdered on August 7, 1996. Katherine was the six year old daughter of Paul Korzilius, a senior figure at Bon Jovi Management.

AUSTRALIAN RECORDING INDUSTRY ASSOCIATION (ARIA)

AUSTRALIAN RECORDING INDUSTRY ASSOCIATION

An organisation which compiles the music charts in Australia. Bon Jovi have broken many records and in 2008, after playing a few shows down under, no less than eight of the band's albums re-entered the Australian Top 100 Albums Chart.

From the lowest selling to the highest: *7800° Fahrenheit* peaked at Number 66 (it never charted when it was first released in 1985); *Bon Jovi* re-entered at Number 59; *These Days* re-entered at Number 58; *Cross Roads* re-entered at Number 57; *New Jersey* re-entered at Number 41; *Keep The Faith* re-entered at Number 39; *Slippery When Wet* re-entered at Number 5 and *Lost Highway* peaked at Number 2 after hitting the Number 5 spot upon its first week of release.

BACKSTAGE WITH JON BON JOVI

The official Jon Bon Jovi fan club website; fans can use the website to join the club and get regular updates on the happenings in JBJ's music. Areas of the website include 'News', 'Board/Chat', 'Merchandise', 'Photos', 'Videos' and 'Tickets.'

Visit *backstagejbj.com*

BALLAD OF YOUTH

A single released from Richie Sambora's first solo album *Stranger In This Town*. It was issued in the UK on September 7, 1991 and only made it to Number 59; while in the States it peaked at a disappointing Number 63 on the *Billboard* Hot 100. The single included a cover of Jimi Hendrix's 'The Wind Cries Mary' as a B-side. 'Ballad Of Youth' was written with Tommy Marolda when Sambora was

BAD MEDICINE

Written by Jon, Richie Sambora and Desmond Child, 'Bad Medicine' was the first single released from the mega-selling *New Jersey* album. It was issued in the UK on September 24, 1988 and hit Number 17 in the charts, but in the States it went to Number 1 on the *Billboard* Hot 100. The song has two music videos: a conventional live video (directed by Wayne Isham) and one featuring the American comedian Sam Kininson and a group of fans with handheld cameras who film the band onstage. The song is one of Bon Jovi's best known numbers, joining the likes of 'Livin' On A Prayer' and 'You Give Love A Bad Name.'

just a teenager. A melodic mid-tempo soft rock song, Sambora sings it with a lot of soul and there are some memorable keys by David Bryan.

BANDIERA, BOBBY

From New Jersey, Bobby Bandiera is a rock guitarist noted for playing with Bruce Springsteen and Southside

Bobby Bandiera with Richie Sambora

Johnny and The Asbury Dukes. He played in Jon Bon Jovi's solo band The Big Dogs in 1997 in support of *Destination Anywhere*. Since 2005 he has played rhythm guitar with Bon Jovi during their live shows and has occasionally filled in for Richie Sambora on lead, most notably during Sambora's stint in rehab.

Visit *bobbandiera.com*

BANGER SISTERS, THE

A 2002 film about ex-rock groupies who get together after 20 years. Suffice to say, their lives have changed considerably. Richie Sambora contributed the song 'One Last Goodbye' to the soundtrack.

BANKATLANTIC CENTER

On April 28, 2008 Bon Jovi had to delay a concert at the BankAtlantic Center in Sunrise, Florida by three hours, because of a bomb scare. It was reported that the police received a call warning that two bombs would go off during the band's gig. Consequently, the venue was cleared of all persons until the police and bomb experts determined that it was safe to proceed with the gig. After the all-clear had been given, the audience were allowed back in to the venue at approximately 9pm. It was certainly a night to remember, if for the wrong reasons…

Crowd outside BankAtlantic Center

BAZILIAN, ERIC

Founding member of the Philadelphia rock band The Hooters and a noted singer-songwriter and musician in his own right. The Hooters formed in 1980, and in 1995 took a long break until their reformation in 2001. In 2007 they released *Time Stand Still*, their first collection of fresh material since '93. Bazilian has also released solo albums: 2000's *The Optimist* and 2002's *A Very Dull Boy*. As a songwriter he has worked with a variety of artists, including Robbie Williams, Scorpions, Ricky Martin, Journey and Cyndi Lauper.

He co-wrote, co-produced and played electric guitar on the track 'Ugly' on Jon's solo album *Destination Anywhere*. On the same album he also played electric guitar on 'It's Just Me.'

With Bon Jovi he also co-wrote 'I Get A Rush' and 'One Man Band', both of which feature in the extensive box-set *100,000,000 Bon Jovi Fans Can't Be Wrong*.

Visit *ericbazilian.com*

BECK, JEFF

Jeff Beck is one of Britain's most revered guitarists. In the sixties he was one of three world-class guitarists to have played in The Yardbirds, the others being Eric Clapton and Jimmy Page. Famously media shy, his career has spanned five decades and he has dabbled in rock, R&B, heavy metal, jazz, blues, instrumental music and even electronica. His band, The Jeff Beck Group, produced just two albums, both of them classics: 1968's *Truth* and 1969's *Beck-ola*. His first solo album, Blow *By Blow,* was released in 1974 and was a Top 10 hit in the States. He has also contributed to a variety of albums by other artists such as Brian May, Stevie Wonder, Tina Turner and Paul Rodgers.

Not only is Beck one of Richie Sambora's idols but Jon is also a fan. Beck contributed to a few songs on Jon's first solo album *Blaze Of Glory*:

'Billy Get Your Guns' – *guitar solo*
'Miracle' – *guitar solo*
'Blaze Of Glory' – *guitar solo*
'Justice In The Barrel' – *guitar solo*
'Never Say Die' – *guitar solo*
'Bang A Drum' – *guitar solo*
'Dyin' Ain't Much Of A Livin''
– *guitars*

Visit *jeffbeck.com*

BED OF ROSES

The second single released from *Keep The Faith*. It was written solely by Jon and released in the UK on January 23, 1993, reaching Number 13 in the Top 40. It managed to climb three places higher on the American *Billboard* Hot 100. The promotional video includes live footage of the band filmed at Stabler Arena in Pennsylvania on December 31, 1992.

(International) Track Listing:
1. 'Bed Of Roses'
2. 'Lay Your Hands On Me' *(Live)*
3. 'Tokyo Road' *(Live)*
4. 'I'll Be There For You' *(Live)*

BEHIND THE MUSIC

A successful and long-running series of documentaries that does exactly as its name suggests. The VH1 show began in 1997 and finished in 2006. Bon Jovi have been the subject of an episode of *Behind The Music,* as have KISS, Aerosmith, Queen, Ozzy Osbourne and Judas Priest and many other artists. Alongside interviews with the featured artists, the show often includes contributions from friends and family, journalists and music business personnel. An obvious criticism to be made is that despite the nature of the documentaries, it is often the case that within less than an hour's running time there is just not enough depth to satisfy knowledgeable music fans. At best, they are entertaining and only occasionally informative.

BIFFY CLYRO

A Scottish alternative rock trio comprised of Simon Neil (lead vocals, guitar), James Johnston (vocals, bass guitar) and Ben Johnston (vocals, drums.) Formed in 1995 they had, by

2007, only released four studios albums, one EP, entitled *thekidswhopop todaywillrocktomorrow* and a collection called *Singles 2001-2005*.

On June 27, 2008, along with a band called Stewart Mac, they supported Bon Jovi at London's Twickenham Stadium on the penultimate night of their UK stadium tour.

Visit *biffyclyro.com*

BIG & RICH

Big Kenny and John Rich are an American country duo. Formed in 1998, their latest album to date, 2007's *Between Raising Hell And Amazing Grace, was* a Number 1 country album in the States.

The duo performed with Bon Jovi on the track 'We Got It Going On' (written by Richie Sambora, Jon Bon Jovi and Big & Rich) which features on the 2007 album *Lost Highway.*

They supported Bon Jovi for two nights (October 28 and 30) in 2007 at the Prudential Center in New Jersey. As quoted on the Prudential Center website (*prucenter.com,*) John Rich said:

"The fact that one of the most popular rock bands of all times has asked us to help open a couple dates of their monstrous 10 day run at the Prudential Center is quite the honour. Kenny and I are going to make sure we give these fans a night they will never forget."

Visit *bigandrich.com*

BILLBOARD HOT 100 SINGLES

The famous American singles chart survey, which has been in circulation in published form since 1958. There are numerous sub-categories such as Mainstream Rock Tracks and Modern Rock Tracks. *Slippery When Wet* had two Number 1 singles in the *Billboard* Hot 100: 'You Give Love A Bad Name' and 'Livin' On A Prayer.' As of 2008, Bon Jovi has had 19 *Billboard* Hot 100 singles.

BILLBOARD 200

Published weekly by *Billboard* magazine, this survey is a list of the best-selling 200 albums in the United States. Previously known as the Top Pop Albums, the survey has been called *Billboard* 200 since 1983. *Slippery When Wet* stayed at the Number 1 position in the *Billboard* 200 for a total of eight weeks after its release in August, 1986. Every Bon Jovi studio album has made it into the *Billboard* 200; the lowest chart positions being the first two albums (*Bon Jovi* and *7800° Fahrenheit*) at Numbers 43 and 37, respectively. *New Jersey* and *Lost Highway* also topped the *Billboard* 200. The compilations and live albums all achieved respectable positions: 1994's *Cross Road* (Number 8), 2001's *One Wild Night Live 1985-2001* (Number 20), 2003's *This Left Feels Right* (Number 14), and even the mammoth 2004 box-set *100,000,000 Bon Jovi Fans Can't Be Wrong* charted at Number 53.

BITTAN, ROY

Otherwise known as The Professor, Roy Bittan is the long time keyboard player in Bruce Springsteen's famous backing group The E Street Band. Bittan also contributed to *Bat Out Of Hell* and subsequent albums by Meat Loaf and Jim Steinman. His curriculum vitae also includes Dire Straits, Bob Seger, Stevie Nicks and Peter Gabriel.

Bittan played the keyboards on Jon's 'Runaway' demo, produced by Billy Squier, in June 1982 which was recorded at New York's Power Station Studios. The demo was instrumental in getting Jon the record deal with PolyGram the following year.

BLACK VELVET

A British independent rock fanzine run by Bon Jovi fan Shari Black, which has featured the band on several occasions.

Black says:

"When you've seen over 220 Bon Jovi shows like I have, all over the UK, USA, Japan and Europe, it's hard to pick just one favourite [show.] I've been going to Bon Jovi shows since they headlined the Monsters Of Rock festival at Castle Donnington in 1987. Their live show blew me away so much at that very first show that I knew I had to see them again and again...and again! Every show, it has to be said, is top quality. The band know how to hold the audiences attention and affect the fans right at the front to the fans in the very last row at the back. The mixture of well known hits with a number of album tracks and then maybe a cover or two for good measure, wrapped up in a set that lasts at least two hours, if not longer, is superbly satisfying for everyone. The band definitely gives the fans their money's worth. Moments such as Jon singing from the back or side of the venue on a small platform within the crowd to having a walkway running through the audience are highlights of the band's actual stage show.

I guess if I had to pick some shows that stood out; most of them would probably be the more intimate shows, where you just felt very privileged to be there, knowing that most folk weren't so lucky...small shows that stand out include a small club show at a venue called Tradewinds in Sea Bright, NJ in April 2000. I was actually on holiday in New York with a friend at the time and then the band announced this small show. It was the night before our flight home, so after the show I had to get a $100 cab back to New York, had about three hours to pack my case and get ready and then flew back to the UK! The venue was tiny and I was very lucky getting a ticket and actually being over there in the first place. Seeing the band's Christmas shows at the Count Basie Theatre in Red Bank, NJ in the early nineties was also a great time for me – especially since my birthday is just before Christmas. They would be like my birthday and Christmas treat combined. One year, I think the show was actually on my birthday and Jon said 'Happy Birthday Shari' during the concert. The Count Basie shows were also great because the band gave proceeds to local charities, so as well as getting to see your fave band you knew you were helping people less fortunate."

Visit *blackvelvetmagazine.com*

BLAZE OF GLORY (ALBUM)

Jon Bon Jovi's debut solo album. Jon was initially approached by John Fusco, a successful Hollywood screenwriter, who wanted to use 'Wanted Dead Or Alive' as the main theme for *Young Guns II,* a western. Jon gave it some thought, but felt that the lyrics weren't entirely suitable for a movie like *Young Guns II,* so he penned a new track entitled 'Blaze Of Glory' and made a trip down to Santa Fe, New Mexico where the film was being shot. Intrigued by the glamour of the movie world, Jon asked the movie producers if he could compose the entire soundtrack. A deal was done.

Produced by Jon and Danny Kortchmar, *Blaze Of Glory* was recorded at A&M Studios in Los Angeles in early 1990. To his credit, Jon brought in the talents of a few music legends. Jeff Beck played guitars on a few songs: 'Billy Get Your Guns,' 'Miracle,' 'Blaze Of Glory,' 'Justice In The Barrel,' 'Never Say Die,' 'Bang A Drum' and 'Dyin' Ain't Much Of A Livin'.' Elton John, one of Jon's main idols, played piano on 'Billy Get Your Guns' and also provided piano and backing vocals on 'Dyin' Ain't Much Of A Livin'.' Little Richard played piano and vocals on 'You Really Got Me Now.' Other personnel included drummer Kenny Aronoff, bassist Randy Jackson, guitarist and keyboardist Aldo Nova, organist Benmont Tench (from Tom Petty's Heartbreakers,) accordion player Phil Parlapiano, bassist Bob Glaub, slide guitarist Waddy Wachtel and backing vocalists Myrna Matthews, Julia Waters, Maxine Waters, and even actor Lou Diamond Phillips, who added backing vocals to 'Justice In The Barrel.' The album's cover includes photography by Mark Weiss and Timothy White.

Blaze Of Glory was released through PolyGram/Vertigo in the UK on August 25, 1990, peaking at an impressive Number 2. In the States it managed the Number 3 position. The single 'Blaze Of Glory' was issued on August 4 in the UK and hit Number 13, while in the States it reached Number 1. 'Miracle' was released on November 10 peaking at Number 29 in the UK and Number 12 in the USA. The album went on to sell over six million copies.

Jerry Ewing reviewed the album in *Metal Forces* #54, saying:

"Jon Bon Jovi may be a talented guy, but it's very clear he [Jon] really needs other people to allow that talent to really shine..."

On the other hand, Jon told writer Mark Day at *Metal Hammer* in 1990:

"To tell you the truth, basically Bon Jovi records are my solo records."

Track Listing:
1. 'Billy Get Your Guns'
2. 'Miracle'
3. 'Blaze Of Glory'
4. 'Blood Money'
5. 'Santa Fe'
6. 'Justice In The Barrel'
7. 'Never Say Die'
8. 'You Really Got Me Now'
9. 'Bang A Drum'
10. 'Dyin' Ain't Much Of A Livin''
11. 'Guano City'

Author's Review:
There's no question about it, Jon Bon Jovi's debut solo album is a well made collection of 11 songs but unlike Sambora's Stranger In This Town *it lacks a personal, introspective touch. The title track could easily fit on any of Bon Jovi's first few albums or act as B-side to the singles, but the rest sound like Jon's attempt at playing Johnny Cash.*

'Billy Get Your Gun' is a rock solid song and a great opening track while

'Miracle' is a fairly competent ballad with only a memorable chorus. 'Blaze Of Glory' is a classic Bon Jovi tune that Bon Jovi never made, if you get my meaning; it's a rock anthem and huge power ballad that Bon Jovi does well. 'Blood Money' is a filler track at best and 'Santa Fe' is an orchestral based song that's actually pretty good although Jon tries too hard to sing the higher notes. 'Justice In The Barrel' starts off with a low misty vibe but then it builds up to a heavy chorus with a short guitar solo from Jeff Beck, whose guitar parts really shine on this album. 'Never Say Die' is one of the heavier songs and quite clearly influenced by Thin Lizzy but with vocals by Bruce Springsteen! Odd. But it works. 'You Really Got Me' is an interesting traditional blues song with some boogie-woogie piano from Little Richard. 'Bang A Drum' is one of the albums weaker numbers; it's just too repetitive. 'Dyin' Ain't Much Of A Livin'' is a slow, yearning track while the closing song 'Guano City' is a grand orchestral composition by Alan Silvestri.

Blaze Of Glory is a decent album but with no surprises. The production is big, and credit must go to Jon for writing all the lyrics and music but there's nothing new or massively inspiring here. A missed opportunity.

Rating **½

BLAZE OF GLORY (SINGLE)

The excellent title-track from Jon's debut solo album and the lead theme for the movie *Young Guns II*; it's not entirely unlike anything Bon Jovi had attempted before. It's a big soaring power ballad with a distinctive western vibe and a catchy melody; and a certain guitarist by the name of Jeff Beck adds a neat solo.

In the States, the single hit the top spot while in Britain it only managed Number 13 after it was released on August 4, 1990. In Australia the song was Number 1 for six weeks. The video was directed by Wayne Isham.

BLUE MURDER

A melodic rock band who supported Bon Jovi in 1989. Formed by John Skyes, formerly guitarist in Whitesnake and the New Wave Of British Heavy Metal band Tygers Of Pan Tang, they released two full studio albums and a live opus prior to their demise in 1994. With the exception of Skyes and bass player Tony Franklin, Blue Murder went through several line-up changes resulting in different players on their initial demo recordings and their officially released studio material. Members who played in the band included singers Ray Gillen and Kelly Keeling, drummers Cozy Powell, Carmine Appice and Tommy O'Steen, keyboardist Nik Green and bassist Marco Mendoza.

Bassist Tony Franklin recalls, *"Blue Murder opened for them [Bon Jovi] for about 10 days in mid 1989. We didn't see too much of the band, though we hung a bit. JBJ is just a few*

days older than me... a fellow Aries. They treated us well, good guys."

BON JOVI (ALBUM)

With a record deal under their belt, the band was good to go. In June 1983 they recorded their debut album at Power Station Studios in NYC with Lance Quinn and Tony Bongiovi. They re-recorded the song 'Runaway', which Jon had previously composed with The All Star Review session band, although those artists (Tim Pierce, Frankie La Roca, Roy Bittan and Hugh McDonald) do make appearances on the album as additional musicians. The bulk of the songwriting was a collaboration between Jon, Richie Sambora and David Bryan. 'Runaway' was co-written by Jon and George Karak; 'She Don't Know' was written solely by the American keyboardist Marc Avsec and 'Shot Through The Heart' was co-written by Jon and Jack Ponti.'

Original Bon Jovi bassist Alec John Such told *RAW* in 1993:

"I never play it! I'm not too fond of either of our first two records, we really didn't get the chance to show what we could do with either of them...To me, it's a solid four out of ten."

On the other hand *Kerrang!* scribe Paul Suter hailed the album as a *"magnificent debut."*

Bon Jovi was released in the UK on April 28, 1984 and peaked at a lowly Number 71 but in the States it managed to make it to Number 43. With constant touring and promotion the album sold around two million copies. The reviews were mostly positive but what was immediately noticeable to fans and critics was the album cover, which depicts Jon, on his own, standing in a street with some woman in the background although the band are featured on the back of the cover sleeve.

Track Listing:
1. 'Runaway'
2. 'Roulette'
3. 'She Don't Know Me'
4. 'Shot Through The Heart'
5. 'Love Lies'
6. 'Breakout'
7. 'Burning For Love'
8. 'Come Back'
9. 'Get Ready'

Author's Review:
Bon Jovi's self-titled debut album is a blast. Sure, there are some teething problems (the songwriting needs a bit of tweaking and Jon's voice sounds a bit shallow) but overall its good fun. 'Runaway' and 'She Don't Know Me' are great melodic rock tracks and the ballad 'Love Lies' is pretty cool. 'Breakout' is probably the album's best track; it's the kind of song that would make Bon Jovi famous later on in the decade: great melody, killing synths, catchy chorus and a good central riff. The lyrics are immature but they reflect the band's youth and the working class kids from New Jersey image that would define them in the early days of their career. With only nine tracks, the album is a bit too short but it's one of those eighties rock albums that can be repeated and repeated without ever tiring out.

Rating * ½**

BON JOVI, JON

He was born John Francis Bongiovi, Jr. on March 2, 1962 in Perth Amboy, New Jersey. As a teen, Jon wanted to be like his hero Bruce Springsteen – a homegrown rock legend - and to all intents and purposes he has achieved that dream. An Italian-American (his father John was a barber and his mother was a Playboy Bunny and then a florist), Jon was raised in Sayreville, New Jersey and had a typical working-class East Coast childhood. He was educated at Union Catholic Regional High School, in Scotch Plains. Afterwards he enrolled at Sayreville War Memorial High School in the Parlin area of New Jersey.

Jon's childhood musical influences include KISS, Bruce Springsteen, Elton John, Thin Lizzy, Elvis and Rush; pretty eclectic stuff, but showing his interest in all styles of popular music. He began learning guitar in 1975, taking lessons from his neighbour Al Parinello, who was not a guitar teacher per se, but who offered some worthwhile tips on how to handle the instrument. It was Jon's aim to learn how to play 'House Of The

Rising Sun,' the song made famous by sixties English pop group The Animals.

It was then up to Jon to get himself involved in the local music scene, so he joined or formed various bands: Raze, Atlantic City Expressway, The Rest, The Leeches and The Wild Ones. Aged 18, he moved to the Big Apple and got himself a $50 a month job at Power Station Studios in Manhattan, a facility co-owned by his cousin Tony Bongiovi. It was basically a minimum wage job doing menial things like fetching coffee for stars like Mick Jagger, sweeping floors, tidying up and running errands. He earned himself some extra pay by continuing to play the clubs with The Wild Ones, featuring guitarist Dave Sabo, and he even sang lead vocals on the track 'R2D2 – We Wish You A Merry Christmas' for the *Star Wars Christmas Album,* which his cousin produced. Years later he endeavoured to stop his cousin from releasing *The Power Station Years*, a collection of songs and demos he made during his years as a janitor at the studios. Some of the pseudonyms he used when he

made demos were Johnny B, Johnny Lightning and Victory.

In June 1982 he recorded the demo 'Runaway' with a host of talented musicians called The All Star Review session band; it was produced by Billy Squier. The demo made its away round local radio stations and become a hit on the Long Island station WAPP FM 103.5. The demo was noticed by executives at Atlantic and PolyGram, and Jon signed to PolyGram on July 1, 1983 as a solo artist. He bought himself a sports car to celebrate.

It was always his intention to get a band together and he did that almost immediately. He located a set of talented musicians: keyboardist David Bryan, bassist Alec John Such, drummer Tico Torres and guitarist Richie Sambora. Jon amended his surname to Bon Jovi and named the band Bon Jovi at the behest of PolyGram's A&R man Derek Shulman, who felt it would be more appropriate to americanise the band's name.

Speaking to *Metal Hammer* in December, 1989, Jon said:

"I put this band together around great guys rather than the greatest players...with no egos in the band."

Bon Jovi released their self-titled debut in 1984 through the PolyGram subsidiary Mercury. Their break-

through album came with their third release *Slippery When Wet*. With Jon's good looks and working class charm, the band became a hit with the ladies and Jon even won the 1985 *Kerrang!* award for 'Sex Object Of The Year.' By the end of the eighties Jon was one of the world's most recognisable rock stars and Bon Jovi were a household name, selling out stadiums everywhere and releasing hit singles. But the main man craved for other things and started to branch out. With Sambora, he wrote songs for Loverboy, Cher, Witness, Gorky Park, Alice Cooper, Paul Young and Ted Nugent.

The *New Jersey Syndicate* tour was so long and draining that Jon had to enlist a vocal coach to help him out before gigs and there was mounting tension in the band. When the tour finished in February, 1990 the band took a break from each other (although they did regroup for some benefit shows.) Jon's first solo endeavour was to compose the soundtrack to the 1990 comedy western *Young Guns II*. His soundtrack ('Songs Written and Performed By Jon Bon Jovi') *Blaze*

Of Glory was a massive commercial success; he achieved an Academy Award Nomination for 'Best Song' for 'Blaze Of Glory' and won a Golden Globe for 'Best Song.' The album includes contributions from Messrs. Little Richard, Elton John and Jeff Beck. *Blaze Of Glory* has sold over six millions copies, a fair achievement by any singer's standards.

His second solo album, *Destination Anywhere,* was released in 1997. It features contributions from Desmond Child, Dave Stewart, David Bryan and Aldo Nova. It was not a big success and failed to reach the Top 30 in the States. However, it has gone on to sell a few million copies worldwide in the decade since its release, helped by a hasty re-release with a bonus live CD. To promote the album Jon took a band on the road with him (dubbing them The Big Dogs,) featuring bassist Hugh McDonald, guitarist Bobby Bandiera, keyboardist Jerry Cohen, percussionist Everett Bradley and drummer Shawn Pelton. They played some small shows in Europe and the States.

Jon still has certain idols that he reveres and from whom he takes ideas, and these would emphatically include Bono, Elvis, Sinatra and Springsteen. Jon has other things besides the band in his CV, as music is not his only passion; he has starred in a number of films after picking up the 'acting bug' in the early nineties. He made an ultra-brief cameo in *Young Guns II* but his first major role was in *Moonlight And Valentino* in 1995. Since then he has appeared in a number of films: *The Leading Man* (1996), *Little City* (1997), *Destination Anywhere* (1997), *No Looking Back* (1998), *Homegrown* (1998), *U-571* (2000), *Pay It Forward* (2000), *Vampires: Los Muertos* (2002), *Cry Wolf* (2005) and *National Lampoon's Pucked* (2006.) Jon has also appeared in some high profile American TV shows beginning with *Sex And The City* in 1999 and continuing with 10 episodes of *Ally McBeal* in 2002, in which he played the character Victor Morrison. In 2006 he appeared in one episode of the highly-acclaimed political drama series *The West Wing.*

Over the years he has committed himself to raising awareness of various charities, for which he has been a major fundraiser. These include the Special Olympics, the American Red Cross and Habitat For Humanity. In

2005, the band donated $1 million to Oprah Winfrey's Angel Network Foundation with the money going to the victims of Hurricane Katrina, which had devastated most of New Orleans. He has won various awards for his charity work, including 'Humanitarian Of The Year' which was handed to him by The Food Bank Of Monmouth & Ocean Counties in NJ. In 2001 he was awarded an Honorary Doctorate in Humanities for his work as a performer and humanitarian by Monmouth University in NJ. Unafraid to talk politics, he is a publicly acknowledged Democrat and has worked with and campaigned for former Vice President Al Gore, Presidential Candidate John Kerry in 2004 and Presidential Candidate Barack Obama in 2008. There are some who think Jon will run for president one day. Arnold Schwarzenegger becoming the 38th Governor of California in 2003 proves that if you're famous in America, anything can happen to you.

A huge sports fan, Jon co-owns the arena football team Philadelphia Soul with Richie Sambora. His love life, unlike that of his guitarist and friend, has been fairly conventional. Aside from a brief separation in the eighties, in which time he dated actress Diane Lane, Jon is happily married to his childhood honey Dorothea Hurley, with whom he has four children. Their marriage ceremony was not exactly lavish by Hollywood standards

or indeed by any standards of the rich and famous; they got hitched at the Graceland Wedding Chapel in Las Vegas on April 29, 1989.

Jon is certainly the leader of the band and he firmly believes that *"what happens in the family, stays in the family"* and his handling of bassist Alec John Such's dismissal from the band in 1994 proves that Jon vehemently sticks by that motto. There are some critics who will eagerly point out that he is full of self-importance (hey, aren't all rock stars?) and that he is not nearly as talented as he makes out. With Jon's dabbling in charity work and politics it certainly appears that he would like to follow in the footsteps of his idol Bono. There's no argument that Jon will go down in the history books as a first rate entertainer and successful rock star. Indeed, credit is due to him for being so tenacious and hard-working. Like fellow New Jersey native Bruce

Springsteen, Jon is proud of his roots and still bases himself in the state after which the band named their 1988 hit album.

Visit *bonjovi.com*

BON JOVI.COM

bonjovi.com is the official band website. It includes all sorts of multimedia additions where fans can download songs, videos and interviews with the band. Areas of the

Vanguard Award at the MTV Video Music Awards in September, 1991 Jon fired manager Doc McGhee because their relationship both personal and professional had deteriorated, probably due to the stressful period the group had been going through at the time. To his credit, McGhee did pull the band back together for the MTV appearance.

Jon formed BJM with former tour manager Paul Korzilius and Margaret

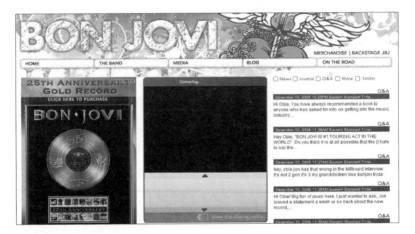

site which include 'Blog', 'The Band', 'Media', 'On The Road', 'Shop' and 'Fan Club.' Fans can access set lists, tour dates, and join the band's mailing list to receive all the latest news.

Visit *bonjovi.com*

BON JOVI MANAGEMENT

Sandwiched between the end of the exhaustive *New Jersey Syndicate* tour in 1990 and the recording of the *Keep The Faith* album in '92, the band was temporarily put on halt as the members were - metaphorically speaking - about to kill each other. Jon and Sambora pursued their solo careers and the other guys also had personal projects.

Shortly after the band met up to accept the Michael Jackson Video

Sterlacci, formerly of McGhee Entertainment Inc. It began as a multi-million dollar company and has continued to grow ever since.

Jon told Malcolm Dome at *Metal Forces* in 1993:

"The company only looks after Bon Jovi. That's what it's there for. And if any member of the band wants help on outside projects, then of course all the facilities would be at his disposal."

As credited in Bon Jovi's latest album *Lost Highway*, Bon Jovi Management is now headed by Paul Korzilius, Scott Casey and Mike Rew.

Visit *bonjovi.com*

BONGIOVI, TONY

His full name is Anthony M. Bongiovi and he was born in Raitan, New Jersey. As a producer and engineer his credits include Aerosmith, Jimi Hendrix, Ozzy Osbourne, Ace Frehley, Scorpions, Ramones and Talking Heads.

He is Jon Bon Jovi's father's cousin, and co-owned the now famous Power Station Studios (now named Avatar Studios) in downtown Manhattan, NYC. He was instrumental in giving Jon's career a much needed boost after seeing him onstage in The Rest, one of Jon's former club bands. Jon worked at Power Station between 1980 and 1984, and it was after he left the studio and found success in Bon Jovi that the pair became entangled in a legal row.

Tony co-produced the band's debut self-titled album, released in 1984, and allegedly helped fund some of Jon's earlier demo recordings. When Bon Jovi, the band, became successful a row over royalties ensued. A settlement was subsequently agreed; in 1988, *Metal Hammer* reported that Tony was *"awarded a producer's credit, a fee and a 1% royalty for both* 7800° Fahrenheit *and* Slippery When Wet.*"

However in the summer of 1997, Jon allegedly tried to stop his cousin Tony from releasing *John Bongiovi: The Power Station Sessions 1980-1983*, which contains some of his earliest recordings. The album was issued in Europe with an extra four tracks on the label Masquerade Records. The CD was re-released in 2001.

Visit *tonybongiovi.com*

BORGATA CASINO & SPA

Bon Jovi used the intimate Borgata Casino and Spa in Atlantic City for two nights on November 15 and 15, 2003 to perform their album *This Left Feels Right* in its entirety. In front of just 1,500 fans (some of whom paid a whopping $5,000 for a ticket) Bon Jovi were joined by Southside Johnny's Everett Bradley and Jeff Kazee. The shows were filmed for a DVD release.

Setlist:
1. 'Love For Sale'
2. 'You Give Love A Bad Name'
3. 'Wanted Dead Or Alive'
4. 'Livin' On A Prayer'
5. 'It's My Life'
6. 'Misunderstood'
7. 'Lay Your Hands On Me'
8. 'Someday I'll Be Saturday Night'
9. 'Last Man Standing'
10. 'Sylvia's Mother'
11. 'Everyday'

BORN TO BE MY BABY

Written by Jon, Richie Sambora and Desmond Child, 'Born To Be My Baby' was the second single released from *New Jersey*. It was issued in the UK on December 10, 1988 and only reached Number 22 in the Top 40, spending seven weeks in the chart. It reached Number 3 in the American *Billboard* Hot 100. The promotional video was shot in black and white and shows the band recording the song live in the studio.

BOUDREAU, RON

Ron Boudreau is an experienced rock photographer who, during the eighties, worked with the likes of Aerosmith, Prince, The Who, Metallica, ZZ Top and even Madonna. From 1987 to 1992 he worked with the revered music photographer Mark Weiss. Known for his photographs of fellow New Jersey band Skid Row, Boudreau got to know Jon and the band during his time working with Weiss, and photographed Jon at his New Jersey home.

Interview:

Do you remember when you first met Jon and the band?

I will never forget the first time I met Jon. I was standing beside his marble pool table in the basement of his house; he came down the stairs and introduced himself. It was October, *1988 the day before the world tour to promote the* New Jersey *album. At the time I was living with Sebastian Bach (Skid Row) in NJ while he was getting ready for debut of Skid Row, and I was working with rock photographer Mark Weiss. Weiss was on assignment to shoot a cover of Jon and Dave "The Snake" Sabo. It would be the first public endorsement of Skid Row by Jon. The photo shoot took place at Jon's house. I had already met everyone else in the band. By the time the shot got started, it became quite funny how many times I got introduced to Jon that day. Weiss was first to tell Jon who I was; as I was the new guy to join the club. Then Snake gave me the next intro, as him and I go back a few years. Next was Tico, and Richie made sure Jon knew me… By that time Jon was telling everyone that him and I go way back.*

How did you get the job of photographing Jon for the first time?

I was Skid Row photographer on tour with Skid Row/Bon Jovi in the summer of 1989. Jon showed up at Skid Row autograph session in Toronto. When Jon came in through the back of the record store I snapped my first photo of him. Later that night after the concert, Skid Row was doing a second show at Sebastian's fave Toronto rock club Rock 'n' Roll Heaven. Towards the end of the Skid Row set, Jon jumped up on stage with the band and I was able to grab a few great shots of Jon and Sebastian!

What was Jon like to work with?

The day I spent at Jon's house was great. Jon was very accommodating and friendly to me. He gave me a bit of tour around his place and showed me where the diet cokes were in the fridge. By the end of the day I was sitting in his office flipping records on

his old phonograph player, I'm sure we were listening to Billie Holiday.

How many times have you photographed Bon Jovi?

I have shot Bon Jovi at least five times, including a magazine cover of Jon.

What is your most memorable photo session with them?

The first is always the best time, but I know getting great shots of Jon and Sebastian at the club are some of my most important photos that I have captured.

What was it like to photograph the band onstage?

The first time I photographed the band, I had to come back with a cover shot of Jon and band photos for the inside of the magazine. I was more concerned with doing a great job; having already met the band a few times it was quite comfortable to do my gig.

Would you work with them again?

Absolutely, they are one of the greatest rock bands ever! Truly the most memorable moment that I recall was during the shoot at Jon's House, when we finally got down to the photo shoot I saw Jon smile for the first time that day. As he was getting ready tour I could tell he had a lot on his mind that day.

Visit *RonBoudreau.com*

BOUNCE (ALBUM)

Post 9/11, many American artists, including Bon Jovi, felt a patriotic desire to write about the devastation that had been caused in New York and wanted to express their thoughts creatively. Evidently the title *Bounce* implies to 'bounce back...' On the other hand, it has also been claimed that the title is about the Bill Belichick, the NFL Head Coach of the New England Patriots, who finally 'bounced back' and won a super bowl.

Preparations for their follow-up studio album to *Crush* began in April, 2002. The songwriting this time around was mainly done by Jon

and Richie Sambora, with contributions from Desmond Child, Billy Falcon and Andreas Carlsson. The album was recorded during the first half of '02 at Jon's personal studio, Sanctuary II, in New Jersey and produced by Luke Ebbin, together with Jon and Sambora. Co-production is also credited to Desmond Child and Andreas Carlsson; mixing was completed by Obie O' Brien. The band had still kept a hard rock edge but at the same time there are a few ballads with very sensitive vocals which reflect the nature of their lyrics, providing moments of light and dark. 'Everyday' (written by Jon, Sambora and Carlsson) was the band's direct response to the 9/11 terrorist attacks and how the country should move forward. 'Undivided' (written by Jon, Sambora and Falcon) was specifical-ly about the destruction caused by the terrorist attacks.

Bounce was released in the UK on October 5, 2002 and reached Number 2 in the Top 40 album chart, spending six weeks in the charts. It was also a Number 2 hit on the American *Billboard* 200. *Bounce* had the band's highest debut in the States at that particular point, and has gone on to sell six million copies worldwide. Three singles were released from the album: 'Everyday,' 'Misunderstood' and 'All About Lovin' You.' None of them were hits in America. 'Bounce' was also released as single in some territories, albeit in a censored version omitting the word 'fuck.'

Ian Fortnam gave the album 3/5 in *Classic Rock* and said:

"...pretty much business as usual. Slick production jobs; chocolate-box

sentiments; the odd smidgen of rock cliché..."

Track Listing:
1. 'Undivided'
2. 'Everyday'
3. 'The Distance'
4. 'Joey'
5. 'Misunderstood'
6. 'All About Lovin' You'
7. 'Hook Me Up'
8. 'Right Side Of Wrong'
9. 'Love Me Back To Life'
10. 'You Had Me From Hello'
11. 'Bounce'
12. 'Open All Night'
13. 'No Regrets' *(Japanese release only)*
14. 'Postcards From The Wasteland' *(Japanese release only)*
(The UK version has track 13 listed as 'Exclusive Bonus Video Footage')

Author's Review

Bounce is an interesting album. There's a strong guitar presence and Jon shifts the tone of his vocals from familiar power ballads like 'The Distance' to a more sensitive side, as heard on 'All About Lovin' You.' The lyrics are probably amongst the most inspired and emotional the band have ever written. There are some heavy riffs that are really quite gritty and distorted ('Hook Me Up') and there is a strong keyboards presence ('Love Me Back To Life.') Again, there are maybe one or two more ballads than there need to be, but the band are more than partial to a love song.

Bounce follows a similar path that began with Crush *in that it shows the band craving a heavier album, but seeming almost scared of alienating those who like the slower tracks. As is often the case with a new Bon Jovi album, this one is a grower. It's got*

some good songs and a strong set of lyrics.

Rating ***½

BOUNCE TOUR (2002-03)

To promote their acclaimed album *Bounce*, Bon Jovi played 84 dates around the world from December 8, 2002 to August 8, 2003.

AUSTRALIAN DATES
December 8, 2002 – Melbourne (Australia)
December 11, 2002 – Brisbane (Australia)
December 14, 2002 - Sydney (Australia)

JAPANESE DATES
January 8, 2003 - Sapporo (Japan)
January 11, 2003 - Osaka (Japan)
January 12, 2003 - Osaka (Japan)
January 14, 2003 - Fukuoka (Japan)
January 16, 2003 - Tokyo (Japan)
January 17, 2003 - Tokyo (Japan)
January 19, 2003 - Yokohama (Japan)
January 21, 2003 - Nagoya (Japan)

NORTH AMERICAN DATES
PART I

February 8, 2003 - University Park, PA (USA)

February 10, 2003 - East Rutherford, NJ (USA)

February 11, 2003 - East Rutherford, NJ (USA)

February 13, 2003 - Atlanta, GA (USA)

February 14, 2003 - Nashville, TN (USA)

February 16, 2003 - Columbus, OH (USA)

February 18, 2003 - Auburn Hills, MI (USA)

February 20, 2003 - Toronto, Ontario (Canada)

February 21, 2003 - Montreal, Quebec (Canada)

February 23, 2003 - Atlantic City, NJ (USA)

February 25, 2003 - Minneapolis, MN (USA)

February 27, 2003 - Milwaukee, WI (USA)

March 1, 2003 - Chicago, IL (USA)

March 3, 2003 - Albany, NY (USA)

March 4, 2003 - Boston, MA (USA)

March 6, 2003 - Uncasville, CT (USA)

March 7, 2003 - Philadelphia, PA (USA)

March 9, 2003 - Washington, D.C (USA)

March 12, 2003 - Houston, TX (USA)

March 14, 2003 - Fort Lauderdale, FL (USA)

March 15, 2003 - Tampa, FL (USA)

March 19, 2003 - Dallas, TX (USA)

March 21, 2003 - Raleigh, NC (USA)

March 22, 2003 - Charlotte, NC (USA)

March 24, 2003 - Pittsburgh, PA (USA)

March 27, 2003 - Buffalo, NY (USA)

March 29, 2003 - Madison, WI (USA)

March 31, 2003 - Cleveland, OH (USA)

April 3, 2003 - Denver, CO (USA)

April 5, 2003 - Salt Lake City, UT (USA)

April 7, 2003 - Phoenix, AZ (USA)

April 9 2003 - Los Angeles, CA (USA)

April 10, 2003 - Anaheim, CA (USA)

April 12, 2003 - San Jose, CA (USA)

April 14, 2003 - Portland, OR (USA)

April 15, 2003 - Seattle, WA (USA)

April 17, 2003 - Sacramento, CA (USA)

April 19, 2003 - Las Vegas, NV (USA)

EUROPEAN DATES

May 20, 2003 – Barcelona (Spain)

May 22, 2003 – Madrid (Spain)

May 25, 2003 – Erfurt (Germany)

May 28, 2003 – Vienna (Austria)

May 30, 2003 – Gelsenkirchen (Germany)

June 1, 2003 – Mannheim (Germany)

June 3, 2003 – Amsterdam (Netherlands)

June 6, 2003 – Bremen (Germany)
June 8, 2003 – Ostend (Belgium)
June 11, 2003 – Zurich (Switzerland)
June 13, 2003 – Munich (Germany)
June 14, 2003 - Imola (Italy -
Heineken Jammin' Festival 2003)
June 17, 2003 – Kiel (Germany)
June 20, 2003 – Dublin (Ireland)
June 22, 2003 – Glasgow (Scotland)
June 24, 2003 – Wolverhampton
(England)
June 26, 2003 – Manchester
(England)
June 28, 2003 – London (England)

NORTH AMERICAN DATES PART II
July 11, 2003 - Tinley Park, IL (USA)
July 12, 2003 - East Troy, WI (USA)
July 15, 2003 - Minneapolis, MN
(USA)

July 17, 2003 - Toronto, Ontario,
(Canada)
July 19, 2003 - Detroit, MI, (USA)
July 22, 2003 - Foxboro, MA, (USA)
July 24, 2003 - Pittsburgh, PA (USA)
July 26, 2003 - Philadelphia, PA
(USA)
July 27, 2003 - Bristow, VA (USA)
July 29, 2003 - Columbus, OH
(USA)
July 30, 2003 - Indianapolis, IN
(USA)
August 1, 2003 - Cincinnati, OH
(USA)
August 3, 2003 - Saratoga Springs,
NY (USA)
August 4, 2003 - Hartford, CT
(USA)
August 7, 2003 - E. Rutherford, NJ
(USA)
August 8, 2003 - E. Rutherford, NJ
(USA)

BRADLEY, EVERETT

An American percussionist from Southside Johnny's band who toured with Richie Sambora during the Japanese leg of his 1998 tour, in support of Sambora's second solo album *Undiscovered Soul*. He also played in Jon Bon Jovi's band The Big Dogs in 1997 in support of *Destination Anywhere*. He has played percussion with Bon Jovi and can be seen on the concert DVD *This Left Feels Right*.

Visit *everettbradley.com*

BREAKOUT: THE SINGLES

Released via PolyGram, this rare 30 minute VHS compilation from 1985 has since been deleted. This six video collection features music from the band's first two albums: *Bon Jovi* and *7800° Fahrenheit*.

Track Listing:
1. 'In And Out Of Love'
2. 'Only Lonely'
3. 'Silent Night'
4. 'She Don't Know Me'
5. 'The Hardest Part Is The Night' *(Live)*
6. 'Runaway'

BRIGHTON CENTRE

Bon Jovi played their first UK gig at this venue on September 30, 1984. They were on a UK tour with KISS.

John Tucker, heavy metal writer and co-author of Biff Byford's autobiography *Never Surrender (Or Nearly Good Looking,)* was in the audience. He vividly remembers the evening's performance:

"Picked up to support KISS on their European tour, Bon Jovi's first UK date was on September 30, 1984 at the Brighton Centre. In truth, the omens

weren't too good; the gig wasn't that well attended even for the headliners (who seemed to know and so used the occasion to road-test a setlist that was then radically changed for later dates,) and Jon Bon Jovi had already lost some of his shine in the eyes of the media. From the off he wanted to be a star, but many writers seemed to think the arrogant young pup had yet to pay his dues. The hacks' knives had been sharpened...

On the night, Bon Jovi were pure 100% entertainment. They were sassy and fun, a talented young Aerosmith for a new generation. Theirs wasn't a lengthy set – a sprint through the cherry-picked best bits of the album which kicked off with 'Breakout' and included short solo spots for both guitarist Richie Sambora and drummer Tico Torres – but they came on, showed off, kicked ass and left again in the time it took most people to select a KISS t-shirt from the merch stand. It was rock 'n' roll, pure and simple, and those that mustered around the crash barriers loved every minute of it. 'Roulette' sent people spinning, and the set rounded off with the obvious 'Runaway'. Kerrang! grudgingly liked what they saw and heard ('not a great singer...but blessed with youth, talent, and the will to succeed,' noted Derek Oliver in Kerrang! *# 79, October 18-31, 1984) but at* Sounds *(October 13, 1984) Dave Roberts,* *catching the band at Manchester three nights later, was singularly unimpressed: 'Their attitude stinks – all 'We're the stars, and we're doing you a big favour...' With their misguided clothes-sense and ass-licking (mis)demeanour, they were about as likeable as a bowl of chewed cornflakes. The guitarist thinks he's Eddie V H, while Jon Bon Jerkoff does a fine Dave Lee Roth/Steve Tyler impersonation, without having that essential ingredient of star quality and prevalent sense of humour.'*

Roberts missed the point that the fans who watched the band knew exactly what they were going to get, and they got it in bucket loads. Bon Jovi was a star in the making, that much was obvious, and in years to come, those who saw those early UK shows were the ones who could say, 'I was there...'"

BRIT AWARDS

Popularly known as The Brits, this British Awards ceremony has been held almost every year since 1997. At the 1994 awards, Bon Jovi performed 'I'll Sleep When I'm Dead', with Dina Carroll on backing vocals; that year's ceremony was held at London's Alexandra Palace. In 1996, Bon Jovi won the award for 'Best International Band', and in 1998 Jon Bon Jovi won the 'Best International Male' award.

BROWN, RAY

Australian-born, American-based designer of rock clothes. Brown was especially famous and successful in the 1980s when he designed clothes for almost every heavy metal and hard rock band, including Judas Priest, Mötley Crüe, Whitesnake, Black Sabbath, Bon Jovi, Ozzy Osbourne and Styx. Although he designs clothes primarily for rock stars

to wear onstage he has also custom tailored clothes for the weddings of Tommy Lee and Heather Locklear as well as for other special occasions, including the weddings of Vince Neil and John Mellencamp.

He worked with Bon Jovi for over a decade, during their most creative and commercially successful period, and also worked with Richie Sambora on his first solo tour.

Interview:

When did you first start working for Bon Jovi?

They'd already had one album out, which was that 7800° Fahrenheit album, and the next album after that was Slippery When Wet; *that's when I first hooked up with them.*

What do you remember about those early years with the band?

Well, that whole time for me was just crazy! The way I got to do Bon Jovi was because I had done Mötley Crüe and they were managed by the same person, Doc McGhee, and so they had me go to New York, meet with Jon and the band, and basically everything from then onwards for

about the next 15 years was all my clothing. The one thing I do remember about them was: everything was badass. That's how they'd describe their clothing; everything was 'bad' or 'badass.' I had a really large workshop; I would just buy fabric that I saw that I liked and they would just pick fabric and just say, 'Make a badass coat out of this or make a badass coat out of that.' They did contribute to a lot of the designs but most guys that are in bands, they have an idea of how they wanna look on stage so it's just a matter of interpreting it for them. A lot of the time, especially with Richie, it was like 'Make me a badass white coat or make me a badass purple coat.'

What was it like to work with them?

They were very open. Basically, they would just pick fabric or just describe something they wanted and just get me to interpret it. They were obviously happy because it went on for a very long time. One of the coats that I made for Jon – that one with the skulls on it, the long patchwork coat – he ended up giving to away to the Smithsonian Museum in New York.

It must be rewarding for you to know that the clothes you made for the band became iconic?

Well, the funny thing about that whole time period, which was basically most of the eighties through to the early nineties, at one point that stuff wasn't cool. The eighties weren't cool up until about seven years ago when all of a sudden the eighties were cool. There's this whole rock fashion thing that's going on in fashion at the moment with all the t-shirts with skulls and crosses on them. That all came out of the eighties. The three bands that I made clothing for that contributed to that look the most were

Mötley Crüe, Bon Jovi and Black Sabbath. Skulls, I don't think had ever been used on clothing before I started using them in the mainstream on Jon. What people wear on stage always finds its way into fashion. It's just even more so now.

You also worked with Richie Sambora on his first solo tour. What was that period like for you?

I actually really liked his music. His first album Stranger In This Town *was a great album; it had some really good stuff on it. And so everything he wore on the solo tour I made for him.*

Richie's look is of the long leather jacket and hat. Was that your idea?

The hat thing was his. Back then all his coats were always long; they were always three-quarter length. Johnny Cash was one of the ways he would describe how he wanted to look. Johnny Cash and Stevie Ray Vaughn type look on stage and he had all his coats made long. I think on that solo tour, he had some velvet jackets I made for him.

Did you actually go on tour with the band?

At that point I was based in LA and if need be, I would go out. If there was a video shoot or something like that I would go out with the clothing and stuff. Most of the video shoots they did over that time period were done in LA anyway. I'd never actually gone on a tour bus with them – that's not my idea of fun! (Laughs.)

At one point did you stop working for the band?

I think I worked out that I'd been with them for about 15 years and I actually had left LA. The main reason I left LA was because I was so busy, I just couldn't take it. Every band you can imagine was calling me. One of the interesting things about the Bon Jovi is: the first pair of lace front pants I ever made was for Jon. I still remember clearly sitting down in a hotel room just throwing ideas out and some how the idea came up about how to make the pants so they lace up. I don't even remember who said it now. But it was basically the first pair I made; I made for him; that's gone on to be copied by...you name it. At that time, all through the eighties, every band was calling me and the first thing they had to have was the lace front pants. It was incredible. Look back at pictures of those old bands: Poison, Cinderella, Warrant, all of them had lace front pants like Jon.

What crosses your mind when you look back to that period?

To see the clothing on stage...obviously if they didn't like the clothes they wouldn't wear them. I've never made the clothing just for the sake of making the money or to say I've dressed Bon Jovi. There were a lot of people in the business at that time that were basically designing just so they could name drop and make money.

What are you most vivid memories from working with Bon Jovi?

My strongest recollections are from those video shoots. They were all day; they were really busy days. Changes of clothing and the whole thing. Another thing that is very interesting: Jon actually took my wife and I to Japan. Him and I had been taking one day and I said: 'No Jon I've never been to Japan, that must be so cool.' He said I'll take you and he put me on the crew list. My wife and I were paid for and we were in Japan for two weeks which was really kind of fun. The promoter had caught on to the fact that 'Hang on, who is this guy?' I had to pretend to work for them for a couple of hours a day. We actually got to see the whole Japanese tour which was really interesting. Japanese audiences are not like American audiences; they basically sit there and just clap. They're a little bit rowdier now. That was a re-

ally fun time; we were basically with the band for the whole two weeks.

The band looks totally different now; what do you think about their image change?

Judas Priest still dress the same. Mötley Crüe has still kept the same vibe about their clothing. The one thing I had noticed about Jon, especially with him, is that he's influenced by a lot of other singers: Springsteen, Bono and the third name is Elvis. I just read recently that he's now got a picture of Frank Sinatra in his dressing room. He had these people that he really admired and at times translated in to the clothing to look like these people. I remember having a discussion with him one time when he said to me: 'Do something like the way Bono looks.' And I go: 'Jon, you're Jon Bon Jovi. You can do it how you wanna look.' And he kind of got annoyed at me. You have your own identity. I remember there was one coat that he had; it was a full length coat that had Elvis paintings on it. I always found that kind of interesting; he was almost like a little bit insecure about his image. I don't know if that was because he did have a lot of admiration poured on him very quickly because of the way he looked. He's a good looking guy and the girls really did go crazy over him.

I actually think that he could look a lot better than he looks at the moment. I see pictures of him now: what are you doing? In one way he really knew how he wanted to look and another way he didn't know. The stuff that I made for him back then always looks really good on him on stage. Whenever he was left to his own devices it kind of went a bit strange. If you look at what those guys looked like before I hooked up with them; the first pictures that were taken for

that album 7800° Fahrenheit. Look at the clothing there; they looked like bad Twisted Sister. It's always baffled me.

People don't associate an image with Jon the way they do with, say, Lemmy or Rob Halford. Is that true?

I think with Jon there's been certain times when I've seen him in clothing and gone 'Oh my god, what are you wearing?!' That leather jacket that he's wearing now almost looks like something he'd wear on a motorbike; I just don't think it's very flattering. He's a really good looking guy. Richie, his style has always stayed the same and David Bryan has pretty much always stayed the same and Jon, it's almost like he just keeps trying to reinvent himself and I'm not really sure why that is. If you look back at how he looked back then he definitely looked like a rock star.

Did you do any other clothing for the band?

I actually did the clothing for him and his wife's wedding as well. They never actually had a full on wedding, it was more like a reception. I made Dorothea's dress and he had a turquoise silk suit that I made for him at the reception in New York.

Anything else?

Around the time just before I stopped working for them...Versace used to follow him a round all the time and it got to the point were they were basically giving him clothing. I refuse to give anybody free clothing. So all of a sudden he started to wear Versace suits and I'm not sure if he had some sort of a deal with them. He's been approached by these people and just given him clothing and that's probably the reason why there's been changes to the way he looks on stage especially with some of the suits and things like that. Obviously the guy has to grow up but you can still look rock.

Visit *raybrownfashion.com*

BRUNO, GIOIA

Born in Italy, Gioia Bruno is a singer and percussionist most famous for being a member of the vocal group Exposé. In 1998 she joined Richie Sambora's band as a singer and percussionist for the Australian leg of his world tour in support of the album *Undiscovered Soul.*

Visit *gioiabruno.com*

BRYAN, DAVID

A long time friend of Jon Bon Jovi, he was born David Bryan Rashbaum on February 7, 1962 in Edison, New Jersey. Classically trained and inspired by his father who was a trumpet player, Bryan took his first piano lesson at the age of seven.

As a teen Bryan became acquainted with progressive rock bands like Yes and shifted his interests towards popular music. He played keyboards in a local high school pop outfit called Transition with bassist Steve Sileo. He joined the ambitious 10 piece rhythm and blues covers band Atlantic City Expressway in 1979. His relationship with Jon would become cemented a few years later. However, Bryan left the band to study classical music at Rutgers University, although he dropped out to join the prestigious Juilliard School of Music located at the Lincoln Center in New York City. He had previously attended Herbert Hoover Junior High School and JP Stevens High School in New Jersey.

In the early eighties when Jon took up a low paid job at Power Station Studios in NYC, he enticed Bryan to join The Wild Ones, a band that he was in with guitarist Dave Sabo. One of the songs they performed at clubs in the city and back home in New Jersey was 'Runaway.' When Jon put a band together after having signed a record deal with PolyGram he asked Bryan if he was interested in the job. Knowing a record deal

with a major label may not be on the cards again, he agreed and joined the band that would become Bon Jovi although it meant quitting his studies and dropping out of Juilliard. He also shortened his name to David Bryan to make him sound more anglicised. Bassist Alec John Such then joined the camp and he in turn recommended drummer Ticco Torres. Richie Sambora replaced temporary guitarist Dave Sabo, and as a five piece band Bon Jovi flew into action

'In These Arms' (with JBJ/RS - *Keep The Faith*)
'Last Cigarette' (with JBJ - *Have A Nice Day*)

His non-Bon Jovi musical endeavours include composing an instrumental soundtrack to the 1991 horror film *Netherworld*. He also went on a quick US tour in 1991 as a member of Richie Sambora's band promoting Sambora's debut solo opus *Stranger In This Town*; Bryan also played keyboards and provided string arrangements on the album. He also co-wrote 'Rest In Peace' and 'Stranger In This Town' with Sambora. Bryan hooked

mid 1983.

As each album progressed Bryan's keyboard and piano skills became evident in the albums the band produced. He also provided backing vocals and has co-written the following songs:

'Breakout' (with JBJ – *Bon Jovi*)
'Love Lies' (with JBJ – *Bon Jovi*)
'(I Don't Wanna Fall) To The Fire' (with JBJ/RS - *7800° Fahrenheit*)
'The Hardest Part Is The Night' (with JBJ/RS - *7800° Fahrenheit*)
'Only Lonely' (with JBJ - *7800° Fahrenheit*)

up with Sambora again in 1998 for the guitarist's second solo album *Undiscovered Soul* and co-wrote the following songs:

'Fallen From Graceland'
(Sambora/Bryan/Supa)
'If God Was A Woman'
(Sambora/Bryan/Supa)
'Downside Of Love'
(Sambora/Bryan/Supa)

Bryan has also written music for the stage, notably the musical *Memphis,* which he co-wrote with the respected playwright Joe DiPietro and for which he composed the song 'Memphis Lives In Me.' This song is included in the box-set *100,000,000 Bon Jovi Fans Can't Be Wrong.* His debut solo album was a 14-track instrumental piece called *On A Full Moon* and was released in 1995 via Ignition Records. In 2000, he released his second opus, *Lunar Eclipse,* through Rounder/

Moon Junction Music. This contains all of the tracks from his first album with the exception of 'Midnight Voodoo' and 'Awakening.' He did, however, record three new songs for it: 'Second Chance,' 'I Can Love' and 'One A Full Moon.'

Bryan also contributed to Jon Bon Jovi's 1997 solo album *Destination Anywhere*, playing piano and accordion on the track 'Staring At Your

Window With A Suitcase In My Hand.'

In 1999, just before Bon Jovi were ready to hit the studio to record *Crush*, Bryan had a nasty accident with an electric power saw. It took some to recover, and his injured hand required extensive therapy. The severity of the accident meant he could

only play the keyboards for short sporadic periods of time and so the recording was delayed.

He's been involved in various charity projects, including Only Make Believe, where he is an honorary board member, and VH1's Save The Music. He has three kids with his ex-

CARLSSON, ANDREAS

Famed Swedish songwriter whose songs have sold over 100 million copies. He has been nominated for five Grammy Awards and has bagged two Emmys. He has written for and with a wide array of pop artists, including Hillary Duff, Westlife, Five and Britney Spears.

Carlsson co-wrote half the songs on *Bounce:* 'Everyday', 'Misunderstood', 'All About Lovin' You', 'Hook Me Up' and 'You Had Me From Hello.' He was also at the recording sessions in New Jersey and Stockholm, Sweden.

Interview:

When did you first meet the band?

I was introduced to Jon and Richie by Desmond Child who was already familiar with writing with Swedes, since Max Martin had co-written 'It's My Life' the year before...The songwriting session happened in different places; 'All About Loving You' was written in Desmond's Miami home, 'Misunderstood' on the Island of Capri and 'Everyday' in New Jersey. When you work with bands I guess you have to be flexible... We also wrote a few songs that became B-sides and bonus songs, like 'Hey I'm Alive' and 'Sad Song Night.'

What was it like to work with the band?

Jon and Richie are like a clock. You can immediately tell that they have been doing this for a long time, and sometimes it's hard to contribute to a machine that is so perfectly in tune. Jon always has a very clear picture

of what he is looking for in a song; he knows exactly what is Bon Jovi and what is not... Jon is the most talented, hardworking celebrity I have ever had the pleasure of working with. He has an amazing drive and has always come back over the years! Staying on top in an ever changing business is hard."

Do you have a favourite track?

I think 'All About Loving You' is my favourite! The video was amazing and the song is classic Bon Jovi, like something off 7800° Fahrenheit *or* Slippery When Wet.

Do you remember anything else?

My standout memory with Bon Jovi was flying in on a private jet to the Olympics in Salt Lake City in 2001. Since 9/11 was literally yesterday, the security was so over the top that we had to be escorted by three US Air Force jets from Vegas!"

Visit *andreascarlsson.se*

CARROLL, DINA

A British soul singer who enjoyed considerable success in the early to mid nineties. Her two hit albums are 1993's *So Close* and 1996's *Only Human*. She was last in the singles charts in 2001 with a cover of the Van Morrison song 'Someone Like You.'

In February 1994 Carroll sang backing vocals during Bon Jovi's performance of 'I'll Sleep When I'm Dead' at the Brit Awards at London's Alexandra Palace.

CASTLE DONINGTON

The home of the original Monsters Of Rock festival, which was first held in 1980 with Rainbow headlining. The village lies in the English Midlands, close to Derby and Nottingham. Download Festival has since replaced Monsters Of Rock. Bon Jovi first played at the grounds in 1985, supporting Marillion and headline act ZZ Top, before returning as headliners themselves in 1987.

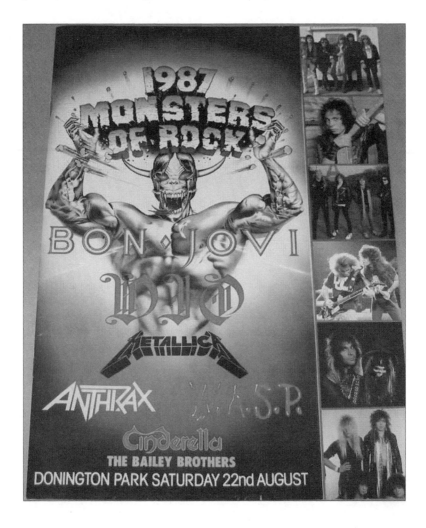

CHARLIE'S ANGELS: FULL THROTTLE

A 2003 comedy directed by McG and starring Cameron Diaz, Drew Barrymore and Lucy Liu. Bon Jovi contributed 'Livin' On A Prayer' to the soundtrack.

CHER

A flamboyant American singer and actress whose most popular songs include 'Believe' and 'If I Could Turn Back Time.' She has also appeared in a number of films such as *Mermaids*, *Moonstruck*, *Tea With Mussolini* and *Suspect*. Like most long-standing entertainers, she has constantly fallen in and out of favour with the public yet she has won just about every major entertainment award: an Emmy, a Grammy, three Golden Globes and even an Academy Award.

She has had a significant role in the world of Bon Jovi.

Tico Torres drummed in Cher's band prior to joining Bon Jovi.

Richie Sambora dated Cher in the late eighties until they split in 1990. During that period Jon and Sambora co-wrote and co-produced Cher's single 'We All Sleep Alone,' which peaked at Number 14 in the US singles chart when it was issued in April of '88. From the same album, 1987's *Cher*, Bon Jovi backed her on a remake of the Sonny and Cher classic 'Bang Bang.' Sambora also collaborated with Cher on the track 'Trail Of Broken Hearts,' which features on the soundtrack to the 1990 Hollywood movie *Days Of Thunder*.

Hugh McDonald played bass in Cher's band prior to replacing Alec John Such in Bon Jovi, appearing on her 1989 album *Heart Of Stone* and her 1991 album *Love Hurts*. McDonald, Dave Amato and Ron

Wikso of Sambora's solo band (during his *Undiscovered Soul* tour) can be seen and heard on her DVD *Live At The Mirage*.

Visit *cher.com*

CHILD, DESMOND

Starting with the group Desmond Child & Rouge in 1973, Child has become one of the most successful producers and songwriters in the music business. His first major brush with success came in the late seventies, when Child co-wrote 'I Was Made For Loving You' with Paul Stanley, which features on the 1979 KISS album *Dynasty*. As a producer and songwriter, Child has collaborated with the likes of Aerosmith, Meat Loaf, Scorpions, Joan Jett, Alice Cooper, Poison, Cher, Michael Bolton and Kelly Clarkson.

The story goes that in '86, on the advice of Paul Stanley of KISS, Jon Bon Jovi and Richie Sambora hooked up with Desmond Child; the trio then wrote the lyrics for 'You Give Love A Bad Name' in the cramped basement of Sambora's parent's house in New Jersey. At the same time they wrote 'Edge Of A Broken Heart', which ended up as the B-side to 'Never Say Goodbye' and which can be found on the box-set *100,000,000 Bon Jovi Fans Can't Be Wrong*. The trio wrote

a number of songs together, and made some demos at New Jersey's Century Productions. Since then Child has worked extensively with the band, co-writing the following songs:

'You Give Love A Bad Name' (with JBJ/RS - *Slippery When Wet*)
'Livin' On A Prayer' (with JBJ/RS - *Slippery When Wet*)
'Without Love' (with JBJ/RS - *Slippery When Wet*)
'Bad Medicine' (with JBJ/RS - *Bad Medicine*)
'Born To Be My Baby' (JBJ/RS - *Bad Medicine*)
'Blood On Blood' (with JBJ/RS - *Bad Medicine*)
'Wild Is The Wind' (with JBJ/RS/ Diane Warren - *Bad Medicine*)
'Keep The Faith' (with JBJ/RS - *Keep The Faith*)
I'll Sleep When I'm Dead' (with JBJ/ RS - *Keep The Faith*)
'Something For The Pain' (with JBJ/ RS - *These Days*)
'This Ain't A Love Song' (with JBJ/ RS - *These Days*)
'Hearts Breaking Even' (with JBJ - *These Days*)
'Diamond Ring' (with JBJ/RS - *These Days*)
'The Distance' (with JBJ/RS – *Bounce*)
'Misunderstood (with JBJ/RS and Andreas Carlsson – *Bounce*)

'All About Lovin' You' (with JBJ/RS and Andreas Carlsson – *Bounce*)
'Hook Me Up' (with JBJ/RS and Andreas Carlsson - *Bounce*)
'Bells Of Freedom' (with JBJ/RS – *Have A Nice Day*)
'Dirty Little Secret' (with JBJ/RS – *Have A Nice Day*)
'(You Want To) Make A Memory' (with JBJ/RS – *Lost Highway*)
'Lonely' (with JBJ and Daryl Brown – *Lost Highway*)

Child co-produced 2002's *Bounce* and was executive producer for 2005's *Have A Nice Day* and 2007's *Lost Highway*. He also had some creative input on Jon's first proper solo album *Destination Anywhere*, co-producing the track 'Ugly' with Eric Bazilian.
Visit *desmondchild.com*

CHRISTMAS IN THE STARS: STAR WARS CHRISTMAS ALBUM

A festive album released in November 1980 and produced by Meco Monardo and Tony Bongiovi at Power Station Studios in NYC. Jon, then John Bongiovi, was working at Power Station as a janitor and was asked by Tony if he wanted to sing on the track 'R2-D2 We Wish You A Merry Christmas.' It was a bit of extra cash for Jon who was struggling with his finances at that time. Jon is

credited on the album under his original name.

CINDERELLA

An American glam rock band formed in Philadelphia, Pennsylvania in 1982 by singer-guitarist Tom Keifer and bassist Eric Brittingham. Their early years involved a slight amendment to the line-up but it wasn't until Jon Bon Jovi came into the picture that guitarist Jeff LaBar and drummer Jim Drnec joined the fold.

One story is that Jon had seen Cinderella play at the Empire Rock Club in Philadelphia and was so psyched that he informed his label about the band. But Derek Shulman, Bon Jovi's former A&R man at PolyGram, explains: *"Jon heard some demos from Tom Keifer about the same time as I did from the same attorney. He thought, as I did, that they sounded great. I went down to Philly to see the band perform. They were OK...but needed a couple of new members to compliment Tom's vision. However, the music Tom had written was incredible. The manager of the band and myself found a new drummer and guitarist to play with Tom and Eric, the bassist. The band rehearsed long and hard. They then completed demos for the first LP. I played these to Jon who thought again as I did that the band sounded great. He was very supportive of mine and the company's work with the band.*

That was the extent of it...he was happy that the label was singing and breaking artists in the rock world."

To clarify, Keifer spoke to *Metal Hammer* in 1987: *"I'll say that he [Jon] definitely speeded things up but Derek Shulman was already interested in the band from a tape that had been brought to him. I know Jon was definitely a major influence in the situation because Derek has a lot of faith in Jon, he respects his opinion."*

Cinderella were signed to PolyGram in 1985 and released their debut album *Night Songs* the following year. In 1987, they supported Bon Jovi for seven months on the final part of the *Slippery When Wet* tour. Both bands performed at the Monsters Of Rock festival at Castle Donington on August 22, 1987 and they also performed at the Moscow Music Peace Festival on August 12-13, 1989.

The current Cinderella line-up is: singer-guitarist Tom Keifer, bassist Eric Brittingham, guitarist Jeff LaBar and drummer Fred Coury.

Visit *cinderella.net*

CITY OF ANGELS

A sequel to the 1994 film *The Crow,* whose star Brandon Lee died during filming. Jon was in the running to play the lead role of Eric Draven, a rock guitarist, but in the end it went to the French film star Vincent Perez. The film was released in 1996.

CITY OF MANCHESTER STADIUM

On Sunday, June 24, 2008 Bon Jovi played a sold out gig at the City of Manchester Stadium in Manchester, England. It was part of their stadium tour of the UK in support of *Lost Highway.* Writing in the city's newspaper the *Manchester Evening News,* one reviewer gave the concert 4/5 and enthused: *"...it is drummer*

Tico Torres that really drives this band. While Sambora's guitar licks and Bon Jovi's vocals grab the (Blaze of) glory it is Torres' unrelenting rhythmic assault at the business end of musical affairs which tee up the band's legendary BIG choruses and sing-along sections."

CLAPTON, ERIC

'Clapton is God' says it all, really. The famous slogan surely helped make Clapton an even bigger star after a fan had spray-painted the phrase on a wall in the Underground station in Islington (London), during Clapton's mid-sixties tenure with John Mayall's Bluesbreakers. As with any artist of his calibre there have been many books written about Clapton, and in 2007 he released his autobiography, simply called *The Autobiography.*

A blues fanatic, Clapton had also played in The Yardbirds in the early sixties (he left as a protest against the pop singles they had began to compose) but Cream was (and still is) his most famous band. Cream formed in 1966 and lasted until '68, after which he formed his next supergroup Blind Faith with Steve Winwood and Cream drummer Ginger Baker; they in turn lasted barely a year together. Another post-Cream musical endeavour was Derek and The Dominoes. His solo career began with a self-titled album in 1970 (when he was still in Derek and The Dominoes), but his career really kicked off in 1974 with the US Number 1 album *461 Ocean Boulevard.* Amongst his many accolades he has been inducted into the US Rock And Roll Hall Of Fame and has been awarded a CBE by the Queen. It's not surprising that the likes of Richie Sambora hold him in such high regard. Throughout his career he has composed many famous songs, including 'Badge' (Cream,) 'Layla' (Derek and The Dominoes) and 'Tears In Heaven' (solo.) His mastery of the guitar has given him the nickname 'Slowhand.'

Clapton is incredibly significant to Richie Sambora; the reason why Sambora picked up a guitar at the age

of 14 and began to play is because of guys like Clapton and Page. Sambora even worked with Clapton on the track 'Mr Bluesman' (from his debut album *Stranger In This Town*); Clapton played lead guitar and a solo while Sambora played the acoustic guitar.

Sambora told Paul Elliot of *Kerrang!* in July, 1993:

"When he [Clapton] came in to play, man, that was one of the best days of my life! It was right up there with being born!"

He even portrayed Clapton in the TV series *American Dreams*.

Visit *ericlapton.com*

CLASSIC ROCK

A glossy monthly magazine dedicated to classic rock and heavy metal. It was first published in 1998 and features on its staff many writers who made their names in magazines like *Sounds* and *Kerrang!* during the late seventies and eighties. Some well-known contributors include Geoff Barton, Dave Ling, Malcolm Dome, Jon Hotten, Pete Makowski, Tommy Udo and Mick Wall. The 100th issue was published in December, 2006.

Bon Jovi have been featured heavily in *Classic Rock* since the magazine was first published. Notable cover features include #3 (March/April, 1999), #25 (March, 2001), #45 (October, 2002), #55 (July, 2003) and #94 (July, 2006).

Visit *classicrockmagazine.com*

CLUB XANADU

Now a gay disco, Club Xanadu in Asbury Park, New Jersey was popular music club in the seventies and early eighties, before dance and disco became popular. Springsteen and Bon Jovi frequented the club, and Springsteen first performed his classic song 'Dancing In The Dark' there.

COLISÉE DE QUEBEC

This is the venue (in Quebec City) where the *Keep The Faith* world tour began on February 8, 1993. They returned there for a second date later on in the tour.

COLLINS, PETER

British born, American based rock producer who is famous for his work with Rush on four of their albums: *Power Windows* (1985), *Hold Your Fire* (1987), *Counterparts* (1993) and *Test For Echo* (1996). He has also produced for **Queensrÿche**, Alice Cooper and Alice In Chains. For Bon Jovi, Collins produced 1995's *These Days* which topped the British, German and Australian charts, and

the singles 'Always' and 'Someday I'll Be Saturday Night', which are featured on the 1994 collection *Cross Road*.

COLONIA

New York born Ticco Torres was raised in the borough of Colonia, in Middlesex County, New Jersey.

COLONIAL STADIUM

The *One Wild Night/Crush* tour began at Melbourne's Colonial Stadium on March 24, 2001. It was a charity gig in aid of the Australian emergency services, who were struggling to cope with natural disasters that were ravaging some rural parts of the country.

CONCERT FOR NEW YORK CITY

On October 20, 2001 Bon Jovi took part in VH1's 9/11 benefit concert, alongside such stellar performers as Paul McCartney, The Who and James Taylor.

COOPER, ALICE

An influential singer, songwriter and live performer, Alice Cooper is the archetypal ROCK LEGEND. The Alice Cooper Band's best-known albums are *Love It To Death, Killer,*

School's Out and *Billion Dollar Babies*. As a solo artist, his hit albums include *Welcome To My Nightmare, Trash* and *Hey Stoopid*. He continues to tour and make albums every couple of years. He has a radio show called *Nights With Alice Cooper*.

Tico Torres drummed for Cooper prior to joining Bon Jovi, and he's not the only member of Bon Jovi to have worked with him; bassist Hugh McDonald, an experienced session and live bass player, played on 1989's smash hit album *Trash* and 1991's *Hey Stoopid*. Jon Bon Jovi and Richie Sambora co-wrote 'Hell Is Living Without You' with Desmond Child and Cooper; the song features on his excellent 1988 album *Trash*.

Visit *alicecooper.com*

COUNT BASIE THEATER

After a series of benefit shows and a brief tour of Japan, the band finished 1991 with a Christmas charity gig on December 21 at the Count Basie Theater in Red Bank, New Jersey. The venue's seating capacity is less than 2,000. The band have played annual Christmas charity concerts over a number of years, and on October 18 and 19, 2001 Bon Jovi took part in a couple of four hour benefit concerts that were held at the Count Basie Theater, whose aim was to help raise money for the charity Alliance Of Neighbors. Bruce Springsteen also took part.

COUNTRY MUSIC

New Jersey rockers Bon Jovi and country music? Is that right? In 2007, they released the country-rock cross over album *Lost Highway* which, despite some mixed reviews, was a commercial hit, mostly due to the discovery of a country fanbase of which they were previously unaware. The album went into the *Billboard* 200 at Number 1, their first stay at the top of the US charts since *New Jersey* way back in 1987. It was a shrewd concept, even though it may have distanced the band from some of their rock fans. During its first week of release in the US, *Lost Highway* sold a credible 292,000 copies.

COUNTRY MUSIC TELEVISION (CMT)

Owned by MTV Networks, Country Music Television is an American cable station that broadcasts programmes and music videos relating to country music. A dedicated awards ceremony began in 2002 and has been held annually since. Bon Jovi won the 'Best Collaborative Video' award in 2006 for the single 'Who Says You Can't Go Home', and have won the 'Collaborative Award Of The Year' for 'Till We Ain't Strangers Anymore'.

COVENT GARDEN

A famous area in Central London, home to The Royal Opera House, market stalls and expensive stores. The area is also frequented by many talented street performers and buskers. On September 7, 1994 Jon and Richie played an acoustic set there to promote *Cross Road*. Approximately 3000 people witnessed their performance.

COWBOY WAY, THE

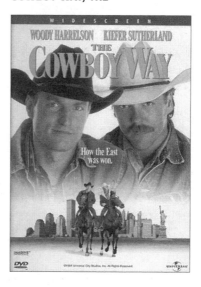

A 1994 comedy western starring Woody Harrelson, Kiefer Sutherland and Dylan McDermott. Bon Jovi contributed 'Good Guys Don't Always Wear White' to the soundtrack.

CRAWFORD, CINDY

Crawford is a famous American supermodel, but she is also a TV personality and actress, who was once married to actor Richard Gere.

Her first film was *Fair Game* with William Baldwin, but it was a huge flop when it was released in 1995.

She appeared in the music video (and on the CD cover) of Bon Jovi's single 'Please Come Home For Christmas', which reached Number 7 in the UK charts in '94 but which failed to chart in the States.

Visit *cindy.com*

CROSS ROAD:
THE BEST OF BON JOVI

Bon Jovi's first compilation album, it also included two new tracks: 'Always' and 'Someday I'll Be Saturday Night.' A special US edition US, featuring a bonus disc, was also released. *Cross Road* was the last Bon Jovi release to feature original bassist Alec John Such on the cover. Apparently, Richie Sambora had joked that they should name the album *Elvis Is Dead But We're Not.*

Cross Road was issued in the UK on October 22, 1994 and hit Number 1, spending an exhaustive 68 weeks in the charts. It became the biggest selling album in Britain in 1994. Elsewhere it reached Number 1 in 18 countries, but in the States it peaked at Number 8 in the *Billboard* 200. It went on to sell over 20 million copies and is still a consistent seller. Coinciding with the CD's original

release, a VHS collection of 16 music videos was also released, bearing the same title; fans were especially pleased as four of those videos had not been released before.

A special deluxe edition box-set was released in 2007. The three disc set features a DVD of the band at Wembley Stadium (*Live In London*), a CD of rarities, B-sides and live tracks, together with the original CD which was released in '94.

Track Listing:
1. 'Living' On A Prayer'
2. 'Keep The Faith'
3. 'Someday I'll Be Saturday Night'
4. 'Always'
5. 'Wanted Dead Or Alive'
6. 'Lay Your Hands On Me'
7. 'You Give Love A Bad Name'
8. 'Bed Of Roses'
9. 'Blaze Of Glory'
10. 'Prayer '94' *(US release)* / 'In These Arms' *(International release)* / 'Tokyo Road' *(Japan release)*
11. 'Bad Medicine'
12. 'I'll Be There For You'
13. 'In And Out Of Love'
14. 'Runaway'
15. 'Never Say Goodbye' *(Bonus track - International release)*

Special Deluxe Edition Bonus CD:

1. 'The Radio Saved My Life Tonight'
2. 'Wild In The Streets'
3. 'Diamond Ring'
4. 'Good Guys Don't Always Wear White'
5. 'The Boys Are Back In Town'
6. 'Edge Of A Broken Heart'
7. 'Postcards From The Wasteland' *(Demo)*
8. 'Blood On Blood' *(Live)*
9. 'Let It Rock'
10. 'Starting All Over Again'

11. 'Blood Money' *(Live)*
12. 'Save A Prayer'
13. 'Lucky' *(Demo)*
14. 'Why Aren't You Dead?'
15. 'Raise Your Hands'

Author's Review:

At best, Cross Road *is a predictable collection of songs. All the ones you'd expect to be here are but as it's a 'best of' rather than a 'greatest hits' the band could have used some imagination and handpicked some obscure gems to spice things up. The special edition is worth getting if you see it on eBay or any other secondhand/auction site because there are some forgotten songs in the mix, as well as some demos and live tracks. Also, it would have been more appropriate to include 'Always' and 'Someday I'll Be Saturday Night' as bonus tracks.*

Nevertheless, it's fun stuff and a neat introduction to newcomers, but 'In These Arms' does not represent the best of Bon Jovi; they've almost entirely forgotten their first two albums, which is a shame.

Rating ***

CROSS ROAD: THE VIDEOS

Released in 1994 to accompany album of the same name, this VHS/Laserdisc collection runs for 80 minutes. It features 16 of the band's music videos, including four previously unreleased ones. It has since been deleted.

Track Listing:
1. 'Livin' On A Prayer'
2. 'Keep The Faith'
3. 'Wanted Dead Or Alive'
4. 'Lay Your Hands On Me'

5. 'You Give Love A Bad Name'
6. 'Bed Of Roses' *(Edited)*
7. 'Blaze Of Glory' *(Previously unreleased)*
8. 'In These Arms'
9. 'Bad Medicine' *(First version)*
10. 'I'll Be There For You'
11. 'Dry County' *(Previously unreleased)*
12. 'Living In Sin'
13. 'Miracle' *(Previously unreleased)*
14. 'I Believe'
15. 'I'll Sleep When I'm Dead'
16. 'Always' *(Previously unreleased)*

CRUSH (ALBUM)

Bon Jovi had released their previous studio album (*These Days*) in 1995; *Crush* was released in 2000. A lot can happen in the music business in five years. By February 2000, *Crush* – which had the working title of *Sex Sells* - had been recorded at Jon's brand new personal studio in New Jersey, Sanctuary II Studio, with producers Luke Ebbin and Desmond Child; Jon and Richie Sambora oversaw the production. The bulk of the songwriting was completed by Jon, Sambora, and famed Swedish songwriters Jay Orpin and Max Martin. Interestingly, the cover sleeve doesn't actually give any songwriting details which afforded some critics the chance to attack the band for relying too much on other songwriters.

To emphasise that Bon Jovi's new album harked back to the past, 'It's My Life' references Jon's fictional characters Tommy and Gina, who were made famous in 'Livin' On A Prayer.' The album's photography was by the acclaimed German lensman Olaf Heine. 'Save The World' was Jon's proposed theme for the movie *Armageddon*, but the produc-

ers had already claimed Aerosmith's 'I Don't Wanna Miss A Thing.'

Crush was released in the UK on June 10, 2000 and hit Number 1, spending 29 weeks in the charts. Given the fact that they had returned to their melodic hard rock roots after a period of "experimentation" with *Keep The Faith* and *These Days*; *Crush* sold considerably well (nine million worldwide), and was a Number 1 smash hit in Denmark, Finland, Switzerland, Italy, Austria, Germany and Belgium. It peaked at Number 9 in the American *Billboard* 200. The success of the album was no doubt helped by its lead single, the European Number 1 hit 'It's My Life', and its accompanying video directed by Wayne Isham. The album had a further two singles releases: 'Say It Isn't So' and 'Thank You For Loving Me.'

A special edition of the album with a bonus disc was also released.

In 2001, *Crush* was nominated for the 'Best Rock Album' at the prestigious Grammy Awards.

Track Listing:
1. 'It's My Life'
2. 'Say It Isn't So'
3. 'Thank You For Loving Me'
4. 'Two Story Town'
5. 'Next 100 Years'
6. 'Just Older'
7. 'Mystery Train'
8. 'Save The World'
9. 'Captain Crash & The Beauty Queen From Mars'
10. 'She's A Mystery'
11. 'I Got The Girl'
12. 'One Wild Night'
13. 'I Could Make A Living Out Of Lovin' You' *(Demo – Feat. on all territories except America)*
14. 'Neurotica' *(Japan and Australia only)* / 'It's My Life' *(Dave*

Bascombe Mix - bonus track on UK edition only)

15. 'Say It Isn't So' *(UK Mix - bonus track on UK edition only)*

Special Edition Bonus CD:
(Live From Osaka)
1. 'Runaway'
2. 'Mystery Train'
3. 'Rockin' In The Free World'
4. 'Just Older'
5. 'It's My Life'
6. 'Someday I'll Be Saturday Night'

Author's Review:

After Keep The Faith *and* These Days *in the nineties it was almost as if Bon Jovi had dumped the melodic rock sound that had made them famous in the previous decade. With* Crush *they had made a conscious decision to divert back to the famil-iar rock sound which would lead the way for* Bounce *and* Have A Nice Day. Crush *is a decent enough album and its lead single, 'It's My Life', has become a fan favourite which will no doubt appear on a future greatest hits collection.*

My main qualm is that there are too many production effects and too few ballsy guitar riffs. 'Thank You for Loving Me' is tedious and slushy and 'Two Story Town' is a forgettable mid-paced ballad. 'Save the World' is just awful; a bland melody and a poor set of lyrics. On the other hand, 'She's A Mystery' is actually quite seductive.

Also, 'Next 100 Years' is a curious song: it begins with a riff that is a step in the right direction but it quickly heads off into the wrong direction (i.e. dull ballad) before Sambora lets rip with a big solo and the song gets faster and heavier. 'Captain Crash & the Beauty Queen from Mars' is a likeable cheeky soft rock tune. 'One Wild Night' and 'I Could Make a Living Out Of Loving You' are good Bon Jovi stadium rock standards.

Crush is an almost even balance of good mid-paced rock songs and average ballads. It will probably be remembered as 'the album that's got 'It's My Life' on it' more than anything else. A good effort but not a patch on the likes of Slippery When Wet.

Rating ***

CRUSH TOUR (2000)

After playing some intimate warm up gigs (including one at the famed House of Blues in Chicago) the *Crush* tour began in Japan on July 12, 2000. Further shows were scheduled in the Far East before the European stint began on August 5 in Finland. By the time the European dates had been completed on September 8, the band had played in Sweden, Germany, Austria and the UK. The North American leg began in October and carried through to the end of the year. They flew through 11 states and played two sold out shows in Canada.

CRUSH TOUR (DVD)

Released on DVD in 2001, *The Crush Tour* is Bon Jovi's second full concert release. The VHS release is a slightly edited version. The show was recorded at Letzigrund Stadion in Zurich, Switzerland on August 30, 2000. The filming was directed by Rudi Dolezal and Hannes Rossacher. The bonus features include the usual gallery and photography bits as well as interviews with the band and music videos for 'It's My Life' and 'Say It Isn't So.'

Track Listing:
1. 'Intro' / 'Livin' On A Prayer'
2. 'You Give Love A Bad Name'
3. 'Captain Crash & The Beauty Queen From Mars'
4. 'Say It Isn't So'
5. 'One Wild Night'
6. 'Born To Be My Baby'
7. 'It's My Life'
8. 'Bed Of Roses'
9. 'Two Story Town'
10. 'Just Older'
11. 'Runaway' *(Acoustic)*
12. 'Lay Your Hands On Me'
12. 'I'll Sleep When I'm Dead'
13. 'Bad Medicine'
14. 'Wanted Dead Or Alive'
15. 'I'll Be There For You'
16. 'Next 100 Years'
17. 'Someday I'll Be Saturday Night'
18. 'Keep The Faith'

CRY WOLF

A predictable 2006 serial killer film directed by Jeff Wadlow, in which Jon Bon Jovi has a supporting role as a teacher of journalism. The film is basically about a killer, known simply as *The Wolf.* The movie was released with little fanfare, although it is interesting to note that it was made after Wadlow had scooped a million dollars at the 2002 Chrysler Film Competition.

D

DAN REED NETWORK

There are two primary connections between Dan Reed Network - a funk rock band from Portland, Oregon led by Dan Reed - and Bon Jovi. Both bands were signed to Mercury Records in the mid-eighties by Derek Shulman, who was Bon Jovi's A&R man at PolyGram at the time. Also, Bruce Fairbairn (who had produced *Slippery When Wet* and *New Jersey*) produced Dan Reed Network's 1988 self-titled debut and 1991's *The Heat*.

Promoting their album *Slam*, Dan Reed Network supported Bon Jovi on some UK and European dates in late 1989 and early 1990 during the *New Jersey Syndicate* tour. Reviewing a show at the Palais des Sports in Paris on December 5, 1989 *RAW* scribe Sylvie Simmons wrote:

"Dan Reed and Co. are a great lot to see live" and Bon Jovi *"somehow managed to keep the magic of playing rock 'n' roll onstage."*

Visit *danreed.com*

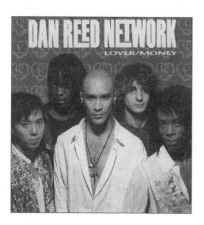

DARKNESS, THE

An English glam rock band from Suffolk, led by brothers Justin and Dan Hawkins. Their 2003 debut album *Permission To Land* was a huge success, reaching Number 1 in the UK charts and achieving sales of 1.5 million copies. They picked up a lot of fans by supporting the likes of Def Leppard and Deep Purple. Their sophomore album, *One Way Ticket To Hell...And Back*, was produced by Roy Thomas Baker, famous

for his work with Queen during the seventies. Despite selling out arenas and even having some success in the States, they were ridiculed by many fellow artists, including Jon Bon Jovi who - as quoted in *Classic Rock* - allegedly said:

"I hate The Darkness. They suck. They're trying to mimic Spinal Tap. I was given their album a while ago. The first time I played it I couldn't believe what I was hearing. I had to play it again. It was just awful."

With Justin Hawkins out of the picture and further changes to the lineup, The Darkness are now known as Stone Gods.

Visit *thedarknessrock.com*

DAUGHTRY

Daughtry is the namesake of former *American Idol* winner Chris Daughtry. They are a five piece band whose self-titled debut album was released in 2006, reaching Number 1 in the *Billboard* Hot 100. Their first two singles, 'It's Not Over' and 'Home', were chart hits in America.

Daughtry supported Bon Jovi on the first North American leg of their 2007/08 *Lost Highway* tour. This road jaunt included some famous gigs. On November 4 and 7, 2007, Daughtry supported them at the Prudential Center in New Jersey to celebrate its opening, and they were also supporting Bon Jovi for their record breaking five sold out nights at Toronto's Air Canada Centre. Those dates were:

December 6, 2007
December 7, 2007

March 10, 2008
March 12, 2008
March 13, 2008

Visit *daughtryofficial.com*

DAVIDBRYAN.COM

This is the official website of Bon Jovi bassist and backing vocalist David Bryan. It's a visually attractive site and features the following pages: 'Welcome', 'News & Press', 'Ask

David', 'Discography', 'Biography', 'Eyecandy', 'Store' and 'Links.'

Visit *davidbryan.com*

DAVIES, RAY

Legendary English singer-songwriter Davies achieved fame as lead singer of revered band The Kinks. He

Duvall and Randy Quaid. The film was directed by Tony Scott and written by Robert Towne.

With Bruce Foster, Richie Sambora co-wrote and produced the song 'Trail Of Broken Hearts' which features on the soundtrack to this film. Cher handles the vocals. Other artists

has also enjoyed a successful solo career: his latest album *Working Man's Café* was released in 2007.

In September, 2002 Ray Davies joined Bon Jovi on stage for at a one-off gig at London's diminutive but famous Shepherd's Bush Empire. Together, they performed an acoustic version of 'Celluloid Heroes,' a hit for The Kinks in 1972. The entire gig was available to download live on a global webcast to 60 countries.

On Saturday 28 June, 2003 Ray Davies joined Bon Jovi on stage in Hyde Park, London, for a rendition of The Kinks classic 'Lola,'

Visit *raydavies.info*

DAYS OF THUNDER

An action-packed 1990 film about NASCAR racing, starring Tom Cruise, Nicole Kidman, Robert

appearing on the soundtrack include Tina Turner, David Coverdale and Guns N' Roses.

DEF LEPPARD

A British rock band, often inaccurately called a heavy metal outfit largely because they rose to fame during the now legendary New Wave Of British Heavy Metal from around 1979-1981; other bands from that period include Saxon, Iron Maiden, Venom and Diamond Head.

Def Leppard formed in Sheffield, a working class city in the North East of England, in 1977; in the eighties their classic albums *Pyromania* (1983) and *Hysteria* (1987) made them the biggest band in the States for a while, and by the end of the decade they had sold more albums than any other band in America. Their best-known songs include 'Bringin' On The Heartbreak', 'Photograph', 'Animal', 'Pour Some Sugar On Me' and 'Love Bites.' The group have been hit by tragedy on two occasions: in 1984, drummer Rick Allen lost his left arm in a car accident yet he re-learned to play the drums using just his right hand and his feet. A specially designed electronic kit was created for him by Simmons, a British drum manufacturer. Then, in 1991 co-lead guitarist Steve Clark died of alcoholism. Their popularity in their home country never quite matched that in the USA. However, in 2008 their album *Songs From The Sparkle Lounge* was a Top 20 hit and

Joe Elliot

their arena tour with Whitesnake was largely sold out.

Def Leppard and Bon Jovi both performed at the Philadelphia Live 8 concert (held at the Museum of Art) on July 2, 2005. It is also well-known that Jon and Def Leppard lead singer Joe Elliot are good friends; Elliot also happens to live in Dublin, Jon's favourite city to play. Both bands were often compared with each other in the eighties, as their particular style of commercial arena rock shared similar traits.

Visit *defleppard.com*

DESTINATION ANYWHERE (ALBUM)

Jon Bon Jovi's second solo album, although as this is an actual album rather than a soundtrack, it could be termed his first "proper" solo release. Many of the songs were written in 1996 when Jon was filming *The Leading Man* in London. With Steve Lironi as producer, the album was recorded at various studios sporadically throughout '96. He also collaborated with a few songwriters notably Dave Stewart and Lironi, as well as Eric Bazilian, Gregg Wells and Mark Hudson.

Jon managed to attract some notable musicians for the project, in-

cluding his Bon Jovi colleagues, bassist Hugh McDonald and pianist and accordion player David Bryan. Other contributors included guitarists Bobby Bandiera, Lance Quinn and Aldo Nova, drummer Kenny Aronoff, and even Desmond Child, who can be heard playing the tuba on 'Ugly.'

Destination Anywhere was released in the UK on June 28, 1997 and peaked at Number 2, although in the States it only managed to make it to Number 31 in the *Billboard* 200. The Japanese release contained 'I Talk To Jesus' as a bonus track, and the French release contained 'Sad Song Night' as a bonus; both are demo versions.

Despite a solo tour, sales were sluggish and a special edition with a live CD was released later on to boost interest in the album. A 45-minute film starring Hollywood actors such as Demi Moore was also released to help promote the album. It has since sold over three million copies, going Platinum in Europe and Gold in Britain.

Track Listing:
1. 'Queen Of New Orleans'
2. 'Janie, Don't Take Your Love To Town'
3. 'Midnight In Chelsea'
4. 'Ugly'
5. 'Staring At Your Window With A Suitcase In My Hand'
6. 'Every Word Was A Piece Of My Heart'
7. 'It's Just Me'
8. 'Destination Anywhere'
9. 'Learning How To Fall'
10. 'Naked'
11. 'Little City'

12. 'August 7, 4:15'
13. 'Cold Hard Heart' *(Demo version)*

Author's Review

I suppose Destination Anywhere *could be termed 'experimental.' The production is unlike any Bon Jovi release; there are some modern sound effects, female backing vocals and drum loops; and instruments like a tuba and accordion are used. All of this has minimal affect because the album lacks charm and excitement. Above all else it's cold and over-produced. Jon sings in a low register and all the songs are mid-paced (or just slow) and a bit too contrived. Some of the album's better songs include the opening track 'Queen Of New Orleans,' which has an interesting melody; the catchy 'Naked' is a worthwhile song; 'Midnight In Chelsea' and 'Ugly' are both well-composed if a little drab; but the prize for the most miserable song goes to 'Cold Hard Heart'. The songwriting is quite strong with some deeply personal and emotional lyrics. Ultimately, it's an album that certainly won't appeal to the average Bon Jovi fan and rock fans will probably detest it. It doesn't engage the listener enough and it's over produced. I suspect he was just trying to steer clear from the typical Bon Jovi sound which he didn't bother doing with* Blaze Of Glory, *so I guess he should not be treated too harshly for that. Nice try but better luck next time...*

Rating **

DESTINATION ANYWHERE: THE FILM

A short film that was made as a companion piece to Jon Bon Jovi's second solo album; the film takes the

basic themes of the album as well as obviously using the music. The film's premise revolves around Jon, played by Jon Bon Jovi, as he struggles to deal with his spiralling debts, gambling addiction and his failing marriage. When he and his wife Janie, a nurse, find an abandoned baby they begin to reassess their troubled life. *Destination Anywhere* was released in 1997 and was directed by Mark Pellington. The film also stars Demi Moore, Kevin Bacon and Whoopi Goldberg. It was released on DVD in 2005.

DESTINATION ANYWHERE TOUR (1997)

To promote his first proper solo album, Jon committed himself to a small

tour playing shows in Europe and North America. The tour was a blend of TV and radio performances and small gigs. His band, The Big Dogs, featured bassist Hugh McDonald, guitarist Bobby Bandiera, keyboardist Jerry Cohen, percussionist Everett Bradley and drummer Shawn Pelton. On August 18, 1997 his tour came to an end so that Jon could return to his movie work. In 1998, he did some charity gigs and made appearances at various awards shows, but much of his time was spent on film sets.

DIDDLEY, BO

Mississippi-born singer and guitarist, recognised as a leading figure in the early years of rock and roll, began his career on the blues circuit. He was born Ellas Otha Bates. Richie Sambora contributed guitars to the tracks 'Can I Walk You Home' and 'Oops! Bo Diddley' on Diddley's 1996 album *A Man Amongst Men*. According to Laura Jackson's biography, as a young guitar novice in 1975, Jon set about trying to learn Didley's 1955 tune 'Bo Diddley'. Finding it too difficult to master the chords, he took up guitar lessons again. Bo Diddley died on June 2, 2008 at the age of 78, after suffering heart failure.

DISTURBED

A metal band from Chicago in Illinois. Their 2005 album *Ten Thousand Fists* kept Bon Jovi's *Have A Nice Day* album from reaching the top spot in the US *Billboard* 200. However, *Have A Nice Day* did manage to make it to the Number 1 spot in eight other countries.

Visit *disturbed1.com*

DOKKEN

A melodic rock band from LA led by Don Dokken. They formed in 1976 and toured with bands like Judas Priest, Ratt, Scorpions and Twisted Sister. The most revered and successful line-up of the band remains the original one: Don Dokken on vocals, George Lynch on lead guitars, Jeff Pilson on bass and Mick Brown on drums. They had their biggest successes in the eighties with such albums as *Tooth And Nail*,

Under Lock And Key and *Back For The Attack*. Although a heavier band than Bon Jovi, they would share a similar fan base. Dokken supported Bon Jovi in 1995.

Don Dokken:

"I knew Jon back in the day when he was just starting out; we hung out at [Ratt drummer] Bobby Blotzer's [place] after their show with Ratt at The Forum in LA. It was the glory days for most of us then, then the nineties came and everything changed...We toured with them in about '95 and their fans didn't care less about us even though we have sold millions as well. It was an eye opener! After the first show Richie says to me, 'It's a whole new world of fans out there.' Of all the bands from our era, Bon

Jovi have survived through all the music changes the best, and I give them a high-five for that. They're still a great band: tight, professional and still nice guys. That's hard to be when your one of the biggest bands on the planet..."

Visit *dokken.net*

DOME, MALCOLM

A respected and very successful rock/metal writer, author and broad-caster, Malcolm Dome has been writing about music on a professional basis since joining *Record Mirror* in 1979. He has written books on Metallica, Van Halen and AC/DC, and his first book on the New Jersey band (and the first ever official band biography) *Bon Jovi: Faith And Glory* was published in 1994 by Sanctuary Publishing Ltd; 144 pages long, it is now out of print.

His collaborative book (written with Mick Wall) *Bon Jovi: All Night Long* was published in 1995 by Omnibus Press. In 1996 the pair published, also through Omnibus Press, not one but two books on the band: *Bon Jovi: Live!* and *The Complete Guide To The Music Of Bon Jovi*. He also provided the liner notes for the unofficial release *The Power Station Years: 1980-1983* by 'John Bongiovi.'

Dome says,

"For me Bon Jovi have had enduring, enormous success, because they're successfully balanced integrity, commercial demands, marketing and musicianship. Few others can claim to have achieved such a balance. I was approached about writ-

ing a Bon Jovi book by Castle in the early part of the 1990s. I asked Bon Jovi themselves whether such a book could have the stamp of official approval - to which they agreed. So that book became the first official Bon Jovi biography."

As well as contributing to *Classic Rock* and *Metal Hammer*, Dome broadcasts on the London-based radio station *Total Rock*.

Visit *totalrock.com*

DOMINION THEATRE

Bon Jovi played their first UK headlining gig at London's Dominion Theatre on May 23, 1985. A ticket for the show cost just £3.50!

John Tucker, author of *Suzie Smiled...The New Wave Of British Heavy Metal*, was in the crowd.

He remembers:

"It wasn't long before Bon Jovi were back in the UK, this time headlining five medium-sized venues. Support came from Lee Aaron, meaning that the package had something for the boys as well as something for the girls! The new album 7800° Fahrenheit *had received a fair mauling in the UK press, with* Kerrang! *awarding it three 'K' out of five ('I can only say that this is a pale imitation of the Bon Jovi we have got to know and learnt to love" commented reviewer Howard Johnson in* Kerrang! #93, *May 2-15 1985), and in* Sounds *(April 27, 1985) Mary Anne Hobbs put the boot in with a two-star review ('...the sad new opus barely bubbles at ten degrees, let alone erupting in the dangerous fashion that its moniker would have us believe...')*

'In And Out Of Love' was the first single, pulled off the album in advance off the tour and flipped with live cuts from the 1984 KISS tour, presumably to show what the band could do on stage. Again, the release received a thumbs-down in Kerrang! ('The crap the Yanks are feeding us now is fast draining my admiration of American rock,' wrote Mark Putterford in Kerrang! #95, May 30-June 12, 1985,) and it was against the backdrop of this media backlash that the band arrived in the UK in May, 1985. Had the tour gone badly, things might have been very different for the future of Jon Bon Jovi and the guys, but the performances wowed the critics and had them lining up behind the band and showering praise once more.

That said, technical difficulties did their best to wreck the showcase show at London's Dominion Theatre. With Jon Bon Jovi's parents and then girlfriend in one of the boxes and a packed house of adoring fans, the

PA blew not once but twice during 'Roulette,' one of the band's trademark songs: the first time led to the customary levels of confusion and an attempt to restart where things left off; on the second occasion Bon Jovi himself seized an acoustic guitar and kept things rolling until the power was restored once more: an act of sheer class. After that, he could do no wrong, and despite the fact that the sound was pretty poor for the rest of the evening, the band were conquering heroes. As far as the UK was concerned, that was the night that made the band, and Steffan Chirazi's observation in Sounds (June 8, 1985) that 'this gig will have been the last time you'll ever pay £3.50 to watch Bon Jovi' hit the nail fair and square on the head."

DRY COUNTY

Written by Jon Bon Jovi, 'Dry County' was issued in the UK on March 26, 1994 and reached Number 9, spending six weeks in the charts. It was the sixth and final single taken from Keep The Faith. The album version runs for nine minutes 52 seconds, although it was edited down to six minutes for the single release. It remains the band's longest song. The UK release consisted of a live version of 'Stranger In This Town' and 'Blood Money.' It was a Number 1 hit in Latin America but was not issued in the United States because of the album's relative lack of success there.

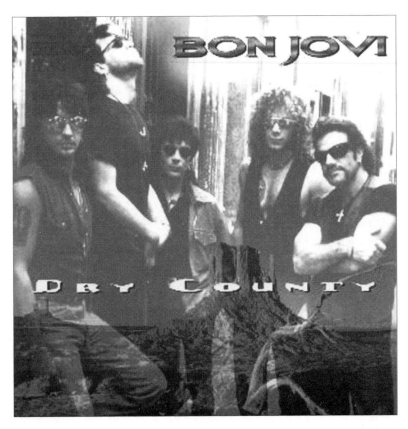

E

EBBIN, LUKE

A famed songwriter and record producer, Luke Ebbin co-produced the album *Crush*, which sold over eight million copies and was nominated for a Grammy in 2001 for 'Best Rock Album'. He also co-produced the twice Grammy-nominated *Bounce*, which has sold over six million copies.

Ebbin has worked with a variety of artists, including Melissa Etheridge, The All-American Rejects, Shannon Noll and Dirty Harry.

EDGE OF A BROKEN HEART

A song which was written and recorded during the making of *Slippery When Wet,* although it never made the final cut, a decision which Jon now regrets. It was, however, released in 1987 as a B-side to the American version of the single 'Never Say Goodbye'. It re-

ceived so much airplay that it became a Top 40 hit in America, peaking at Number 38 in the *Billboard* Hot 100. Understandably it has since become a firm fan favourite. It was included in the soundtrack to the 1987 comedy *Disorderlies*, starring The Fat Boys and Ralph Bellamy. It is also included in the box-set *100,000,000 Bon Jovi Fans Can't Be Wrong* and the two disc special edition of *Cross Road.*

EDISON

A small city in Middlesex County, New Jersey where David Bryan was raised. It is apparently one of the safest cities in the whole of America.

EDTV

Directed by Ron Howard and released in 1999, *EdTV* is a film about a video store clerk (played by Matthew McConaughey) who agrees to have his life filmed for 24 hours. The soundtrack features the Bon Jovi song 'Real Life.'

ESTES, WILL

An American TV and film actor who appeared in the music video to the Bon Jovi single 'It's My Life'. He has starred in *American Dreams* and *Law & Order*, and his film credits include *Mimic 2* and *U-571*, which also starred Jon Bon Jovi.

EVERYDAY

The first single from the 2002 album *Bounce*. Written by Jon, Richie Sambora and Andreas Carlsson, it reflects the band's response to the 9/11 terrorist attacks on New York City. It was issued in the UK on September 28, 2002 and peaked at Number 5, spending six weeks in the charts. The song did not chart in the *Billboard* Hot 100 but it made it to Number 38 in the Adult Contemporary Chart and was a Number 1 hit in Canada. In 2003 'Everyday' won a Grammy nomination for 'Best Rock Performance By Duo/Group.' The music video was directed by Joseph Kahn.

Track Listing:
1. 'Everyday'
2. 'Lucky'

3. 'No Regrets'
4. 'Standing'

EXTREME

A rock band from Massachusetts. Extreme supported Bon Jovi during the American leg of their 1993 *Keep The Faith* tour, beginning on June 24 at the Open Air Theater in San Diego. The tour finished on August 8 at the Merriweather Post Pavilion in Columbia, Maryland.

Extreme released four albums between forming in 1985 and splitting up in 1996. Their 1990 album *Pornograffitti* was undoubtedly their biggest mainstream success. Extreme's most famous song is the ballad 'More Than Words,' released in the States on March 23, 1991. Their lead singer Gary Cherone later had a brief sojourn in Van Halen for the unpopular *Van Halen III* album. Extreme reformed in 2007.

F

FAIRBAIRN, BRUCE

The late Bruce Fairbairn was a revered Canadian rock producer who came to prominence in 1977 as the producer of Prism's self-titled debut album. He went on to produce their next three albums and also played horn in the band; incidentally he brought horn arrangements into much of his work with other bands. But he is perhaps better known for his work with Canadian melodic rockers Loverboy, and also with Blue Öyster Cult, whose 1983 album *The Revölution By Night* is an absolute classic. He has also produced albums by KISS, AC/DC, INXS, Chicago, Dan Reed Network and Aerosmith.

Fairbairn played an integral role in the early years of Bon Jovi's career. Impressed by his collaborations with Loverboy, Fairbairn was hired by Bon Jovi to produce their third opus, *Slippery When Wet*. After the disappointment of *7800° Fahrenheit,* they needed to make an album that would blow their fans away and for that they had to have the right producer. The recording took place over a two month period at Little Mountain

Sound Studios in Vancouver, Canada. Fairbairn's protégé was studio engineer Bob Rock, who would later find enormous success as a record producer in his own right.

Keen to make a similar album, the band hired Fairbairn to produce their follow-up album *New Jersey,* which was recorded during a three month period in early '88, again at Fairbairn's favourite studio in Vancouver. Finally, Fairbairn teamed up with the band for a third time in January, 1999 to produce the single 'Real Life' which was composed specifically for the film *EdTV,* directed by Ron Howard and starring Matthew McConaughey and Rob Reiner.

Sadly, Fairbairn died on May 17, 1999 at his home in Vancouver. He was found by Jon Anderson of Yes; they had been recording the Yes album *The Ladder* at his Armoury Studios. He was 49 years old when he died, and the exact cause of his death is still unclear. He was given a posthumous award by the Canadian Music Hall of Fame in 2000.

Commenting on his character, former Scorpions drummer Herman Rarebell, says:

"It was amazing to work with Bruce. He gave us so many good suggestions for recording; it was really amazing. Like 'try this,' or 'try that.' I'm sad he's not with us anymore!"

Marc Storace of the heavy metal band Krokus also recalls:

"One afternoon, whilst tinkering away in my garden, I experienced a mild flashback of Bruce throwing karate-kicks at the punch-bag he had rigged up in the Little Mountain Sound Studios in Vancouver, Canada way back in '84. I also pictured us

sitting round the table at his home whilst his dear wife served us the most delicious dinner. He was a fine human being.

He was clever enough to organise a schedule so that those musicians who did not need to be in the studio that day felt free to check out the city and it's whereabouts or do whatever they fancied! Vancouver is a pretty cool place to hang out and we even drove over to revisit Seattle one day. Another time when my ex-wife Alice flew in, he let the two of us borrow his apartment up in the mountains, so we could enjoy a cool weekend alone skiing down the famous Whistler!'

FALCON, BILLY

Falcon is a Nashville-based singer-songwriter who has worked with such esteemed artists as Cher, Stevie Nicks, Manfred Mann's Earth Band and Bon Jovi. He is also a solo artist in his own right, having released his debut *Billy Falcon's Burning Rose* in 1977. His latest release, *Burning Man,* was issued in 2006.

Jon and Falcon co-wrote 'Sometimes It's A Bitch', the opening track on Stevie Nicks' 1991 collection *Timespace - The Best of Stevie Nicks.* Jon Bon Jovi co-produced Falcon's 1991 album *Pretty Blue World* which

was released on Jon's own label Jambco. The album's lead song, 'Power Windows', remains Falcon's sole hit single in the *Billboard* Hot 100.

The track listing for *Pretty Blue World* is:
1. 'Power Windows'
2. 'Heaven's Highest Hill'
3. 'What She Will'
4. 'Pretty Blue World'
5. 'Die Twice'
6. 'Still Got A Prayer'
7. 'Not Funny Anymore'
8. 'My New Girlfriend'
9. 'This Burning Love'
10. 'Getting' Married In The Morning'
11. 'Oh Boy'

Falcon has also co-written the following songs with Bon Jovi:

'Undivided' (from *Bounce*)
'Bounce' (from *Bounce*)
'Last Man Standing' (from *Have A Nice Day*)
'Complicated' (from *Have A Nice Day*)
'Story Of My Life' (from *Have A Nice Day*)
'Everybody's Broken' (from *Lost Highway*)
'I Love This Town' (from *Lost Highway*)

Visit *billyfalcon.com*

FARM AID

Although initially conceived as a one-off concert, Farm Aid is now a benefit organisation that holds a yearly concert to raise awareness of the importance of American family farmers especially in the rural midwest and the south. The first concert was organised by John Mellencamp, Willie Nelson and Neil Young in the wake of Live Aid in 1985. They felt

strongly that it was important to raise public awareness of the problems facing American farmers, and aimed to raise funds to enable practical to be offered. Bon Jovi performed at the following Farm Aid concerts:

September 22, 1985 – Memorial Stadium in Champaign, Illinois
July 4, 1986 – Manor Downs Racetrack in Manor, Texas

FASTLANE

A famous New Jersey bar/club which opened in 1974. Despite being under the legal drinking age at the time Jon Bon Jovi frequently visited Fastlane to perform and to watch the local bands.

On one occasion, whilst in the Atlantic City Expressway, Bruce Springsteen reportedly joined Jon, David Bryan and their eight other band members onstage for a song or two.

FEELING, THE

The Feeling is a successful five-piece rock band from the south of England. Their first two albums, *Twelve Stops And Home* (2006) and *Join With Us* (2008) were critical and commercial hits. They have managed to capture the attention of classic and melodic rock fans as well as a modern indie crowd. Two of their most popular singles are 'I Love It When You Call' and 'I Thought It Was Over.'

They supported Bon Jovi with the Scottish rock band Logan on June 21, 2008 at Hampden Park in Glasgow, Scotland, before an audience of some 25,000-30,000 fans. On June 22, they supported Bon Jovi with Heaven's

Basement at the City of Manchester Stadium in England; on June 24, they supported Bon Jovi again but this time at the Ricoh Arena in Coventry with a band called Richlife; and finally, they supported Bon Jovi on the last night of the UK leg of the *Lost Highway Tour* on June 28 at Twickenham Stadium in London with a band called Ivyrise.

Visit *thefeeling.co.uk*

FIRE DOWN BELOW

Directed by Félix Enríquez Alcalá, *Fire Down Below* is a typical Steven Segal action film. Richie Sambora contributed the song 'Long Way

Around' to the soundtrack; it features in the final scene of the 1997 film.

FM

Often touted as Britain's answer to Bon Jovi, FM were a popular melodic rock/AOR band throughout the eighties. Their debut album, *Indiscreet,* was released in 1986 and spawned the popular power ballad 'Frozen Heart.' As well as supporting other big names like Meat Loaf, Tina Turner and Gary Moore, they supported Bon Jovi in Britain in November, 1986 at the start of the *Slippery When Wet* tour.

Jon told *Kerrang!* before the tour commenced:

"We actually wanted Vinnie Vincent Invasion to open the shows in Britain

but they couldn't get their work papers together in time...FM will be doing most of the shows with Queensrÿche taking over on a couple in London and one in the North. Britain will be the start of the endless tour!"

Drummer Pete Jupp remembers:

"...it was a really exciting time; it was just when they'd absolutely ex- ploded worldwide. They treated us absolutely brilliantly on the tour; we couldn't have asked for anything more. I think what had happened, they'd come of a tour with Ratt - and they were opening for Ratt - and I think Ratt absolutely treated them like shit. I think they said, 'Well, we're not going to treat any bands that open for us like that.' It's true. They were great. I remember one night, I think their soundcheck had overrun, and the old bass player Alec [John Such] was there saying, 'No, no. Hold the doors, hold the doors. Let them [FM] do a quick soundcheck.' They were brilliant.

I remember when we did Bradford Queen's Hall; that was the first time I'd experienced someone screaming at us. The whole tour was brilliant. We'd done a lot of other tours with other people but they couldn't have treated us any better...a really nice bunch of guys."

Despite their successes, FM split up in 1995 but reformed for the 2007 Firefest IV – *"the UK's premier Me- lodicrock and AOR festival"* -held at Nottingham Rock City. The band comprises vocalist/guitarist Steve Overland, bassist Merv Goldswor- thy, guitarist Andy Barnett, keyboard player Gem Davis and drummer Pete Jupp.

Visit *fmofficial.com*

FORD, LITA

Lita Ford is probably one of the most iconic female rock stars of all time. British born, Ford and her family moved to the States when she was four years old. In the seventies she was a member of the legendary all-female rock group The Runaways, along with Joan Jet t, Micki Steele, Sandy West, Cherie Currie, Jackie Fox, Vicki Blue and Laurie McAllister. Their best-known songs are undoubtedly 'Cherry Bomb', 'Born To Be Bad' and 'Queens Of Noise'. The group folded in 1979.

Ford went on to achieve huge popularity as a solo artist during the 1980s with the albums *Lita* and *Stiletto*. Her most famous and successful singles include 'Kiss Me Deadly,' 'Back To The Cave,' 'Hungary,' 'Lisa' and the Ozzy Osbourne duet 'Close My Eyes Forever.' After a long break from the music business, Ford returned in 2008 with a new band.

Ford supported Bon Jovi in 1988 on a tour of Europe, although due to ill health she had to miss the Birmingham NEC show (melodic rockers Shy stepping in as the opening act). The tour started at the RDS Hall in Dublin and progressed around the UK and Europe, playing in Germany, Switzerland, France, the Netherlands and Scandinavia.

Bon Jovi bassist Hugh McDonald has also worked with Ford; he played bass on her 1984 album *Dancin' On The Edge*.

Visit *myspace.com/litaford*

FOSTER, BRUCE

Grammy nominated singer-song-writer-producer Bruce Foster has had a long professional association with Richie Sambora. The pair were in a pre-Bon Jovi band called Shark Frenzy. They co-wrote the song 'Trail Of Broken Hearts' (sung by Cher) for the Hollywood film *Days Of Thunder* and in 1995 they worked together on Foster's solo album *Reality Game*, having co-written 'The Answer' and 'One Night Of Peace.' It is also worth noting that bassist Hugh McDonald played bass on Foster's 1977 album *After The Show*.

In his own words, Foster remembers when he first met Richie Sambora:

"Richie Sambora merged with my life and career in an East Brunswick, New Jersey nightclub in late 1978. I was there with my trio which

was Tom Marolda on bass (Tom has had an illustrious career that continues to this day, recently working with Elton John and The Killers) and on drums was Steve Mosley (having toured and recorded with Phoebe Snow, David Bromberg, Gladys Knight and others.) Then, a miracle happened...Tom got food poisoning and could not come back in to perform after our break.

I jokingly addressed the audience: 'Is there a bass player in the house? Mine is busy retching in the parking lot ...'

Amidst the laughter, an 18 year old Richie Sambora, sitting close to the stage, said: 'I'm a guitar player... I've never even HELD a bass, but I'll give it a try...'

There was something immediately likeable about him so I handed him Tom's bass. We played five or six songs and Richie was absolutely dreadful, but every time he played a really bad note he looked up and gave the most endearing good natured laugh. When we finally gave up and called it a night. Richie said: 'Hey, I know I was terrible on bass, but I really can play the guitar. I'd like to come back next week with my guitar and redeem myself.'

Something made me say an unprecedented 'Okay.' By the next week, I had totally forgotten about Richie, but he showed up mid way into the evening and took a beautiful Les Paul Custom guitar out of a case. It's pretty cool that Les and Richie are now close comrades! I called Richie up for 'a single song' so he knew he had just one shot to make good. I went into 'Kansas City,' a popular three chord tune that ever musician knew. Richie's Rhythm playing was alright so I told him to take a solo. A small part of rock history was made at that

moment when he confidently hit the toggle switch on his guitar to the solo setting. I expected him to hit a barrage of fast meaningless notes or a series of scales he had practiced at home to impress me. Instead, he hit a solitary note. He bent the string from a C up to a D with a sustained and beautiful vibrato that sounded like a fine violin. Before he played the second note, I leaned into him and said: 'You're in the band!'

Well, a week later we were a quartet and Richie instantly became a true brother to all of us. I can probably say for the whole band that the next two years of music and camaraderie was the peak of unfettered roaring good times in our entire musical careers."

Visit *brucefoster.com*

FRANKE AND THE KNOCKOUTS

Hailing from New Jersey, the original version of Franke and The Knockouts consisted of: Franke Previte (lead vocals), Billy Elworthy (lead and rhythm guitars), Blake Levinsohn (keyboards), Leigh Foxx (bass) and Claude LeHenaff (drums). Despite some hit US singles, including the Number 10 hit 'Sweetheart,' the band didn't last long. Tico Torres was their drummer in the early eighties; it was when he teamed up with Jon

and joined the band that became Bon Jovi that his life changed rather dramatically. Franke and The Knockouts split in 1986 after just three albums.

Visit *frankeandtheknockouts.com*

FREEHOLD RACEWAY

A popular New Jersey club which was frequented by members of Bon Jovi during the seventies.

FRIEND, LONN

A noted heavy metal fan and journalist. Friend edited the famous magazine *RIP* in the eighties and early nineties. He came up with an idea

of making a magazine dedicated to heavy metal when he worked for *Hustler* publisher Larry Flynt. Friend documented his experience working with Bon Jovi and other bands in his entertaining autobiography *Life On Planet Rock*. The chapter 'Ballad Of Jon And Richie' is an enlightening account of what Bon Jovi were experiencing between the albums *New Jersey* and *Keep The Faith* with some personal comments from Friend about the shaky relationship between Jon and Richie at that point. It was Friend who wrote the December 1992 *RIP* cover story 'Bon Jovi: Born

Again', published to coincide with the band's "mature" comeback album *Keep The Faith*. Friend also appeared in the VH1 *Behind The Music* episode on Bon Jovi, broadcast in 2000, and at the personal request of Jon sold a special limited edition *Bounce* live DVD (filmed at a concert in San Jose on April 13, 2003) on the American shopping channel QVC. It's all in his book. It's worth a read.

Visit *myspace.com/lonnsworld*

FUSCO, JOHN

An American screenwriter, Fusco's credits include *Crossroads, Thunderheart, Hidalgo* and *Spirit: Stallion Of The Cimarron.*

Fusco wrote the screenplay for *Young Guns II*, for which Jon Bon Jovi wrote the score. Apparently Fusco was keen to use the Bon Jovi track 'Wanted Dead Or Alive' from *Slippery When Wet*. Jon, however, felt that the lyrics were not relevant to the film so he opted to write an original lead song – 'Blaze Of Glory.' Consequently, Jon signed a deal to compose the entire soundtrack to the film, the result of which was *Blaze Of Glory*, his first solo album.

G

GELDOF, BOB

Geldof is the former singer with The Boomtown Rats, whose best-known song, 'I Don't Like Mondays', spent four weeks at the top of the UK singles chart in 1979.

He is now more famous for his philanthropic work, having organised Live Aid in 1985 and Live 8 in 2005. Geldof also has various business, journalistic and other media interests.

On June 25, 1995, during Bon Jovi's *These Days* tour, Bob Geldof joined the band on stage at Wembley Stadium for an encore of 'I Don't Like Mondays,' which can be heard on the live album *One Wild Night Live 1985-2001*.

Bon Jovi performed at the Live 8 concert in Philadelphia on July 2 2005.

Visit *bobgeldof.info*

GIANTS STADIUM

Situated in East Rutherford, New Jersey, this world-famous stadium is home to the New York Giants American football team. Bon Jovi played there for the first time on June 11, 1989, an especially potent occasion as Jon is a long-time Giants fan. The existing stadium is due to be demolished in 2010 and replaced by a new construction.

George Martin, and features a collection Gershwin songs interpreted by contemporary artists, including Bon Jovi, who performed 'How Long Has This Been Going On?'. Many other stars took part, including Meat Loaf, Robert Palmer, Elvis Costello and Kate Bush.

Richie Sambora told Jason Arnopp at *Kerrang!*:

"It was a big challenge for a rock 'n' roll player".

GLASGOW SECC

The Scottish Exhibition and Conference Centre is a famous Glasgow venue. After a brief stay in Russia to plan for the following year's Moscow Music Peace Festival, Bon Jovi began their British tour here on December 2 1988, just as their single 'Born To Be My Baby' was entering the UK chart.

GOLD DISC

In the UK, a Gold Disc is awarded by the British Phonographic Industry to an artist whose album achieves sales of 100,000 copies.

The following Bon Jovi albums have gone Gold:

One Wild Night Live 1985-2001 (2001)
Bounce (2002)
This Left Feels Right (2003)
Have A Nice Day (2005)
Lost Highway (2007)

GOLDEN GLOBE AWARDS

A hugely popular and revered American awards ceremony for artists who work in cinema and television. The Globes, as they are known, are considered to be a precursor to the Oscars. In 1991, Jon Bon Jovi was the winner in the 'Best Original Song'

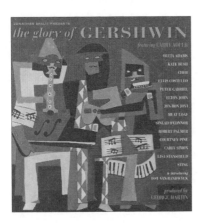

GLORY OF GERSHWIN, THE

This album of songs by the American composer George Gershwin was created to celebrate the 80th birthday of legendary harmonica player Larry Adler. It was produced by the great

category for 'Blaze Of Glory' from the soundtrack to *Young Guns II*.

GORE, AL

Al Gore was Vice President of the United States from 1993 to 2001 under President Bill Clinton. An active politician since 1997, Gore failed in his bid to become President in 2000/01; the popular vote went to the Republican candidate George W. Bush. Jon Bon Jovi has close ties to the Democratic Party and even helped raise cash for Al Gore's Presidential campaign in 2000 and followed Gore on his campaign trail drumming up support.

Gore now dedicates much of his time to environmental concerns, and in 2007 was awarded the prestigious Nobel Peace Prize. His 2006 documentary on global warming *An Inconvenient Truth* was widely praised and won two Academy Awards for 'Best Original Song' and 'Best Documentary Feature.' A book was also released to accompany the film: *An Inconvenient Truth: The Planetary Emergency Of Global Warming And What We Can Do About It* was a Number 1 *New York Times* bestseller. His wife, Tipper Gore, co-founded the Parents Music Resource Center (PMRC) in 1985 with fellow politicians' wives, collectively known as the 'Washington Wives'. The organisation blamed rock/metal music for contributing to social problems in America, such as rape, teenage drunkenness and rising crime levels. On their "hit list" were Judas Priest, AC/DC, Black Sabbath and others. Their aim was the prevent heavy metal/rock from "brainwashing" the youth of America.

* On September 14, 2000 at New York City's Radio City Music Hall Jon Bon Jovi performed at The Concert

For Al Gore, which also featured Paul Simon, Sheryl Crow, Don Henley and others. Jon sang 'Wanted Dead Or Alive' in his solo spot and joined in with others to sing The Beatles classic 'Revolution.'

* On October 4, 2000 Jon played host to a fundraising event at his mansion in Middletown, New Jersey. It was not cheap: invitees had to pay $25,000 to attend. The event, attended by Al Gore, raised over $1 million.

* Bon Jovi played at the Live 8 fundraiser which was partly organised by Al Gore.

Asked by *Time Magazine* if he'd encourage Gore to run again, he said:

"I may have been the first one in that line, but there are a lot of people behind me trying to say the same thing. I think I have spoken my piece politically with Have A Nice Day. *I find I can get a lot more done personally through philanthropy than I can stumping for either side of the aisle."*

Visit *algore.com*

GORKY PARK

A Russian glam metal band formed in 1987, they were signed by Mercury Records in the US after Jon Bon Jovi and Richie Sambora allegedly put a word in for them with label bosses. Their singer and guitarist also produced the track 'Peace In Our Time' which features on Gorky Park's self-titled 1989 debut album. On August 12-13 1989, they played at the Moscow Music Peace Festival, at which Bon Jovi headlined. Gorky Park have been mostly inactive in recent years.

GRACELAND CHAPEL

A famous wedding chapel in Las Vegas which has been a part of the

Vegas strip for over 50 years. Bon Jovi married his childhood sweetheart Dorothea here on April 29, 1989. In 2001, Jon gave a concert in the chapel's parking lot in front of 75 couples who renewed their vows alongside himself and his wife. Other rock stars to marry at Graceland Chapel include members of Def Leppard, KISS and Deep Purple.

GRAMMY AWARDS

The prestigious American award in the form of a diminutive golden gramophone, which is given for outstanding achievement in the recording industry. Organised by the National Academy of Recording Arts and Sciences of the United States, The Grammy Awards (known as The Grammys) held its 50th anniversary show in February 2007.

Bon Jovi have received considerable recognition from the Grammys, bagging one award and several nominations.

In 1991, Jon Bon Jovi was nominated for a Grammy for the song 'Blaze Of Glory' (from the film *Young Guns II*) in the category 'Best Song Written Specifically For A Motion Picture Or For Television.'

In 1997, the band was nominated for a Grammy for *Live From London,* which comes under the category of 'Best Music Video – Long Form.'

For the 2000 album *Crush* they were nominated for 'Best Rock Album', and for the title-track (released as a single) they were nominated for 'Best Rock Performance By Duo/Group.'

In 2003, the single 'Everyday' was nominated for 'Best Rock Performance By Duo/Group.'

Finally, in 2007, they won a Grammy for 'Who Says You Can't Go Home' in the category of 'Best Country Collaboration.'

GRUNGE

Grunge and Bon Jovi have nothing in common. However, just as in the late seventies, when Punk made Heavy Metal and Progressive Rock look outdated and meaningless (not necessarily to everyone but to a certain proportion of British and American youth), Grunge metaphorically spat in the face of Glam and Hair Metal, decrying it for having no emotion, political meaning or social substance.

Grunge is a style of gritty alternative-rock that originates in Washington State in the North West of the USA. Although the beginnings of Grunge date back to the mid-1980s, it was in the early nineties that the genre achieved commercial success.

While many of their peers struggled to sell records during this period, Bon Jovi continued to do surprisingly well, especially considering that they took a break between 1990 and 1992. They then returned with the mammoth-selling *Keep The Faith* at the tail-end of '92.

The melodic rock singer Don Dokken believes:

"I thought the first band that would take a hit [in the nineties] was Bon Jovi but they went to Europe and broke out there, which I thought would be impossible because they're too pop for the Europeans. But they did it and came back to the States stronger that ever."

The most famous grunge bands include Nirvana, Soundgarden, Alice In Chains and Pearl Jam.

GUSKIN, HAROLD

A revered American acting coach who has privately given classes to such renowned thespians as David Suchet, Glenn Close, James Gandolfini, Bridget Fonda and Kevin Kline. He is the author of *How To Stop Acting*, published by Faber & Faber in 2003.

Prior to his first major acting role in 1995s *Moonlight And Valentino*, Jon Bon Jovi took private one-to-one acting lessons with Guskin in New York City. In interviews, Jon has publicly acknowledged Guskin's help.

H

HABITAT FOR HUMANITY INTERNATIONAL

Founded in 1976, Habitat For Humanity International is non-profit making and non-governmental project which uses voluntary labour to build affordable homes for poor people in some 100 countries around the world. After becoming associated with HFHI in 2005, Jon Bon Jovi became their first ambassador a year later. He has helped to provide homes for poor people in Philadelphia and in '06 he made a $1 million donation to help build 28 homes in Louisiana in the aftermath of Hurricane Katrina. The video for 'Who Says You Can't Go Home' documents the construction of those HFHI homes.

Visit *habitatforhumanity.org.uk*

HACK, EMERY

It was under the 13 year tutelage of Juilliard Professor Emery Hack that David Bryan was able to realise the full extent of his talents on piano and keyboards. Hack was mentor to the young Bryan before he returned to pop music and hooked up with Jon to form Bon Jovi.

HAIR METAL

Hair Metal is a style of commercial music that fused familiar traits of glam rock with seventies heavy metal to make a catchy and highly enjoyable style of eighties American arena rock music.

Frankie Banali, the drummer in the legendary hair metal band Quiet Riot, says:

"Hair Metal: 90% hair, 10% hair spray, 100% attitude! I rest my case…"

How does hair metal relate to Bon Jovi? Hmm…it is certainly controversial to label Bon Jovi a hair metal band per se but certainly their image during the eighties and their two biggest selling albums *Slippery When Wet* and *New Jersey* display common traits of the genre. The single (and its accompanying video) 'Livin' On A Prayer' is certainly a typical example of eighties American hair metal.

Famous characteristics of hair metal include spandex, tight leather or denim trousers, ripped shirts, headbands and obviously large hair and even make-up. Just check out the band on the back of the album cover to *7800° Fahrenheit*! In terms of the music, hair metal is famous for pow-

Quiet Riot

er ballads, anthemic singles, melodic choruses and memorable guitar riffs.

Loathed by many but adored by more, hair metal had a rough ride during the 1990s after grunge temporarily 'killed it off' but has returned in style as bands like Whitesnake, Mötley Crüe and Van Halen have re-formed to tour the world yet again; although their images are toned down compared to what they looked like at the zenith of hair metal's popularity. In the new millennium, most bands of Bon Jovi's popularity tend to distance themselves from the term as it is associated with a particular style of MTV style commercial rock; these days they strive to be taken more seriously. That doesn't apply to all bands, of course, some use the term to cash in on their past.

Even the self-proclaimed heavy metal gods Judas Priest had a stab at the hair metal thing with their 1986 album *Turbo*, as did Alice Cooper with his brilliant album *Trash* and Aerosmith with their Bruce Fairbairn produced classic *Permanent Vacation*.

Other hair metal bands of the era include: Ratt, Cinderella, W.A.S.P., Twisted Sister, Dokken, Helix, Poison, Warrant, Winger and Skid Row. European hair metal bands such as Europe, Hanoi Rocks and Def Leppard were tremendously popular both at home and abroad. All of these bands are still touring and making new albums although their fan bases have dwindled considerably over the years. Bon Jovi remain hugely popular and these days they certainly look and sound a lot different. One thing is for sure: they wouldn't even dare to call themselves a *hair* metal band.

Currently, hair metal seems to have morphed into sleaze metal as played by bands such as Backyard Babies, Fatal Smile and Hardcore Superstar.

HALFIN, ROSS

Undoubtedly one of the most successful photographers in the music business, Halfin is also a popular diarist who often makes witty yet scathing verbal attacks on the artists he shoots, and especially their managers and PR people. He started working for *Sounds* in the seventies on a freelance basis and moved on to other publications, including *Kerrang!, Mojo, Q* and *Classic Rock*. Halfin has photographed some of the biggest bands in the world including Led Zeppelin, The Who, Guns N' Roses, Iron Maiden, The Police, Rush and KISS. He also has quite a few pictorial books to his name notably on Metallica, The Who and Iron Maiden.

Halfin has also photographed Bon Jovi in the past but is no longer allowed to work for them...

On his website, he once wrote:

"Heard I've just been banned from shooting JBJ. Because his office thinks I make him look too old. Quite amazing really... as the pictures you see are all approved by Jon. If you look on the contract sheets you can

even see where he signed them, JBJ (his way of approving photos.) The strange thing about Jon is when you meet him he's always friendly and he's easy to shoot, yet his office insists on signing contracts which are in the league of Tom Cruise. They really enforce a 'Jersey Sopranos' us against them bullshit... Sad really... as a photographer, whenever you get very friendly with an artist someone in his office always feels threatened... A shame, I've always liked Jon."

On June 26, 2008 after photographing Whitesnake and Def Leppard at Wembley Arena, Halfin wrote on his website:

"Jimmy Page came with Richie Sambora. Richie said hello - I asked him, 'Does Jon allow you to speak to someone who's banned?' 'I have no idea why that is and I'm going to find out,' he said. Seemed genuine - maybe JBJ will fire him for asking."

Interview:

Do you remember when you first met the band?

Jon came to a Mötley Crüe show in Hartford, Connecticut. Nikki Sixx introduced him as a new singer Doc McGhee had signed.

Were you a fan before you worked with them?

No, I thought they were a Def Leppard copy band, but Jon was a really good front man. They always seemed a bit too Vegas.

Roughly, how many times have you photographed Bon Jovi?

No idea, shot them on every tour up to the late '90s...lots.

What is your most memorable photo session with them?

Shot Jon at his house in Malibu for a magazine. I got him to pose on an old cross; he borrowed his kid's nanny's sunglasses. It looked great, as if he was in Mexico. Then his management demanded I let them use the photo for FREE for press. Remember this was at the time he was a million selling artist. I said no, and then things became 'difficult'...

Another time was over New Year 1989. On New Year's Day in Tokyo or Osaka, can't remember, I did a shoot with him and Richie Sambora except neither was talking to each other. We drove for an hour with them both looking out opposite windows, not saying a word. Skid Row were not talking to him as they felt he'd ripped him off with a production deal. It wasn't a fun trip at all.

What were they like to work with?

When you get Jon in front of you he gets on with it, always easy.

Would you say Jon is a difficult person to please?

Jon NEVER seems happy. I even asked Doc [McGhee] this recently. There is always something wrong. I think he feels everybody is out to scam him.

What do you recall about working with Richie Sambora?

Richie is always nice. When his solo record came out I was shooting him in LA; before he would do photos, his PA pulled out a contract saying they own the copyright - I refused to sign it. I asked him why I was banned recently, he said he'd find out and let me know. Of course, I've never heard from him.

Why are you "banned" from photographing them?

I have no idea why I'm banned - maybe I won't play by JBJ's rules contracts-control. I saw him at the

Mojo *awards last year; he came with Elton John, he hugged me as if he was my best friend. I thought about saying something then thought fuck it, life's too short.*

Anything else?

Q *magazine do a feature this year; my name came up to do the photos - absolutely not, came the reply from Jon's office....*

Visit *rosshalfin.com*

HALL & OATES

Daryl Hall and John Oates are a famous American duo popular for a distinctive brand of rock and roll merged with traditional American R&B. Their chart success began to wane in the nineties, but over a career spanning 40 years they have had six Number 1 US hit singles and 34 singles in the *Billboard* Hot 100, which is a pretty decent record. The acclaimed American writer of both fiction and non-fiction, Nick Tosches, wrote *Dangerous Dances: The Authorized Biography* which was published by St. Martin's Press in 1984. Their debut album *Whole Oats* was released in 1972 and their latest album *Home For Christmas* was released in 2006.

Jon Bon Jovi co-wrote their song 'So Close', which peaked at Number 11 in the US *Billboard* Hot 100 in 1990. It features on the album *Change*

Of Season, released in America on November 13, 1990 via Arista.

Visit *hallandoates.com*

HAMMERSMITH ODEON

A famous West London venue now known as the Hammersmith Apollo. Many great bands have performed there, including AC/DC, Queen, Iron Maiden and Dire Straits. Although Motörhead never actually recorded their famous live album at the Odeon, they released *No Sleep 'Til Hammersmith* in 1981.

Bon Jovi played a series of four dates at the Hammersmith Odeon in November, 1986. Noted heavy metal writer John Tucker was there on the 17th.

His personal review states:

"Almost overnight, Bon Jovi have become a household name in Britain, and it's doubtful whether the albums and tours of the previous two years had done anything to prepare the band for the adulation they've received since their arrival here. Two hit singles have paved the way for TV appearances and tabloid coverage which in turn have boosted sales of Slippery When Wet *and turned what may have been a perfunctory UK tour into a massive sold-out success.*

Tonight was the first of four – count 'em! – nights at Hammersmith Odeon, and although it's great to see a band getting the acclaim it richly deserves, one glance around the audience showed it to be mainly composed of recent converts of the Slippery When Wet *kind; and success built on singles can be short-lived as the record-buying public move swiftly on to the next 'in' thing. So it came as no surprise that the set featured more songs from the new album than from its two predecessors combined, and for the biggest applause of the night*

to go to the two singles 'You Give Love A Bad Name' and 'Livin' On A Prayer.' But from the opening strains of 'Raise Your Hands' to the last few bars of a rocked-up 'Get Ready' Jon Bon Jovi had the capacity crowd in the palm of his hand, a puppet master pulling the strings of four thousand eager marionettes. The set itself drew largely on the best of the new album supported by three old favourites apiece from the band's self-titled debut and 7800° Fahrenheit, the only personal low-spots being the all-too-bland 'Silent Night' and the horrendous 'Wild In The Streets.'

As ever though, the best was saved till last, the first encore producing a soul-searching rendition of 'Wanted Dead Or Alive' – perhaps the finest showcase of the band's song-writing abilities – and a cover of Thin Lizzy's 'The Boys Are Back In Town' as a tribute to Phil Lynott RIP. Called back for more, Bon Jovi – complete with brass trio – ripped through the excellent 'Social Disease' and a lively version of the otherwise ordinary 'Get Ready.' It was a great night, believe me."

Bon Jovi had become a huge touring band by the end of the eighties but on Wednesday, January 10, 1990, they returned to the West London

venue for a special charity show with the proceeds being donated to Nordoff-Robbins Music Therapy. The setlist included acoustic renditions of 'Wanted Dead Or Alive,' 'Livin' On A Prayer' and a cover of Bad Company's 'Shooting Star.' Other songs played included 'Wild In The Streets,' 'You Give Love A Bad Name,' 'Blood On Blood' and 'Bad Medicine.' They also threw in a few covers, including Little Richard's 'Good Golly Miss Molly,' 'Travellin' Band' by Creedence Clearwater Revival and a medley of two songs by The Animals: 'It's My Life' and 'We've Gotta Get Out Of This Place.' Jimmy Page joined the band onstage for a version of 'Train Kept A-Rollin'' and 'With A Little Help From My Friends.'

They played another six shows, finishing on January 16.

HARD ROCK CAFÉ

The Hard Rock Café, on London's Hyde Park Corner, was the first of a series of international cafés that cel-

ebrate rock and roll via merchandise, wall displays and even holding rock concerts and press conferences.

One of Richie Sambora's guitars, used on the *Bounce* tour, is displayed there.

HARD TIMES COME EASY

The first single from Richie Sambora's second solo album was issued in the UK on March 7, 1998. It just made it into the UK Top 40 at Number 37, spending two weeks in the charts. It's a soft rock anthem with a splendid melody and some effective backing vocals which give it an almost gospel feel. It was written with the noted songwriter Richie Supa.

HARDEST PART IS THE NIGHT, THE

The only single released in the UK from the band's second album *7800° Fahrenheit,* it was the band's debut single in Britain. Issued on August 31 1985, it peaked at Number 68 in the Top 40. It was their second single release in the States, but failed to chart in the *Billboard* Hot 100.

HARLEY DAVIDSON AND THE MARLBORO MAN

A 1991 mob related bank caper starring Mickey Rourke, Don Johnson, Vanessa Williams and Daniel Baldwin. The film was directed by Simon

Wincer. Bon Jovi's 'Wanted Dead Or Alive' features in the soundtrack.

HAVE A NICE DAY (ALBUM)

Okay, so the band had stumbled slightly with the re-recorded greatest hits set *This Left Feels Right* (2003) but afterwards they returned to a harder edged sound with *Have A Nice Day*. It's a heavier album than both *Crush* (2000) and *Bounce* (2002.)

Have A Nice Day as supposed to be recorded by mid-2004, with the intention of releasing it in early '05 but that didn't happen, allegedly because of record company politics. A pre-release version of the album had already been distributed by the time the band had began re-recording and writing more tracks for the newer version.

Some tracks that didn't make the final cut of the second version include 'Unbreakable' and 'These Open Arms,' which were included in territories as bonus tracks. A song called 'Nothing' was also set aside although it was recorded and retitled 'Nothing Without You' by the 2005 *American Idol* contestant Bo Bice. 'Who Say's You Can't Go Home' was originally recorded with Keith Urban, the New Zealand born country singer, but it was thought that his voice was too similar to Jon's. The song was re-recorded with Jennifer Nettles in a country rock format and released in the States as a single and a bonus track on the US/Canadian edition of the album, but the actual album version of the song just features Jon's singing. The band's own version is known as the 'rock version' while the Nettles collaboration is evidently known as the 'country rock version.'

Have A Nice Day had been recorded at Jon's personal recording facility Sanctuary II Studios in New Jer-

sey, with additional recording being completed at Henson Studios in LA. It was produced by John Shanks, Jon and Sambora, with Desmond Child as executive producer. Rick Parashar (producer of Alice In Chains and Pearl Jam) also co-produced some tracks with Jon and Sambora ('Wildflower,' 'Last Cigarette,' 'Novocaine' and 'Story'); the idea was probably to give the album an even harder and contemporary rock sound. It worked.

On the songwriting side of things, *Have A Nice Day* sees Jon and Richie Sambora collaborating with John Shanks, Billy Falcon, Desmond Child, Max Martin and even keyboardist David Bryan, who co-penned 'Last Cigarette.'

Have A Nice Day was released in the UK on October 1, 2005 and peaked at Number 2, spending over four weeks in the charts. It sold seven million copies worldwide and showcased the band's tenacity as a popular rock band in the 21st Century. The album was also a Number 2 hit in the American *Billboard* 200, but reached Number 1 in over five countries, including Canada. Three singles were released from the album: 'Have A Nice Day,' 'Who Says You Can't Go Home' and 'Welcome To Wherever Your Are.'

Awarding the album 8/10, Malcolm Dome wrote in *Classic Rock*:

"...arguably the band's best studio album since 1992s Keep The Faith... *it's an improvement on the old model...*Have A Nice Day *is among the most generous, well-crafted, thought-provoking rock records of 2005"*

A special edition version of the album was released with a bonus DVD of five live tracks that had been recorded at a show in Atlantic City in November, 2004.

Track Listing:

1. 'Have A Nice Day'
2. 'I Want To Be Loved'
3. 'Welcome To Wherever You Are'
4. 'Who Says You Can't Go Home'
5. 'Last Man Standing'
6. 'Bells Of Freedom'
7. 'Wildflower'
8. 'Last Cigarette'
9. 'I Am'
10. 'Complicated'
11. 'Novocaine'
12. 'Story Of My Life'
13. 'Dirty Little Secret' *(Bonus track on the Japanese, UK, Australian and Asian versions)* / 'Who Says You Can't Go Home' *(duet version with Jennifer Nettles – bonus track on the North American version)*
14. 'Unbreakable' *(Bonus track on the Japanese, UK, Australian and Asian versions)*
15. 'These Open Arms' *(Bonus track on the Japanese version)*

Special Edition Bonus DVD:

1. 'Everyday'
2. 'Miss Fourth Of July'
3. 'I Get A Rush'
4. 'These Arms Are Open All Night'
5. 'The Radio Saved My Life Tonight'

Author's Review:

Have A Nice Day *begins with the gritty lead riff of the title-track before the thumping drums of Tico Torres come into action. It's a terrific rock song and amongst the heaviest singles the band had released in years. There's no question about it,* Have A Nice Day *is their best album since*

their glorious rock days of the eighties. With John Shanks and Rick Parashar, they got themselves a good set of producers to give their sound a harder, and even grunge-like, edge.

Crush *and* Bounce *were good commercial rock albums and a step in the right direction but this is a different beast, a more thrilling one with fewer production effects and distorted guitars. Jon even sounds pretty annoyed on some songs and it's cool to hear the talk-box on 'I Want To Be Loved' which adds some characterisation to the track. Surprisingly, the ballads are slightly heavier than usual ('Welcome To Wherever Your Are') and even the soppy 'Wildflower' is quite catchy. The stand out rock track is without question 'Last Man Standing' which has a killer riff delivered by Sambora. 'Last Cigarette' has a good melody although the lyrics are just too repetitive, but 'Complicated' builds up to a solid grove. 'Novocaine' and 'Story Of My Life' have got some heavy guitars and infectious choruses.*

On the whole, Have A Nice Day *is a well made and thoroughly likeable rock album for the charts. It's undoubtedly their best set of songs since* New Jersey. *This is what Bon Jovi does well and they should stick to it.*

Rating ****

HAVE A NICE DAY (SINGLE)

The title track (and the first single) taken from the album of the same name. It was issued in the UK on September 24, 2005 and peaked at Number 6 in the Top 40. It was less successful in the States reaching Number 53 on the *Billboard* Hot 100. The lyrics were penned by Jon Bon Jovi, Richie Sambora and John Shanks.

HAVE A NICE DAY TOUR (2005-06)

To promote *Have A Nice Day*, Bon Jovi played 89 shows between November 2, 2005 and July 29, 2006. The setlist was often tweaked so they could play the entire album during the run of the tour. It was the third most financially successful tour of 2006 with the Rolling Stones *A Bigger Bang Tour* topping the poll and Madonna's *Confessions Tour* in second place. Bon Jovi played to over two million fans.

Simon Bradley at *Classic Rock* reviewed the band's show at St. Mary's Stadium in Southampton on June 9, 2006. He wrote:

> *"...although the music and spectacle are certainly above contempt, this was a disjointed show."*

HAVE A NICE DAY TOUR

NORTH AMERICAN DATES (& VENUES) PART I

November 2, 2005 - Wells Fargo Arena, Des Moines, IA (USA)

November 4, 2005 - United Center, Chicago, IL (USA)

November 5, 2005 - United Center, Chicago, IL (USA)

November 8, 2005 - Quicken Loans Arena, Cleveland, OH (USA)

November 9, 2005 - Value City Arena, Columbus, OH (USA)

November 11, 2005 - Target Center, Minneapolis, MN (USA)

November 12, 2005 - Qwest Center, Omaha, NE (USA)

November 16, 2005 - Kohl Center, Madison, WI (USA)

November 18, 2005 - Palace of Auburn Hills, Auburn Hills, MI (USA)

November 19, 2005 - Palace of Auburn Hills, Auburn Hills, MI (USA)

November 26, 2005 - Mohegan Sun, Uncasville, CT (USA)

November 28, 2005 - Madison Square Garden, New York, NY (USA)

November 29, 2005 - Madison Square Garden, New York, NY (USA)

December 2, 2005 - Wachovia Center, Philadelphia, PA (USA)

December 3, 2005 - Wachovia Center, Philadelphia, PA (USA)

December 6, 2005 - Mellon Arena, Pittsburgh, PA (USA)

December 7, 2005 - Nassau Coliseum, Uniondale, NY (USA)

December 9, 2005 - TD Banknorth Garden, Boston, MA (USA)

December 10, 2005 - TD Banknorth Garden, Boston, MA (USA)

December 12, 2005 - Pepsi Arena, Albany, NY (USA)

December 14, 2005 - Bell Centre, Montreal, QB (Canada)

December 15, 2005 - Bell Centre, Montreal, QB (Canada)

December 17, 2005 - Verizon Center, Washington, DC (USA)

December 19, 2005 - Izod Center, East Rutherford, NJ (USA)

December 21, 2005 - Izod Center, East Rutherford, NJ (USA)

December 22, 2005 - Izod Center, East Rutherford, NJ (USA)

January 14, 2005 - Ford Center, Oklahoma City, OK (USA)

January 15, 2006 - American Airlines Center, Dallas, TX (USA)

January 17, 2006 - Philips Arena, Atlanta, GA (USA)

January 18, 2006 - Charlotte Bobcats Arena, Charlotte, NC (USA)

January 20, 2006 - HSBC Arena, Buffalo, NY (USA)

January 21, 2006 - Air Canada Centre, Toronto, ON (Canada)

January 23, 2006 - Air Canada Centre, Toronto, ON (Canada)

January 24, 2006 - Air Canada Centre, Toronto, ON (Canada)

January 27, 2006 - Xcel Energy Center, St. Paul, MN (USA)

January 28, 2006 - Bradley Center, Milwaukee, WI (USA)

January 30, 2006 - Air Canada Centre, Toronto, ON (Canada)

February 1, 2006 - Mohegan Sun Arena, Uncasville, CT (USA)

February 2, 2006 - Verizon Center, Washington, DC (USA)

February 4, 2006 - Boardwalk Hall, Atlantic City, NJ (USA)

February 8, 2006 - BI-LO Center, Greenville, SC (USA)
February 10, 2006 – Bank Atlantic Center, Sunrise, FL (USA)
February 14, 2006 - Sommet Center, Nashville, TN (USA)
February 15, 2006 - Gwinnett Center, Atlanta, GA (USA)
February 16, 2006 - BankAtlantic Center, Sunrise, FL (USA)
February 17, 2006 - St. Pete Times Forum, Tampa, FL (USA)
February 18, 2006 - St. Pete Times Forum,Tampa, FL (USA)
February 21, 2006 - Toyota Center, Houston, TX (USA)
February 23, 2006 - Pepsi Center, Denver, CO (USA)
February 25, 2006 - Honda Center, Anaheim, CA (USA)
February 27, 2006 - HP Pavilion, San Jose CA (USA)
March 1, 2006 - Save Mart Center, Fresno, CA (USA)
March 3, 2006 - Staples Center, Los Angeles, CA (USA)
March 5, 2006 - Rose Garden Arena, Portland, OR (USA)
March 6, 2006 - Key Arena, Seattle, WA (USA)

March 9, 2006 - Glendale Arena, Glendale, AZ (USA)
March 11, 2006 - MGM Grand Arena, Las Vegas, NV (USA)

JAPANESE DATES (& VENUES)

April 8, 2006 - Tokyo Dome, Tokyo (Japan)
April 9, 2006 - Tokyo Dome, Tokyo (Japan)
April 12, 2006 - Nagoya Dome, Nagoya (Japan)
April 14, 2006 - Osaka Dome, Osaka (Japan)
April 15, 2006 - Osaka Dome, Osaka (Japan)
April 18, 2006 - Sapporo Dome, Sapporo (Japan)

EUROPEAN DATES (& VENUES)

May 13, 2006 - LTU Arena, Düsseldorf (Germany)
May 15, 2006 - Linzer Stadion, Linz (Austria)
May 17, 2006 - Schloßplatz, Koblenz (Germany)
May 20, 2006 - Cork Park, Dublin (Ireland)

JAPAN TOUR EDITION

May 24, 2006 – Hessentag, Hessisch
Lichtenau (Germany)
May 25, 2006 - Goffert Park,
Nijmegen (Netherlands)
May 27, 2006 - Cannstatter Wasen,
Stuttgart (Germany)
May 28, 2006 - München Stadion,
München (Germany)
May 30, 2006 - Olympia Stadium,
Innsbruck (Austria)
May 31, 2006 - Stade de Suisse,
Berne (Switzerland)
June 3, 2006 - Hampden Park,
Glasgow (Scotland)
June 4, 2006 - City of Manchester
Stadium, Manchester (England)
June 7, 2006 - Ricoh Arena,
Coventry (England)
June 9, 2006 - St. Mary's Stadium,
Southampton (England)
June 10, 2006 - National Bowl,
Milton Keynes (England)
June 11, 2006 - National Bowl,
Milton Keynes (England)
June 13, 2006 - KC Stadium,
Kingston Upon Hull (England)

**NORTH AMERICAN DATES
(& VENUES) PART II**

July 10, 2006 - Seminole Hard Rock
Live, Fort Lauderdale, FL (USA)
July 13, 2006 - Parc Jean-Drapeau,
Montreal, QC (Canada)
July 15, 2006 - Citizens Bank Park,
Philadelphia, PA (USA)
July 18, 2006 - Giants Stadium, East
Rutherford, NJ (USA)
July 19, 2006 - Giants Stadium, East
Rutherford, NJ (USA)
July 21, 2006 - Soldier Field,
Chicago, IL (USA)
July 23, 2006 - Heinz Field,
Pittsburgh, PA (USA)
July 27, 2006 - Gillette Stadium,
Foxboro, MA (USA)
July 29, 2006 - Giants Stadium, East
Rutherford, NJ (USA)

HEAT

Written and directed by Michael
Mann, *Heat* is basically a remake of
the 1989 TV movie *LA Takedown,*
and stars Al Pacino and Robert De-
Niro. Apparently, Jon auditioned for
the part of the youngest of a group of
bank robbers, a role that Val Kilmer

ultimately played. The film was released to universal acclaim in 1995.

HEATLEY, MICHAEL

An author, publisher and editor, Michael Heatley has written over 30 biographies of rock stars and celebrities on subjects as diverse as Deep Purple and Rolf Harris. His book *Bon Jovi: In Their Own Words* was published in 1997 by Omnibus Press as part of a popular series of that name. The book gathers together interviews the band have given over the years, to tell their story in, well, their own words. It's a good point of reference but is now out of print. In '98 he put together a 32 page illustrated history (including a pull-out poster) of Jon simply called *Jon Bon Jovi* – this title was also published through Omnibus,

Heatley runs his long-established 'specialist' publishers Northdown Publishing.

Visit *northdown.demon.co.uk*

HEAVEN'S BASEMENT

Formally known as Hurricane's Party and Roadstar, this British rock band have built up a loyal fanbase across the UK after supporting the likes of Meat Loaf and Thunder and through lots of hard work at various rock festivals. Heaven's Basement comprises singer Richie Hevanz,

guitarist Sid Glover, rhythm guitarist Johnny Rocker, drummer Chris Rivers and bassist Rob Randell.

They supported Bon Jovi on June 22, 2008 at the City of Manchester Stadium. Johnny Rocker says,

"It was a great day from start to finish and it couldn't have gone any better for us. We found out we were playing with them about three days before the show, so we didn't have a chance to get nervous or worry too much about it. The timing of it was perfect for us too as we were on tour at the time so we were ready for anything. It was by far the biggest crowd we'd played to, around 60,000 I think it was; and they were great to us. The only shame of the day was not getting to meet the guys from Bon Jovi, they turned up in time for the gig and left as soon as they came off so we didn't get the chance to thank them for letting us play. We're not too worried though, hopefully it won't be the last time we get to share the stage with them or hang out someplace with them."

Visit *myspace.com/ heavensbasementofficial*

HEDLEY

The lead singer of Hedley, Jacob Hoggard, came third in the 2004 season of *Canadian Idol*, a reality TV show that is essentially the same format as *American Idol* and Britain's *The X Factor*. The band was formed

in 2004 and have released two albums thus far: 2005's self-titled debut and 2007s *Famous Last Words*. The name derives from the town of Hedley in British Columbia, Canada.

Hedley supported Bon Jovi on the Canadian leg of the 2007 *Lost Highway Tour*. The dates ran from November 14, to December 16, 2007.

Visit *hedleyonline.com*

HEINE, OLAF

Famed German photographer who has worked with advertisers, film stars and musicians of the calibre of Sting, Iggy Pop, Depeche Mode and Tom Jones He has also directed music videos and commercials. Heine did the photography for the Bon Jovi albums *Crush* (2000) and *Have A Nice Day* (2005.)

Visit *olafheine.com*

HELL IS LIVING WITHOUT YOU

Jon Bon Jovi and Richie Sambora co-wrote this track with Desmond Child and Alice Cooper. It features on the shock rocker's 1988 "comeback" album *Trash*.

HERBERT HOOVER JUNIOR HIGH SCHOOL

A "Middle School" in Edison, New Jersey which David Bryan attended. It was here that Bryan played keyboards in a band called Transition.

HERZIGOVA, EVA

A Czech born model and actress. She married Tico Torres in September 1996 in an expensive Hollywood style wedding that included celebrities such as Donald Trump. They divorced in June 2000.

Visit *evaherzigova.com*

HEY GOD

The fifth and final single release taken from *These Days*. It was issued in the UK on July 6, 1996 and peaked at Number 13, spending five weeks in the chart. It's a powerful song written by Jon and Sambora, concerning the breakdown mental health and tackling issues of despair and depression.

HOBART, CHIP

A successful radio broadcaster who has worked for stations all over the East Coast. Was he is responsible for giving Jon his first major break? In 1982 Jon handed the 'Runaway' demo to DJ Chip Hobart of the Long Island based WAPP FM 103.5. Hobart consequently entered it in the 'Rock To Riches' competition and, guess what, it won the regional part! The song appeared on the WAPP compilation of unsigned acts, *New York Rocks 1983*, subsequently picking up popularity amongst DJs on the East Coast.

HOLLYWOOD SALUTES ARNOLD SCHWARZENEGGER: AN AMERICAN CINEMATHEQUE TRIBUTE

A ceremony held in honour of Arnold Schwarzenegger. Tim Allen, James Cameron and George Clooney were among the many Hollywood stars who attended. Jon Bon Jovi performed 'It's Only Make Believe' at the event.

HOMEGROWN

Directed by Stephen Gyllenhaal, this 1998 comedy thriller stars John Lithgow, Ryan Phillippe, Billy Bob

Thornton and Jon Bon Jovi. The film surrounds three characters Jack, Carter and Harlan as they run a marijuana farm and become embroiled in murder and scandal. Jon plays a secondary character called Danny.

HOT COUNTRY SONGS

As with all singles charts, *Billboard* magazine's Hot Country Songs is published on a weekly basis, and lists the biggest selling country singles in America. In 2006, Bon Jovi had a Number 1 'Hot Country Song' with 'Who Says You Can't Go Home' featuring singer Jennifer Nettles of Sugarland. In the same year the Hot Country Songs chart had nine Number 1 singles from newcomers to the genre, something which hadn't happened since 1991. Those nine artists were: Bon Jovi, Carrie Underwood,

Josh Turner, Jack Ingram, Jason Aldean, Rodney Atkins, The Wreckers, Heartland and Sugarland.

HUDSON, MARK

Based in Los Angeles, Hudson is a successful record producer, songwrit-

er and musician. He has worked with Ringo Starr, Aerosmith and Hanson.

With Greg Wells and Jon Bon Jovi, Hudson co-wrote 'Naked' which was included on the 1997 album *Destination Anywhere*.

Visit *markhudson.net*

HUEYMCDONALD.COM

The official cyberspace domain of Bon Jovi bassist Hugh McDonald. It features the following pages: 'Updates', 'Bassics', 'Just Ask', 'Pictures', 'Meetings', 'Post Board,' 'Bass Tab', 'Fun Stuff' and 'Links.' It also has current tour dates and previous updates.

Visit *hueymcdonald.com*

HUMANITARIANISM

The 2006 *Collins English Dictionary & Thesaurus* (published by HarperCollins) defines humanitarianism as "having the interests of mankind at heart."

Bon Jovi have received widespread acclaim for their commitment to helping others. In 2001, they took part in the Twenty Years With AIDS festival, playing alongside Elton John,

Bon Jovi Boulevard

Matchbox Twenty and Sting. After appearing on the *Oprah Winfrey Show* in 2005, the band donated $1 million to Winfrey's Angel Network Foundation. Winfrey used the money to make BON JOVI BOULEVARD in Louisiana. Obviously, the band made a public performance at the Live 8 charity concert in Philadelphia in 2005.

Jon Bon Jovi has proven he is eager to help various international charities, for which work he has won several awards.

In 2001, he was honoured for his charitable work in his home state of New Jersey; he was handed the 'Humanitarian Of The Year' award by The Food Bank of Monmouth and Ocean Counties. In the same year, Jon Bon Jovi proved that you don't have to go to university or college to get a degree: he was awarded an 'Honorary Doctorate In Humanities' from New Jersey's Monmouth University for his commitment to humanitarian aid. In 2006, the organisation HELP USA publicly recognised his relationship with Habitat For Humanity International (HFHI,) a non-profit making organisation that endeavours to build affordable homes for poor people around the world. He became the first ambassador to HFHI.

He has also been associated with a number of charities: the American Red Cross, the Special Olympics and the Elizabeth Glaser Pediatric AIDS Foundation. He works closely with the fashion designer Kenneth Cole on various charitable causes.

Asked about which "social ill" he would prevent if he had the power to do so, Jon told *Time Magazine*:

"In this, the richest country in the history of the world, I think not addressing poverty, domestically, is the one issue that I would really like to point a finger at. Community service as it pertains to affordable housing is what I'm really focused on. Volunteerism in your community is something that is really rewarding and I find it has given me more personal satisfaction than any accolade that my profession brings me. You never know, the people that you're helping may be the next leaders of the free world. It's always great to give someone the opportunity to have a hand up."

Richie Sambora has also worked closely with various charities, including the Michael J. Fox Parkinson's Charity, Dream Street and the Steve Young Foundation.

David Bryan is involved with VH-1's Save The Music charity and is an honorary board member of Only Make Believe, a non-profit making organisation that gives free theatrical workshops to disabled and ill children. Bryan composed their signature song 'Rockin' All Over The World.'

HURLEY, DOROTHEA

Jon Bon Jovi's wife and childhood sweetheart. They split up briefly in the mid-eighties, during which time Jon famously dated actress Diane Lane for around 10 months. But they rekindled their relationship and eventually married (in secret) on April 29, 1989 at the Graceland Wedding Chapel in Las Vegas, Nevada. The wedding took place during some time out from the *New Jersey Syndicate* tour. They have four children together: Stephanie Rose (May 31, 1993,) Jesse James Louis (February 19, 1995,) Jacob Hurley (May 7, 2002) and Romeo Jon (March 29, 2004.)

HYDE PARK

With an audience of 90,000+ and supported by the Pennsylvania band Live, Bon Jovi played a gig (the culmination of a four date UK tour) on a scorching hot day at Hyde Park in Central London on Saturday, 28 June, 2003.

The press reviews of the Hyde Park gig were average; most critics claimed that despite the size and spectacle of the show the band were predictable. The author was at this particular show and recalls that it ran for over three hours breaking the 11 o'clock curfew, and with a good mix of greatest hits and songs from *Bounce*, the gig was thoroughly enjoyable. Ray Davies of The Kinks even joined the band on stage for a version of 'Lola.'

The Guardian writer Sharon O'Connell awarded the concert three stars out of five, calling their greatest hits *"cheap, portentous and cataclysmically clichéd"* although one could hardly claim this particular critic captured the energy and excitement of the show in her rather biased review.

Setlist:
1. 'Bounce'
2. 'You Give Love A Bad Name'
3. 'Runaway'
4. 'Everyday'
5. 'Livin' On A Prayer'
6. 'Undivided'
7. 'Keep The Faith' (with 'Sympathy For The Devil')
8. 'Wanted Dead Or Alive'
9. 'Lay Your Hands On Me'
10. 'The Distance'
11. 'It's My Life'
12. 'Misunderstood'
13. 'Someday I'll Be Saturday Night'
14. 'Just Older'
15. 'I'll Be There For You'
16. 'In These Arms'
17. 'Born To Be My Baby'
18. 'I'll Sleep When I'm Dead' (with 'Dancing In The Street' and 'Rocking All Over The World')
19. 'Raise Your Hands'
20. 'These Days'
21. 'I Got The Girl'
22. 'Lola'
23. 'Blood On Blood'
24. 'Shout'
25. 'Captain Crash & The Beauty Queen From Mars'
26. 'Bad Medicine'
27. 'Twist And Shout'
28. 'Never Say Goodbye'

I

I BELIEVE

Written by Jon Bon Jovi, 'I Believe' is the opening track on *Keep The Faith* and it was the fifth single taken from that album. It was issued in the UK on October 2, 1993 and peaked at Number 11, spending six weeks in the charts. It was not released in the US because the album had not been a big success there.

(UK) Track Listing:
1. 'I Believe' *(Clearmountain Mix)*
2. 'Runaway' *(Live)*
3. 'Livin' On A Prayer' *(Live)*
4. 'Wanted Dead Or Alive' *(Live)*

IDOL, BILLY

English punk rock singer whose band Generation X was one of the first wave of punk bands in the late seventies. Idol has also had an extensive solo career with hits like 'White Wedding' and 'Rebel Yell.' His comeback album *Devil's Playground* was released to critical acclaim in 2005.

Along with Little Angels and the Manic Street Preachers, Idol supported Bon Jovi at the Milton Keynes Na-

tional Bowl on September 18 and 19, 1993.

Visit *billyidol.com*

I'LL BE THERE FOR YOU

The third single release from *New Jersey* was written by Jon and Sambora. It was issued in the UK on April 29, 1989 and reached Number 18, but in the States it was a Number 1 smash hit. The video (directed by Wayne Isham) is merely a live performance by the band, with the black and white segments filmed at London's Wembley Arena.

I'LL SLEEP WHEN I'M DEAD

The fourth single released from *Keep The Faith* was penned by Jon, Richie Sambora and Desmond Child. It was issued in the UK on August 7, 1993 and peaked at Number 17, spending five weeks in the charts. It reached Number 97 in the *Billboard* Hot 100, which is the band's lowest ever singles chart position. The track listings of the American and British release differed:

US Release:
1. 'I'll Sleep When I'm Dead'
2. 'I'll Sleep When I'm Dead' *(Live)*

UK Release:
1. 'I'll Sleep When I'm Dead'
2. 'Blaze Of Glory' *(Live)*
3. 'Wild In The Streets' *(Live)*

IN AND OUT OF LOVE

The second single from the band's second album *7800° Fahrenheit*. It was not issued in the UK but it was released in America in July, 1985 where it peaked at Number 69 in the *Billboard* Hot 100. The original version appears on the 1994 collection *Cross Road*, while a live version (recorded April 28, 1985 in Tokyo, Japan) is included in *One Wild Night Live 1985-2001.*

IN IT FOR LOVE

The second single taken from Richie Sambora's second solo album was issued in the UK on August 1, 1998, peaking at Number 58. It was written with revered songwriter Richie Supa. 'In It For Love' is an acoustic based track, whose opening notes sound not too dissimilar to Eric Clapton's 'Tears In Heaven.' It's just a bit too low-key and twee. Sure, Sambora is a good singer but this track will make you yawn more than once.

IN THESE ARMS

Written by Jon, Richie Sambora and David Bryan, 'In These Arms' was the third single released from *Keep The Faith*. It was issued in the UK on May 15, 1993 and peaked at Number 9, spending a total of seven weeks in the charts. In the States it sold less, reaching Number 27 in the *Billboard* Hot 100. The promotional video consists of live performances by the band, filmed at Stabler Arena in Bethlehem, Pennsylvania on December 31, 1992 and Dane County Coliseum in Madison, Wisconsin on March 1993.

ISCHGL

An Austrian ski resort on the border with Switzerland. An end of skiing season concert, the Top Of The Mountain Concert, is held here every year. Jon Bon Jovi played a solo gig here in 1998, and other stars to have played there include Elton John, Tina Turner and Bob Dylan. *Black Velvet* editor Shari Black attended Jon's gig. A decade later, she recalls:

"One of the shows that will stand out in my memory for being 'different' and 'something I'll never forget' was a Jon Bon Jovi solo show. In May, 1998 Jon Bon Jovi toured with The Big Dogs in Europe, and one of the shows was in Ischgl in Austria. Ischgl was a ski resort and the show was up the top of a mountain! You had to get a ski lift up to the mountain for the show and then back down afterwards. They started letting fans up at 7am in the morning as the show was to be around midday/1pm. Naturally there was snow everywhere and the funniest thing was that instead of a metal barrier at the front, the barrier was a huge five foot block of ice! Insane!"

ISHAM, WAYNE

A renowned director of music videos, Isham's credits include Judas Priest, Mötley Crüe, Queensrÿche, Megadeth, Metallica, Ozzy Osbourne, Pink Floyd and Skid Row. He has also worked with such pop stars as Michael and Janet Jackson, Billy Joel, Madonna and Whitney Houston.

He directed *all* the music videos for the *New Jersey* album, which can be found the on VHS collection *New Jersey: The Videos*. Isham made a film of the three day Moscow Music Peace Festival in 1989, and also directed the video for Jon's solo release 'Blaze Of

Glory.' Years later, he directed the video for the 'It's My Life' single. He is a close friend of the band.

IT'S MY LIFE

The hit single taken from Bon Jovi's 2000 rock album *Crush*; it was written by Jon and Richie Sambora, together with the revered Swedish songwriters Jay Ordin and Max Martin. The song references Jon's fictional characters Tommy and Gina who were made famous in the classic Bon Jovi song 'Livin' On A Prayer'.

Preceding the album's release, it was issued in the UK on June 3, 2000 and hit Number 3, spending 13 weeks in the charts. It spent four weeks on top of the European singles chart. In the States, the band were pleased to learn that 'It's My Life' made it to Number 33 on the *Billboard* Hot 100, making it their first Top 40 single in five years. The song is notable for its references to Frank Sinatra and Jon's film *U-571* and for Sambora's use of the talk-box musical device.

It was nominated for two Grammys, namely 'Best Rock Performance By A Duo Or Group With Vocal' and 'Best Rock Song.' However, it did win the 'Video Of The Year' at the VH1 My Music Awards. The video was directed by Wayne Isham and stars actors Will Estes as Tommy and Shiri Appleby as Gina. Jon actually invited 1,000 fans to appear in the video, which was filmed in LA.

J

JACKSON, LAURA

Laura Jackson is a British author of popular biographies of rock stars and celebrities, including Queen, Brian May, Mick Jagger and The Eagles. Her 256- page hardback biography of Jon Bon Jovi was published in 2003 via Portrait. The paperback version is still in print.

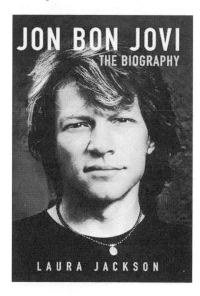

JANIE, DON'T TAKE YOUR LOVE TO TOWN

The third and final single from Jon's solo album *Destination Anywhere* was released in the UK on November 15 1997, and reached Number 13 in the singles chart. It was recorded at Jon's personal recording facility Sanctuary II Studios in New Jersey during August, 1996.

Track Listing:
1. 'Janie, Don't Take Your Love To Town' *(Radio edit)*

2. 'Talk To Jesus' *(Demo)*
3. 'Billy Get Your Guns' *(Live)*
4. 'Janie, Don't Take Your Love To Town'

JAMBCO

A record label formed by Jon Bon Jovi in the late 1980s. The name Jambco stood for Jon, Anthony, Matt Bongiovi Company. Jambco's releases were distributed through Mercury Records, who also handled Bon Jovi's albums. The label released Billy Falcon's *Pretty Blue World* and Aldo Nova's *Blood Other Bricks,* and Skid Row and Colour Me Badd were also on the roster. *New Jersey, Keep The Faith* and the EP *Bed Of Roses* were also released via Jambco in certain territories. The label is no longer in operation, having folded allegedly

due to a lack of commercial success with its releases.

JAY AND SILENT BOB STRIKE BACK

Written and directed by Kevin Smith, *Jay And Silent Bob Strike Back* is a comedy about two unlucky pop-culture lovin' characters named Jay and Silent Bob. The film features the classic Bon Jovi anthem 'Bad Medicine.'

JEFFRIES, NEIL

An established rock writer and occasional author, Neil Jeffries currently writes for *Classic Rock* and has

previously contributed to rock magazines such as *Kerrang!* His detailed 299 page hardback book *Bon Jovi: A Biography* was published in 1996 by Sidgwick & Jackson Ltd. A paperback version was issued in 1997 but is sadly now out of print.

JFK MEMORIAL HIGH SCHOOL

Ticco Torres attended this high school in Iselin, New Jersey.

JOHN, ELTON

Undoubtedly one of the world's most famous, iconic and successful rock stars, Elton John is, in a word, legendary. Incredibly prolific, many critics regard his 1970s albums as his best work. His 1973 double album *Goodbye Yellow Brick Road* was a childhood favourite of Jon Bon Jovi.

In 1989, during the first of four Bon Jovi concerts at Wembley Arena in London, Elton John, Brian May and a few other rock stars who attended the gig joined the band on stage for an encore of The Beatles song 'Get Back.'

Elton John collaborated with Jon on his debut solo album *Blaze Of Glory*; he played piano on 'Billy Get Your Gun' and supplied piano and backing vocals on 'Dyin' Ain't Much Of A Livin'.' In 2001, Bon Jovi took part in the Twenty Years With AIDS festival playing alongside Elton John. Both Elton John and Jon Bon Jovi appeared in the US show *Ally McBeal*.

Visit *eltonjohn.com*

J.P. STEVENS HIGH SCHOOL

David Bryan attended this high school in Edison, New Jersey.

JUDAS PRIEST

Legendary heavy metal band from the English West Midlands. Their most iconic albums include *British Steel*, *Screaming For Vengeance* and *Painkiller*. The most famous line-up of the band is: singer Rob Halford, guitarists KK Downing and Glenn Tipton and bassist Ian Hill.

Bon Jovi supported the self-proclaimed Metal Gods during their tour of Canada in July, 1986. The dates were:

July 14 – PNE Coliseum, Vancouver
July 17 – Northlands Coliseum,
Edmonton
July 19 – The Arena, Winnipeg
July 22 – Maple Leaf Gardens,
Toronto
July 23 – The Forum, Montreal
July 24 – Quebec Coliseum, Quebec
July 27 – Ontario Civic Center,
Ottawa

At the time Priest were on the road promoting their pop-metal album *Turbo*. The North American tour was controversial amongst Priest fans because the band hired ex-Legs Diamond drummer Jonathan Valen to support their own drummer Dave Holland, and thus bolster their live sound. They attempted to "hide" Valen inside the stage so the audience wouldn't notice they had extra support; but after seeing the band in LA, *Kerrang!*'s Derek Oliver reported the story of a "secret" drummer and Valen was consequently dropped after the tour.

Jonathan Valen:

"...Bon Jovi was probably the most professional support band I encountered during that period. The crew all wore custom shirts with embroidered flags of different countries on them. We had toured with them through Canada when Slippery When Wet *hit the charts and the rest is history. We knew they were going on to greatness. Those boys deserve all the success they achieved."*

Visit *judaspriest.com*

JUILLIARD SCHOOL OF MUSIC

Based at the Lincoln Center in New York City, Juilliard is one of the world's premier schools of dance, drama, music and the performing

K

KALODNER, JOHN

A highly successful A&R man, John Kalodner has worked with Bon Jovi, Journey, Heart, REO Speedwagon and Aerosmith, amongst many others. He worked at Atlantic Records in the seventies before moving on to Geffen in the eighties. He retired in 2006.

Visit *johnkalodner.com*

KARAKOGLOU, GEORGE

An acquaintance of Jon Bon Jovi's who co-wrote the track 'Runaway.'

The airplay this song had on a rock station in Long Island, New York brought it to the attention of Poly-Gram A&R man Derek Shulman, who was so impressed that he persuaded fellow executives to sign Jon to their label.

KAZEE, JEFF

Based in New York, Jeff Kazee is an American keyboardist and singer who has played with Southside Johnny and The Asbury Dukes, The Blues Brothers and has even appeared on *The Late Show with David Letterman,* filling in for the show's usual band leader Paul Schaffer. He has

played onstage with Bon Jovi and can be seen on the live DVD *This Left Feels Right.*

Visit *myspace.com/jeffkazeemusic*

KEAN UNIVERSITY

A state university in Union County, New Jersey. Richie Sambora abandoned his studies at this very University during his first year to become a professional musician. He was, however, awarded an 'Honorary Doctorate Of Letters' by the university in May, 2004.

Visit *kean.edu*

KEEP THE FAITH (ALBUM)

After the sheer exhaustion of the *New Jersey Syndicate* tour, Bon Jovi took a well-earned sabbatical. During that time (1990-91) Grunge had exploded onto the scene and become the new musical trend. Would a band like Bon Jovi be popular again when so many of their peers no longer seemed relevant?

In January, 1992 the band hooked up with each other on the Caribbean Island of St. Thomas. On the songwriting front the lyrics were handled by Jon, Richie Sambora, Desmond Child and even keyboardist David Bryan, who co-wrote 'In These Arms.' Over a period of time they penned some 30 songs. Desmond Child co-wrote just two numbers: 'Keep The Faith' and 'I'll Sleep When I'm Dead.'

They recorded *Keep The Faith* with producer Bob Rock, who had been the sound engineer on the band's previous two albums, *Slippery When Wet* and *New Jersey*. Recording took place at Little Mountain Sound Studios in Vancouver, Canada between December, 1991 and August, 1992. Mixing was done by Randy Straub and the engineering was done by Straub and Rock.

Speaking to Malcolm Dome at *Metal Forces* in 1993, Jon said:

"This is a Bon Jovi record for the '90s. You know, I can never repeat old formulae. There is no point in going backwards, that's just bullshit...I made this record for myself."

Keep The Faith was released in the UK on November 14, 1992 and hit Number 1, making it their second consecutive Number 1 in the UK; it spent 70 weeks in the charts. It also went onto become the biggest selling album of 1993 in Europe and the band's fourth biggest-selling album of all time. It was a Number 1 hit in Finland and Australia. However, in the States it only managed to make it to Number 5 (their two previous albums had been Number 1's) in the *Billboard* 200 so evidently the grunge/alternative rock scene had affected their sales. The album had six singles: 'Keep The Faith,' 'Bed Of Roses,' 'In These Arms,' 'I'll Sleep When I'm Dead,' 'I Believe' and 'Dry County.'

Reviewing the album in *Kerrang!* (October, 1992) Paul Elliot had some scathing comments:

"These days, when Bon Jovi play straightforward hard rock, it's without passion or conviction." But he ended his mixed review by saying, *"...Keep The Faith has something for everyone; rock, ballads, pop, whatever."*

The recent remastered version comes with an enhanced CD video of a live performance of 'Keep The Faith,' directed by David Mallet. It should also be noted that on the UK remastered version, the song 'Blame It On The love Of Rock & Roll' is misspelt as 'Blame *In* On The Love Of Rock & Roll.'

Keep The Faith is also the last studio album to feature the original bassist Alec John Such, who was allegedly dismissed from the band because of inadequate musical talent and for speaking to the press about the inner workings of the band.

Track Listing:
1. 'I Believe'
2. 'Keep The Faith'
3. 'I'll Sleep When I'm Dead'
4. 'In These Arms'
5. 'Bed Of Roses'
6. 'If I Was Your Mother'
7. 'Dry County'
8. 'Woman In Love'
9. 'Fear'
10. 'I Want You'
11. 'Blame It On The Love Of Rock & Roll'
12. 'Little Bit Of Soul'

(Some versions of the album have the bonus tracks 'Save A Prayer' and 'Starting All Over Again.')

Author's Review:
Well, this Bon Jovi album sounds like no other and it was obviously an intentional plan. As they entered a

new decade and put their differences behind them, they decided a change in sound and image was in order. The poodle-haired pop-metal boys from NJ thing was in the past. It's almost as if they wanted to sound like U2, a band Jon rates very highly. There's lots of piano, extended guitar solos and soaring power ballads. There's little of the melodic rock that made albums like Slippery When Wet so enjoyable. Take the first song 'I Believe,' it's a great track with a funky rhythm and even better than that is the excellent 'I'll Sleep When I'm Dead'.

It was a bold move to make this kind of album especially considering the state of the rock world at the time with the explosion of the grunge scene. Perhaps the nine minute 'Dry County' is just too ambitious and there are other times when the band are try-

ing to be too clever. 'In These Arms' is definitely inspired by U2 and there are moments when it sounds like Jon is doing his best Bono impression. No thanks. The production is typically polished and as a result predictable and almost unspectacular; they tried having a grittier sound on their second album and they weren't keen with the results. 'If I Was Your Mother' is an underrated song with a sturdy riff and a thumping chorus; it is unquestionably the most rockin' song on the album. 'Woman In Love' must have one of the most irresistible melodies the band have ever made; ditto 'Fear,' which is surprisingly heavy. 'Blame It On The Love Of Rock & Roll' is fun but could have been made by any eighties rock band.

Overall, there are too many ballads here; it's a grower and you can't

doubt the quality of the music. It was a good idea to allow the enviable talents of David Bryan to come up front as it were. Hmm...no matter how many times I listen to this I am still undecided. I think it's among their best set of lyrics and they do sound "mature" but a dollop of the old hard rockin' Bon Jovi would have been fun. It's a curious release but lacks consistent power.

Rating ***

KEEP THE FAITH (SINGLE)

The first single released from the album of the same name. Written by Jon, Richie Sambora and Desmond Child, it was issued in the UK on October 24, 1992 and hit Number 5. It peaked at a disappointing Number 25 in the US *Billboard* Hot 100, their lowest chart position in over seven years.

KEEP THE FAITH: AN EVENING WITH BON JOVI

Pre-publicity for *Keep The Faith* - Bon Jovi's follow-up to *New Jersey* - included this intimate performance which was first broadcast on MTV in 1992, preceding the album's release in November. The set included covers of The Beatles 'A Little Help From My Friends', Errol Brown's 'Brother

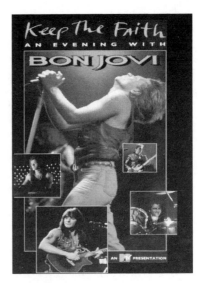

Louie', the classic rock and roll track 'Fever', The Animals' 'We Gotta Get Out Of This Place' and 'It's My Life. Issued on VHS and Laserdisc in 1993, it is now deleted.

Track Listing:
1. 'With A Little Help From My Friends'
2. 'Love For Sale'
3. 'Lay Your Hands On Me'
4. 'Blaze Of Glory'
5. 'Little Bit Of Soul'
6. 'Brother Louie'
7. 'Bed Of Roses'
8. 'Livin' On A Prayer'
9. 'Fever'
10. 'We Gotta Get Out Of This Place'
11. 'It's My Life'
12. 'Wanted Dead Or Alive'
13. 'I'll Sleep When I'm Dead'
14. 'Bad Medicine'
15. 'Keep The Faith'

KEEP THE FAITH: THE VIDEOS

Running for 90 minutes and released in 1994 via Mercury, *Keep The Faith: The Videos* features all the music videos from said album with the exception of 'Dry County', although there is an exclusive video for 'If I Was Your Mother'. There are also interviews and behind the scenes snippets. This VHS/Laserdisc collection has since been deleted.

Track Listing:
1. 'Keep The Faith'
2. 'Bed Of Roses'
3. 'In These Arms'
4. 'If I Was Your Mother'
5. 'I'll Sleep When I'm Dead'
6. 'I Believe'
7. 'I Wish Everyday Could Be Like Christmas'
8. 'Bed Of Roses'
9. 'Ballad Of Youth'
10. 'Dyin' Ain't Much Of A Livin''
11. 'I'll Sleep When I'm Dead'
(Acoustic)

KEEP THE FAITH TOUR (1993)

With memories of the *New Jersey Syndicate* tour far behind them, Bon Jovi went on the road to promote their hit album *Keep The Faith*. The tour commenced at the Colisée de Quebec

in Quebec City (Canada) on February 8, 1993. The North American leg of the tour lasted six weeks, covering most of the major venues. They hit Europe/UK in April and May.

Kerrang! scribe Steve Beebee reviewed the band's gig at the Birmingham NEC on May 10. He wrote: *"Bon Jovi's arena presence entails an almost unique atmospheric magic...Bon Jovi are large than life, and yet so very real."*

Following Europe they headed over to Japan, before it was time to fly back to America in June for another round of dates. On the second US leg, they were supported by the Boston funk rock band Extreme. The second European leg began in Berlin (the tour's 126th gig) in August, and from there they hit all the hot spots in Germany, Switzerland, Poland, Hungary, Austria, Czechoslovakia, Italy, Greece, Turkey, France and England. And then it was on to the Far East, playing in places like Taiwan, Hong Kong, Bangkok, the Philippines and Singapore. An Australian tour followed in October and then it was off to South America before they finally flew back to the States to finish the tour in their homeland in December, '93.

KERRANG!

The first issue of the famed heavy metal magazine *Kerrang*! was published on June 6, 1981; it was edited by Geoff Barton. It was originally a one-off supplement in the weekly music rag *Sounds* but due to its popularity it eventually became a weekly magazine in its own right. Many long-standing rock fans believe its heyday was in the 1980s when it had on its staff such writers as Mick Wall, Malcolm Dome, Dave Ling, Paul Suter, Dave Reynolds, Geoff Barton,

Steve Gett and Gary Bushell. Dome actually penned the first official Bon Jovi book *Faith And Glory* in '94.

Bon Jovi have featured in *Kerrang!* many times over the years, especially during the eighties and early nineties. Speaking about some internal issues in the band after the *New Jersey Syndicate* tour finished in 1990, Jon told Sylvie Simmons at *Kerrang!* in 1994:

"Truth is, Kerrang! *started this whole f**king fiasco. A lot of things had been printed out of context, and that added fuel to the fire."*

Some notable *Kerrang!* covers to feature Bon Jovi include: #253 (1989,) #264 (1989,) #271 (1990,) #300 (1990,) #336 (1991,) #412 (1992,) #440 (1993,) #459 (1993,) #483 (1994,) #500 (1994.)

In terms of the end of year polls, Bon Jovi did not score too badly in the eighties. In 1984, *Bon Jovi* was ranked as the eleventh best album, with Van Halen's *1984* sitting on the top spot. They climbed higher in 1986 with *Slippery When Wet* at number four. *Bad Medicine* was the fourteenth best album of 1988. In the 1990s, when grunge became massively popular, *Kerrang!*'s fan base changed dramatically, but the magazine continued to cover Bon Jovi. These days Bon Jovi would not re-

ally hold much appeal for *Kerrang!* readers.

Visit *kerrang.com*

KINGDOM COME

A melodic rock band that was formed in the States but which now features a complete German line-up. Main man Lenny Wolf was born in Hamburg and has been in the band since it began in 1987. They were signed to Polydor by Derek Shulman, who is well known to fans of Bon Jovi's first few albums. Also, Kingdom Come's self-titled debut album was recorded at Little Mountain Sound Studios in Vancouver with the über-producer Bob Rock. Their latest album, *Ain't Crying For The Moon,* was released in 2006. It was during Bon Jovi's *New Jersey Syndicate* tour that Ratt and Kingdom Come supported the band at some shows in Japan in late December/January, 1988.

Lenny Wolf:

"The promoter from Japan by the name of Udo invited us to play the New Year's Eve show in Tokyo, and to play a few follow-up headline shows throughout Japan later on. A wonderful experience. One funny story keeps popping up in my mind: I remember back in the early eighties, when I was still playing with Stone Fury, my LA band before I started Kingdom Come, a Japanese magazine started a contest questioning who is cuter: Jon or me. I'll never understand why, but I

think John won. (Laughs). We only shared the stage in Tokyo once. Jon seemed to be a charming perfection- ist just like me. And sharing the ele- vator with Ritchie Sambora and our sweethearts did not leave much time to discuss life in general. Looking back after all those years, they must have done something right!"

Visit *lennywolf.com*

KISS

Formed in 1973 in New York City, KISS remains one of America's most popular rock bands, less popular in Britain but huge in North America and Australia. They are famous not just for their music but also for their image, a glam look with painted fac- es like comic book characters. KISS have gone through several line-ups but the original version remains the most popular and by far the most re- spected: Paul Stanley (vocals and rhythm guitar), Gene Simmons (vo- cals and bass guitar), Ace Frehley (lead guitar and vocals) and Peter Criss (drums, percussion and vocals). They did a reunion tour in 1996-97. Like many rock bands from their time, KISS have a long and convolut- ed history; their most successful al- bums include *Destroyer* (1976), *Love Gun* (1977), *Dynasty* (1979), *Crazy Nights* (1987) and *Revenge* (1992). Their 1975 *Alive!* album is without question a classic live album. KISS has also been turned into a franchise with all kinds of memorabilia and items being produced.

A few important facts link KISS and Bon Jovi, aside from having their origins in two cities that are divided only by the Hudson River.

In one of Jon's high school bands, Raze, they played a cover of KISS's 'Strutter' for a talent contest at the

school Sayreville War Memorial. They didn't win.

KISS provided Bon Jovi with one of the biggest stepping stones in their career: on their first trip to Europe in 1984, Bon Jovi supported KISS on a British tour, beginning on Septem- ber 30 at Brighton Centre. The tour finished with two nights at Wembley Arena in London in mid-October.

Jon Bon Jovi told Sylvie Simmons at *Kerrang!* in 1994:

"I remember real well how Gene would go out of his way to be nice to everybody...I went to see them as a kid, and suddenly we were playing with them!"

On August 22, 1987 at the Monsters Of Rock festival at Donington, Gene Simmons and Paul Stanley joined Bon Jovi onstage for an encore of 'Travelin' Band' by Creedence Clear- water Revival and 'We're An Amer- ican Band', with Iron Maiden singer Bruce Dickinson. It was a headlining set from Bon Jovi:

Bruce Kulick was a guitarist in KISS from 1984 to 1996:

Interview:

So what do you recall about the Bon Jovi/KISS tour?

We enjoyed Bon Jovi, but at the time I think they were still finding their sound. So we referred to them as a New Jersey band...working hard to get to the top in other words. We knew that Jon was a star and that the band had huge potential. I remember meeting Jon at a club in the UK and he was so proud to have press on him in Kerrang!, etc. He seemed to be genuine and ambitious.

How did Bon Jovi go down with the KISS audiences?

I remember the crowd liking them. It was a great bill.

Were you impressed with their stage act?

I didn't see them as much as heard them from backstage!

Had you heard their first two albums before they supported KISS?

No...I heard about them though.

Are you surprised by how popular they have become?

Not at all! I am very impressed with the continued massive success, and they deserve it for sure.

Have you met any of the guys in Bon Jovi since then?

I have not seen them much over the years. I loved Richie's first solo disc and I was a guest at the listening party up at Griffith Park Observatory in Hollywood MANY years ago!

Bruce Kulick

Do you have any anecdotes /stories?

I had some friends that dated Richie! One girl from the label was totally into him, but you know he was hard to settle down. I knew about the bass player issues. Using a studio guy and replacing him in time.

Anything else?

I was happy to get to work with Desmond Child as well who, of course, was so important in their career. And Doc McGhee has always been cool to me and I met him originally from Bon Jovi.

Recently I did a favour for a friend who needed some talk-box guitar stuff like 'Livin' On A Prayer,' so that was a trip. And in retrospect there was a song I did with Eric Carr that wound up on his Rockology CD that was strongly reminiscent of the band. So they definitely have been an influence for me.

Bruce Kulick's website: *kulick.net*
Visit *kissonline.com* and *kissontour.com*

KNIGHT, HOLLY

A successful and highly sought after singer, songwriter and musician who is based in Southern California. She has worked with some of the biggest names in the business: Tina Turner, Aerosmith, Meat Loaf, KISS, Ozzy Osbourne, Rod Stewart and Heart, amongst others.

Knight co-wrote 'Stick To Your Guns' on the *New Jersey* album.

Interview:

How did you become acquainted with Bon Jovi? Did they approach you to collaborate?

I met Jon one night at The Rainbow in Hollywood. He was sitting at *a booth with a table of friends, musicians. My friend, Phil Soussan, who was the bass player at the time in Ozzy's [band] knew him, and introduced me to him. Jon stood up and told everyone to please clear the table and then he asked me to sit down. His first words to me were: 'Why haven't we met? And why haven't we worked together?' I was very flattered.*

What do you remember about the recording session for 'Stick To Your Guns?'

I wasn't there for the master recordings of 'Stick To Your Guns,' but we did do the demo in my studio, which I still have, only it's on one inch tape, before the days of Protools. I would say it's very similar to the final version except without the real drums and bass.

You're credited as co-writer of 'Stick To Your Guns'; essentially, what is the song about?

'Stick To Your Guns' is about believing in something and not being swayed by outside opinions and influences even if you have to go to the point of pissing someone off. It has to do with personal integrity...the only person you have to answer to is yourself.

What was the writing process like for that particular song? Jon and Richie are also credited as songwriters.

Jon and Ritchie are also credited as songwriters. Ritchie played guitar. I think I played on a keyboard; I mentioned the title to them. It's a phrase my mother used to say to me growing up and the ironic part is she's the person I mostly had to stick to my guns about! As far as I can remember most of it was written in the first day

What was it like working with the band?

I never had the opportunity to work with the whole band, which is often the case. I usually work with one or two band members, away from the band.

'Stick To Your Guns' features on the album *New Jersey*; did you have any inkling that it would be such a massive success?

Well, let's just say, Bon Jovi was already massive so there was a good chance the album was going to do well.

Have you meet up with them since then?

No, I haven't met up with them recently and they are the nicest guys. Jon was very unpretentious and down to earth. They all were .The band seemed more like a family than a band, which you don't see often. Who knows, maybe they can't stand each other by now! (Laughs.)

Visit *hollyknight.com*

KORTCHMAR, DANNY

A famed singer-songwriter-guitarist-producer, Kortchmar's CV reads like a who's who of popular music. He has worked with Billy Joel, Don Henley, Carole King, Neil Young, Stevie Nicks and James Taylor, amongst others.

Kortchmar co-produced Jon Bon Jovi's debut solo album *Blaze Of Glo-*

ry and even organised the studio band. The pair also co-produced the hit Hall and Oates single 'So Close', which features on the 1990 album *Change Of Season*.

Visit *dannykortchmar.com*

KORZILIUS, PETER

Ex-tour manager, Korzilius is now a key member of Bon Jovi Management. The song 'August 7, 4:15' (on *Destination Anywhere*) was written by Jon about the tragic death of Korzilius' six year old daughter, Katherine, who was murdered on August 7, 1996.

Visit *bonjovi.com*

L

LAGUNA BEACH PD

The police and rock stars go hand in hand, with hardly a month going by without some rock star getting arrested. Richie Sambora was collared by the Laguna Beach PD on March 25, 2008 for driving erratically, with an adult female and two female minors in his vehicle. As reported in the press, Sgt. Jason Kravitz said:

"We did ask for a misdemeanour child endangerment charge to be filed against him...We also recommended they charge him with misdemeanour DUI."

He was actually arrested for DUI (Driving Under The Influence) after failing some on the spot sobriety tests, but because he was not considered to be dangerous he was not charged with child endangerment.

LANE, DIANE

An American actress who has never quite been an A-list star despite nominations for a host of thespian awards, including an Academy Award, two Golden Globes, a Screen Actors Guild Award and an Emmy.

Some of her films of the eighties include *The Outsiders, Rumble Fish* and *The Cotton Club.* In the 1990s she starred in *Chaplin* and *Murder At 1600,* and more recently in *Hollywoodland* and *Jumper.* She dated Jon Bon Jovi in the mid eighties during his temporary split from Dorothea Hurley, who is now his wife. Their relationship is still talked about in the celebrity tabloids.

Visit *dianelane.com*

LAROCA, FRANK

Also known as Frankie LaRocka, he was an American drummer who is probably best known for his extensive tours with Bryan Adams during the eighties, as well as his work with John Waite, Patty Smyth and Scandal.

LaRocha contributed drums to Jon's 'Runaway' demo, recorded at

New York's Power Station Studios in June, 1982 with producer Billy Squier, keyboardist Roy Bittan, bassist Hugh McDonald and guitarist Tim Pierce. This session band was dubbed The All Star Review, and the demo in question ultimately led to Jon's recording deal with PolyGram in '83. LaRoca died of pneumonia on May 12, 2005, aged 51.

LAY YOUR HANDS ON ME

Written by Jon and Richie Sambora, 'Lay Your Hands On Me' is the first track on the hugely successful *New Jersey* album and the album's fourth single release. It was issued in the UK on August 26, 1989 and reached Number 18, spending six weeks in the charts. It hit Number 7 in the *Billboard* Hot 100. As Bon Jovi were so busy on tour promoting the album, the video (directed by Wayne Isham) for this song is merely a montage of live shots from Tacoma Dome in Washington and the Memorial Coliseum in Regan. The song is a live favourite of both fans and the band.

LEADING MAN, THE

A 1996 film starring Jon Bon Jovi as Robin George, a successful Hollywood actor who arrives in London to make his West End debut in the play *The Hit Man*; he becomes entangled in a love affair between the play's writer and leading actress. Filming took place in the English capital, with Jon and his family basing themselves in a rented house near Wandsworth Common. During the actual filming, however, Jon stayed in a trailer in Borough Market, South London. The film was directed by John Duigan and premièred at the '96 Toronto Film Festival. The tagline ran: *"Inde-*

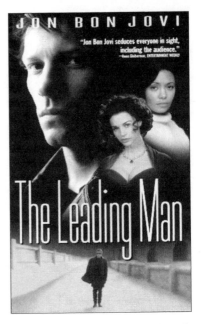

cent. Immoral. Irresitible. It's the role he was born to play."

LEECHES, THE

A pub band (also known as Johnny and The Leeches) formed by Jon Bon Jovi in the early eighties. The Leeches never got further than the clubs of New York and New Jersey, but gave Jon the chance to hone his craft in front of a live audience.

LEONARD, PATRICK

A former member of the Chicago rock band Trillion (which also fea-

tured former Toto singer Dennis 'Fergie' Fredriksen), Patrick Leonard is an American producer, keyboardist and songwriter. He is known for his work with Madonna and Roger Waters. He produced Bon Jovi's 2003 album *This Left Feels Right*.

LESS THAN JAKE

Less Than Jake formed in 1992 in Florida. Never major league players in the rock world, they nevertheless acquired a loyal following. Between 1995 and 2008 they released seven albums, their biggest US hit being the 1996 album *Losing Streak*.

They were one of the guest bands to support Bon Jovi on the American leg of their 2000 *Crush* tour. That particular part of the world tour began on November 3 at the Independence Arena in Charlotte, North Carolina and continued for a month, playing 15 venues in 11 States.

Visit *lessthanjake.com*

LEVIN, TONY

Tony Levin is a distinguished American bass player, who has worked with such luminaries as Yes, Pink Floyd, King Crimson, Cher, Alice Cooper, John Lennon and Todd Rundgren. He joined Richie Sambo-

ra's band for his short tour of America in support of *Stranger In This Town*.

Visit *tonylevin.com*

LEVON

This Bernie Taupin-Elton John song was covered by Jon Bon Jovi for the 1991 album *Two Rooms,* which celebrates the back catalogue of the famed English songwriting duo. Other artists who appeared on the album include Kate Bush, Rod Stewart and Phil Collins.

LEWIS, BLAKE

A runner-up on the sixth season of the smash hit TV show *American Idol*, Lewis is known as a singer-songwriter and beatboxer. Beatboxing is a vocal style that is mostly used in Hip Hop and Rap music, in which the vocalist uses his mouth to

produce various sounds such as drum beats and rhythms.

During *American Idol* he sang an altered version of 'You Give Love A Bad Name,' adding beatboxing parts. Jon Bon Jovi was the mentor for that particular episode and said on TV that Lewis was *"rolling the dice."* Beatboxing has become Lewis' signature vocal style. According to sales figures from *SoundScan*, the network system that tracks sales of digital downloads, Lewis' version of the Bon Jovi song sold 192,000 copies on *iTunes* during its first few weeks of release, consequently featuring in several US charts.

Visit *blakelewisofficial.com*

LIE TO ME

The third single release from *These Days*, written by Jon and Sambora. It was issued in the UK on November 25, 1995 and reached Number 10, spending eight weeks in the charts. Meanwhile, in the *Billboard* Hot 100, it managed a lowly Number 76.

LIGHT OF DAY

A 1987 film written and directed by Paul Schrader and starring Michael J. Fox and Gena Rowlands. The soundtrack features the original Bon Jovi track 'Only Lonely.'

LIRONI, STEVE

A former member of Scottish pop band Altered Images, Steve Lironi is a highly talented producer who has produced hits for the likes of Black Grape, Fun Lovin' Criminals, Happy Mondays and Hanson. He is married to Scottish actress and Altered Images singer Clare Grogan.

Lironi is credited as a co-producer of Jon Bon Jovi's solo opus *Destination Anywhere* along with Jon, Dave Stewart, Desmond Child and Eric Bazilian. He co-produced the following tracks:

'Janie, Don't Take Your Love To Town'
Recorded at Sanctuary II Studio, New Jersey; August, 1996.
(Co-producer and programmer)
'Staring At Your Window'
Recorded at Sanctuary II Studio, New Jersey; 1996.
(Co-producer, loops/keyboards)
'Every Word Was A Piece Of My Heart'
Recorded at Sanctuary II Studio, New Jersey; January, 1997.
(Co-producer, programming and electric guitar)
'Destination Anywhere'
Recorded at Sanctuary II Studio, New Jersey; 1996.
(Co-producer, synths, electric guitar and programming)
'Learning How To Fall'
Recorded at Sanctuary II Studio, New Jersey; August, 1996.
(Co-producer, acoustic guitar, synths, loops and programming)
'Naked'
Recorded at Sanctuary II Studio, New Jersey; January, 1997.
(Co-producer, acoustic guitar, loops and programming)
'Little City'

*Recorded at Sanctuary II Studio,
New Jersey; January, 1997.
(Co-producer, synths and
programming)*

LITTLE ANGELS

Formed in 1984 in Scarborough, England, Little Angels had some modest success with 1991's *Young Gods* and 1993's UK Number 1 smash hit *Jam*. The band folded in 1994. Little Angels supported Bon Jovi for two nights (along with fellow support bands Billy Idol and the Manic Street Preachers) at Milton Keynes National Bowl on September 18 and 19, 1993.

Visit *tobyjepson.com*

LITTLE CITY

Directed by Roberto Benabib, Little City is a romantic comedy that was released in 1997 and went straight to VHS. The film follows the complicated love lives and egos of a group of inhabitants of San Francisco. Jon Bon Jovi plays bartender and womaniser Kevin.

LITTLE MOUNTAIN SOUND STUDIOS

Situated in Vancouver, British Columbia (Canada), Little Mountain Sound Studios is one of the most popular recording facilities in the North America, and has attracted some of the biggest names in rock, including AC/DC, Mötley Crüe, Aerosmith, Whitesnake, Scorpions and The Cult.

Revered producer Bruce Fairbairn produced Prism's debut album there in 1977, and he used Little Mountain Sound Studios for most of his career. Together with his protégé Bob Rock, he turned Little Mountain Sound Studios into one of the most sought after facilities in the business.

Some famous albums that have been recorded at Little Mountain Sound Studios include:

AC/DC – *The Razor's Edge* (1990)
Bryan Adams – *Reckless* (1984)
Aerosmith – *Permanent Vacation* (1987), *Pump* (1989) and *Get A Grip* (1993)
Mötley Crüe – *Dr. Feelgood* (1989)
Poison – *Flesh And Blood* (1990)

Bon Jovi recorded three albums at Little Sound Studios: 1986's *Slippery When Wet* (produced by Bruce Fairbairn), 1988's *New Jersey* (also produced by Bruce Fairbairn) and 1992's *Keep The Faith* (produced by Bob Rock).

LIVE 8

A series of charity concerts held around the world on July 2, 2005 on the eve of the international G8 Summit. Live 8 was the brainchild of Sir Bob Geldof and Midge Ure, organisers of 1985's Live Aid concerts at Wembley Stadium in London and JFK Stadium in Philadelphia. Bon Jovi performed at the Philadelphia concert, alongside such eclectic names as Def Leppard, Jay Z and Destiny's Child.

In a press statement, Jon Bon Jovi said:

"We're excited to be part of such a great line-up of artists for these shows...And we're honoured to help fulfil Bob's vision. The impact he

made in Africa 20 years ago is still the benchmark by which all charitable music events are measured."

Visit *live8live.com*

LIVE FROM LONDON

Directed by the esteemed concert music director David Mallet, and released on video in 1995, *Live From London* was recorded at Wembley Stadium on June 25, 1995 and was

the band's first full concert video release. It was issued on DVD in 2003. The actual concert footage was edited for both releases and runs for 90 minutes.

Track Listing:
1. 'Livin' On A Prayer'
2. 'You Give Love A Bad Name'
3. 'Keep The Faith'
4. 'Always'
5. 'Blaze Of Glory'
6. 'Lay Your Hands On Me'
7. 'I'll Sleep When I'm Dead' / 'Papa Was A Rolling Stone'
8. 'Bad Medicine' / 'Shout'
9. 'Hey God'
10. 'Wanted Dead Or Alive'
11. 'This Ain't A Love Song'
12. 'These Days' *(Bonus video)*

LIVIN' ON A PRAYER

The second single release from *Slippery When Wet* was written by Jon, Sambora and Desmond Child. It was released in the UK on October 25, 1986 and peaked at Number 4, spending 15 weeks in the charts. In the States it was the second single from the album to hit Number 1 in the *Billboard* Hot 100. During the recording of the album Jon was unimpressed with the song and tried to encourage the band to dump it; Sambora, however, was adamant it would be a hit and so they re-recorded it. The song is known for its use of the talk-box musical device. The original version can be located as a hidden track on the box-set *100,000,000 Bon Jovi Fans Can't Be Wrong*. The song is said to have been inspired by the American working classes and the Labour Unions during the Reagan era. 'Livin' On A Prayer' also references Jon's fictional characters Tommy and Gina who would later be mentioned in the hit single 'It's My Life'. The promotional video, filmed at the Mayo Civic Center in Rochester, Minnesota, won the 'Best Performance' award at the MTV Music Awards in California in 1987.

LIVING IN SIN

The fifth and final single release from *New Jersey* was issued in the UK on December 9, 1989 and peaked at Number 35, but in the States it reached Number 9 in the *Billboard* Hot 100. The song was solely written by Jon Bon Jovi. Similarly to the video to 'Born To Be My Baby,' the video for 'Living In Sin' (directed by Wayne Isham) was filmed in black and white, presumably due to budget constraints.

LL COOL J

A popular American rapper and occasional actor whose real name is James Todd Smith. He has had a stream of hit singles notably 'Mama Said Knock You Out', '4, 3, 2, 1', 'I Need Love' and 'Hey Lover'. His film credits include *Toys, S.W.A.T., Any Given Sunday* and *Charlie's Angels*.

Richie Sambora guested on the song 'Baby' on LL Cool J's 2008 album *Exit 13*, his last for Def Jam Records. Other guest stars include 50 Cent, Wyclef Jean and The-Dream.

Visit *myspace.com/llcoolj*

LOCKLEAR, HEATHER

An American actress who these days is more famous for marrying rock stars than for her acting. Previously married to Mötley Crüe drummer Tommy Lee, Locklear married Richie Sambora on December 15, 1994 in Red Bank, New Jersey. Their formal wedding was held a couple of days later at the American Cathedral Episcopal Church in Paris. The couple had one daughter, and divorced in 2007. Locklear has starred in a number of high-profile TV shows,

including *Dynasty*, *T.J. Hooker* and *Melrose Place*. Her films include *Wayne's World 3*, *The First Wives Club* and *The Perfect Man*.

LOGAN

Hailing from Glasgow, Scotland, Logan is a five-piece rock outfit which formed in 2003. Their debut album, *First Leaf Fallen,* followed in 2004. They managed to acquire a fan base in the States before achieving any popularity in Britain. Given their hard rock, post-grunge sound, they have been likened to Alter Bridge, Creed, Nickelback and bands of that ilk.

They supported Bon Jovi with The Feeling on June 21, 2008 at Hampden Park, Glasgow, before an audience of 25,000-30,000 fans. Guitarist Mick Coll says:

"I can tell you that opening for Bon Jovi was an incredible experience for us. It opened Logan's sound up to a mass audience that wouldn't otherwise have been aware of us. The impact of the show was immediate and can clearly be seen in ticket sales, album sales and website hits."

Visit *logan-net.com*

LOST HIGHWAY (ALBUM)

Inspired by their collaboration with Jennifer Nettles of Sugarland on the country crossover track 'Who Say's Who Can't Go Home,' Bon Jovi decided to make an album of Nashville influenced songs.

Lost Highway was recorded at Henson Recording Studios in LA, NRG Recording in Hollywood and Starstruck Studios in Nashville in early 2006.

The following tracks were produced by Dann Huff: '(You Want To) Make A Memory', 'We Got It Going On', 'Any Other Day', 'Seat Next To You', 'Till We Ain't Strangers Anymore' and 'I Love This Town.' The following tracks were produced by John Shanks: 'Lost Highway', 'Summertime', 'Whole Lot Of Leavin'', 'Everybody's Broken', 'The Last Night', 'One Step Closer' and 'Lonely.' Desmond Child was the executive producer of the album.

On the songwriting side, there are contributions from Jon, Richie Sambora, John Shanks and Desmond Child; Billy Falcon co-wrote 'Everybody's Broken' with Jon; 'Seat Next To You' was written by Jon, Sambora and Hillary Lindsey; 'Lonely' was written by Jon, Desmond Child and Daryl Brown and 'Any Other Day' was co-written by Jon, Sambora and Geordie Sampson.

Clearly the band's collaboration with Jennifer Nettles influenced them to work with other country artists: 'We Got It Going On' is a duet with Big & Rich, and the country duo also co-wrote the track with Jon and Sambora. Country starlet LeAnn Rimes shares the vocals with Jon on 'Till We Ain't Strangers Anymore', which was written by Jon, Sambora and the country singer-songwriter Brett James.

Lost Highway was released in the UK on June 11, 2007 and peaked at Number 2 in the Top 40 but in the States it was a Number 1 hit on the *Billboard* 200, making it the band's third US Number 1 after *Slippery When Wet* and *New Jersey*. At the 2008 Grammy Awards, *Lost Highway* was nominated for 'Best Pop Vocal Album'. *Lost Highway* is one of Bon Jovi's most commercially successful albums; it has sold almost four million copies around the world.

In the States, fans buying the album from Walmart stores had the chance to buy bonus DVDs featuring soundcheck performances, and in Australia and Japan a tour edition of the album featuring a second disc of six live performances was released on January 12, 2008.

Track Listing:
1. 'Lost Highway'
2. 'Summertime'
3. '(You Want To) Make A Memory'
4. 'Whole Lot Of Leavin''
5. 'We Got It Going On' *(Feat. Big & Rich)*
6. 'Any Other Day'
7. 'Seat Next To You'
8. 'Everybody's Broken'
9. 'Till We Ain't Strangers Anymore' *(Feat. LeAnn Rimes)*
10. 'The Last Night'
11. 'One Step Closer'
12. 'I Love This Town'
13. 'Lonely'
14. 'Put The Boy Back In Cowboy' *(Bonus track on the Japanese version only)*

Author's Review:
This is an odd one: the idea of a Nashville style rock album by Bon

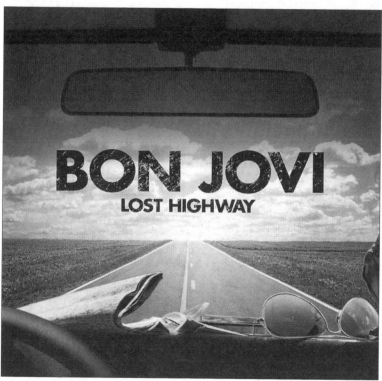

Jovi is not greeted with open enthusi-asm by my ears. There's a fair selec-tion of neatly composed melodies but the biggest problem is not the coun-try thing (which is actually not that dominant) but a complete lack of ex-citement and energy. The songs are too laid back and either slow or mid-paced. The sleepy 'Till We Ain't Stran-gers Anymore' and the dull 'Whole Lot Of Leavin'' are primary reasons why country music doesn't often work well with pop/soft rock bands; there's no real connection there. 'We Got It Going On' is actually a decent track helped by Sambora's use of the talk-box and a groovy riff.

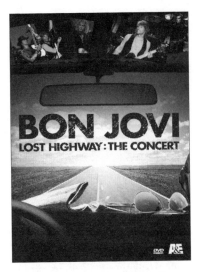

So it's a bold venture on behalf of the band and I'm completely flabber-gasted as to why this album has been so commercially successful. To use a cliché, Lost Highway *is a middle of the road album for housewives on a Sunday afternoon. Frankly, it's dull and tedious and lacks decent riffs and a couple of forceful singles.*

Rating **

LOST HIGHWAY (SINGLE)

The second single release in the UK from the album of the same name. It was issued on December 3, 2007 and only made it to Number 117 in the UK Top 40 the worst ever position for the band in the UK singles chart. The song was written by Jon, Richie Sam-bora and John Shanks.

LOST HIGHWAY: THE CONCERT

Released on DVD in 2007, *Lost Highway: The Concert* is the band's third full concert release and sees them performing the entire album in front of just 400 fans in Chicago. It is the first time they have ever per-formed a complete album. The bonus material includes interviews with the band and the usual gallery, discog-raphy and photography additions as well as bonus performances of 'Halle-lujah', '(You Want To) Make A Mem-ory', 'Lost Highway', 'Wanted Dead Or Alive', 'Who Says You Can't Go Home' and 'Whole Lot Of Leavin''.

Track Listing:
1. 'Lost Highway'
2. 'Summertime'
3. '(You Want To) Make A Memory'
4. 'Whole Lot Of Leavin''
5. 'We Got It Going On'
6. 'Any Other Day'
7. 'Seat Next To You'
8. 'Everybody's Broken'
9. 'Till We Ain't Strangers Anymore'
10. 'The Last Night'
11. 'One Step Closer'
12. 'I Love This Town'
13. 'It's My Life'
14. 'Wanted Dead Or Alive'
15. 'Who Says You Can't Go Home'

LOST HIGHWAY TOUR (2007-08)

To support *Lost Highway*, their U.S. Number 1 album, Bon Jovi hit the road for a mammoth tour that ran from October 25, 2007 to 15 July, 2008. They also played a handful of charity concerts prior to the tour. During the tour, they gave fans special treats by performing the original versions of 'Hey God' and 'Always' which hadn't been played since the *These Days* tour. Many bands supported Bon Jovi throughout the tour, mostly unknown bands from areas local to the venues at which they happened to be performing. They broke many records during the tour, including a 10 night stint at new Prudential Center in Newark, New Jersey. They played five sold out nights at Toronto's Air Canada Center and a FREE concert at New York's Central Park, dubbed 'All-Star Concert In Central Park'.

NORTH AMERICAN DATES (& VENUES) PART I

October 25, 2007 - Prudential Center, Newark, NJ (USA)
October 26, 2007 - Prudential Center, Newark, NJ (USA)
October 28, 2007 - Prudential Center, Newark, NJ (USA)

October 30, 2007 - Prudential Center, Newark, NJ (USA)
November 1, 2007 - Prudential Center, Newark, NJ (USA)
November 3, 2007 - Prudential Center, Newark, NJ (USA)
November 4, 2007 - Prudential Center, Newark, NJ (USA)
November 7, 2007 - Prudential Center, Newark, NJ (USA)
November 9, 2007 - Prudential Center, Newark, NJ (USA)
November 10, 2007 - Prudential Center, Newark, NJ (USA)
November 14, 2007 - Bell Centre, Montreal, Quebec (Canada)
November 15, 2007 - Bell Centre, Montreal, Quebec (Canada)
November 17, 2007 - Scotiabank Place, Ottawa, Ontario (Canada)
November 19, 2007 - John Labatt Centre, London, Ontario (Canada)
December 6, 2007 - Air Canada Centre, Toronto, Ontario (Canada)
December 7, 2007 - Air Canada Centre, Toronto, Ontario (Canada)
December 9, 2007 - MTS Centre, Winnipeg, Manitoba (Canada)
December 10, 2007 - Credit Union Centre, Saskatoon, Saskatchewan (Canada)
December 12, 2007 - Rexall Place, Edmonton, Alberta (Canada)
December 13, 2007 - Pengrowth Saddledome, Calgary, Alberta (Canada)

December 15, 2007 - General Motors Place, Vancouver, British Columbia (Canada)
December 16, 2007 - General Motors Place, Vancouver, British Columbia (Canada)

JAPANESE DATES (& VENUES)

January 11, 2008 - Nagoya Dome, Nagoya (Japan)
January 13, 2008 - Tokyo Dome, Tokyo (Japan)
January 14, 2008 - Tokyo Dome, Tokyo (Japan)
January 16, 2008 - Kyocera Dome, Osaka (Japan)

AUSTRALIAN & NEW ZEALAND DATES (& VENUES)

January 19, 2008 - Sidney Myer Music Bowl, Melbourne (Australia)
January 21, 2008 - Acer Arena, Sydney, New South Wales (Australia)

January 22, 2008 - Acer Arena, Sydney, New South Wales (Australia)
January 25, 2008 - Subiaco Oval, Perth, Western Australia (Australia)
January 27, 2008 - AMI Stadium, Christchurch (New Zealand)

NORTH AMERICAN DATES (& VENUES) PART II

February 18, 2008 - Qwest Center, Omaha, NE (USA)
February 20, 2008 - The Palace of Auburn Hills, Detroit, MI (USA)
February 21, 2008 - Bradley Center, Milwaukee, WI (USA)
February 23, 2008 - United Center, Chicago, IL (USA)
February 24, 2008 - United Center, Chicago, IL (USA)
February 26, 2008 - United Center, Chicago, IL (USA)
February 28, 2008 - Verizon Center, Washington, DC (USA)
March 2, 2008 - Wachovia Center, Philadelphia, PA (USA)

March 3, 2008 - Wachovia Center, Philadelphia, PA (USA)
March 5, 2008 - Mellon Arena, Pittsburgh, PA (USA)
March 7, 2008 - Mohegan Sun Arena, Uncasville, CT (USA)
March 8, 2008 - Mohegan Sun Arena, Uncasville, CT (USA)
March 10, 2008 - Air Canada Centre, Toronto, Ontario (Canada)
March 12, 2008 - Air Canada Centre, Toronto, Ontario (Canada)
March 13, 2008 - Air Canada Centre, Toronto, Ontario (Canada)
March 15, 2008 - Mellon Arena, Pittsburgh, PA (USA)
March 16, 2008 - Greensboro Coliseum, Greensboro, NC (USA)
March 18, 2008 - Xcel Energy Center, Saint Paul, MN (USA)
March 19, 2008 - Xcel Energy Center, Saint Paul, MN (USA)
March 31, 2008 - Pepsi Center, Denver, CO (USA)
April 2, 2008 - HP Pavilion, San Jose, CA (USA)
April 4, 2008 - Honda Center, Anaheim, CA (USA)
April 5, 2008 - Honda Center, Anaheim, CA (USA)
April 8, 2008 - HP Pavilion, San Jose, CA (USA)
April 9, 2008 - Staples Center, Los Angeles, CA (USA)
April 11, 2008 - Jobing.com Arena, Glendale, AZ (USA)
April 12, 2008 - MGM Grand Garden Arena, Las Vegas, NV (USA)
April 14, 2008 - American Airlines Center, Dallas, TX (USA)
April 15, 2008 - Ford Center, Oklahoma City, OK (USA)
April 17, 2008 - Sprint Center, Kansas City, MO (USA)
April 19, 2008 - Fargodome, Fargo, ND (USA)

April 20, 2008 - Wells Fargo Arena, Des Moines, IA (USA)
April 22, 2008 - Sprint Center, Kansas City, MO (USA)
April 24, 2008 - Sommet Center, Nashville, TN (USA)
April 26, 2008 - BankAtlantic Center, Fort Lauderdale, FL (USA)
April 27, 2008 - St. Pete Times Forum, Tampa, FL (USA)
April 30, 2008 - Philips Arena, Atlanta, GA (USA)
May 1, 2008 - Philips Arena, Atlanta, GA (USA)

MIDDLE EASTERN & EUROPEAN DATES (& VENUES)

May 20, 2008 - Emirates Palace, Abu Dhabi (United Arab Emirates)
May 22, 2008 - Veltins-Arena, Gelsenkirchen (Germany)
May 24, 2008 - Olympiastadion, Munich (Germany)
May 25, 2008 - Zentralstadion, Leipzig (Germany)
May 28, 2008 - HSH Nordbank Arena, Hamburg (Germany)
May 29, 2008 – Gottlieb Daimler Stadion, Stuttgart (Germany)
May 31, 2008 - Parque da Bela Vista, Lisbon (Portugal - Rock In Rio Lisboa)
June 1, 2008 - Estadi Olímpic Lluís Companys, Barcelona (Spain)
June 3, 2008 - Commerzbank-Arena, Frankfurt (Germany)
June 4, 2008 - Magna Racino, Ebreichsdorf (Germany)
June 7, 2008 - Punchestown Racecourse, Kildare (Ireland)
June 11, 2008 - St Mary's Stadium, Southampton (England)
June 13, 2008 - Amsterdam Arena, Amsterdam (Netherlands)
June 14, 2008 - King Baudouin Stadium, Brussels (Belgium)

June 16, 2008 - Olympiastadion, Helsinki (Finland)
June 18, 2008 - Ullevaal Stadion, Oslo (Norway)
June 19, 2008 - Gammel Estrup, Randers (Denmark)
June 21, 2008 - Hampden Park, Glasgow (Scotland)
June 22, 2008 - City of Manchester Stadium, Manchester (England)
June 24, 2008 - Ricoh Arena, Coventry (England)
June 25, 2008 - Ashton Gate, Bristol (England)
June 27, 2008 - Twickenham Stadium, London (England)
June 28, 2008 - Twickenham Stadium, London (England)

NORTH AMERICAN DATES (& VENUES) PART III

July 6, 2008 - Sarnia Bayfest, Centennial Park, Sarnia, Ontario (Canada)
July 7, 2008 - The Palace of Auburn Hills, Detroit, MI (USA)
July 9, 2008 - TD Banknorth Garden, Boston, MA (USA)
July 10, 2008 - TD Banknorth Garden, Boston, MA (USA)
July 12, 2008 - Central Park, New York City, NY (USA)
July 14, 2008 - Madison Square Garden, New York City, NY (USA)
July 15, 2008 - Madison Square Garden, New York City, NY (USA)

LOT LIKE LOVE, A

Released in 2005, *A Lot Like Love* is a romantic comedy starring Ashton Kutcher. The film's tagline runs: *"There's nothing better than a great romance...to ruin a perfectly good friendship."* The soundtrack features Bon Jovi's 'I'll Be There For You.'

LUNAR ECLIPSE

Released in 2000 via Rounder/ Moon Junction Music, *Lunar Eclipse* is the second solo album by Bon Jovi keyboardist David Bryan, following on from 1995's *On A Full Moon.* It has to be said that *Lunar Eclipse* is something of a cheat, especially for those who had already purchased his first album: it is essentially the same album as *On A Full Moon,* although it omits two tracks ('Midnight Voodoo' and 'Awakening') and includes three *brand new* tracks ('Second Chance', 'I Can Love' and 'On A Full Moon'). In 1999, Bryan had suffered a nasty accident with an electric power saw, which caused him to require extensive therapy on an injured hand. His playing on this album is exemplary.

Track Listing:
1. 'Second Chance'
2. 'I Can Love'
3. 'It's A Long Road'
4. 'On A Full Moon'
5. 'April'
6. 'Kissed By An Angel'
7. 'Endless Horizon'
8. 'Lullaby For Two Moons'
9. 'Interlude'
10. 'Room Full Of Blues'
11. 'Hear Our Prayer'
12. 'Summer Of Dreams'
13. 'Up The River'
14. 'Netherworld Waltz'
15. 'In These Arms'

David Bryan lunar eclipse

M

MANDEL, TOMMY

Born in New York City, Tommy Mandel was the keyboards player in Bryan Adams' band from 1981 to 1998. He has also worked with The Clash, Dire Straits, Tina Turner, Ian Hunter and The Pretenders, amongst others.

He contributed synthesizers to *7800° Fahrenheit;* interestingly Tommy Mandel described his role in the making of the album in his memoirs, which are as yet only viewable online at *tommymandel.com/mybookch3*

He also toured with Richie Sambora during the guitarist's 1998 *Undiscovered Soul* tour, playing to audiences in Japan, Australia and Europe.

In his own words, Tommy Mandel says:

"Richie was one of the nicest, most musical, generous guys I ever worked for. And I hear he's one of the world's great lovers, although I don't know that from personal experience. He loves all kinds of music, and you can listen to him tell stories of meeting the great and the strange of our planet, for hours. He could do stand up if he weren't such a musical force. Playing in his band was a trip. His best bud-dy, David Bryan, had hurt his hand before the tour, so Kasim Sulton reminded Richie of me, (since we'd done a bit of work together on Bon Jovi's second album, mostly programming...) and the next thing I knew, I was flying out to LA (from NYC) to rehearse. It was a pleasure, almost like a perpetual jam session with the best cats: Everett Bradley and Gioia Bruno on percussion and vocals, Kasim, Richie, Ron Wikso, and Richie Supa - the songs were pretty deep, so we just played them with respect, and Richie did his soulful thing out front. After playing in Bryan Adams' band for so many years, I appreciated the free interplay between the musicians, or maybe it was just the change. Bryan's band was smaller, and playing with Bryan is an insane amount of fun too, but going into Richie's band was like putting on a different pair of shoes after 10 years in one pair, even if it was the best ones you could imagine - the change was fun. Plus the styles: sort of like going from AC/DC into Steely Dan. But better of course! Ha. And the guy whose parts I was recreating was Bill Preston! It was an education too".

Visit *tommymandel.com*

MANIC STREET PREACHERS

Welsh rock band who supported Bon Jovi at Milton Keynes National Bowl on September 18 and 19, 1993, alongside Little Angels and Billy Idol.

The band's lead singer Richey Edwards famously disappeared in 1995 and his whereabouts are still unknown. The remaining band members, James Dean Bradfield, Nicky Wire and Sean Moore carried on without him. Despite a lack of success in the States, the Manics are one of Britain's most treasured bands. Visit *manicstreetpreachers.com*

MAROLDA, TOMMY

After over three decades in the business Las Vegas based Tommy Morolda is a chief songwriter, musician and producer. He has worked on several soundtracks, including *Staying Alive* and *Days Of Thunder,* and has collaborated with such artists as Cher and the Bee Gees.

Marolda has a long friendship with Richie Sambora, the pair having worked together on some good songs over the years. On 1991's *Strangers In This Town* they co-wrote 'Ballad Of Youth' with Tom Marolda and 'One Light Burning', which was also co-written with Sambora's former Shark Frenzy band mate Bruce Foster. On 1998's *Undiscovered Soul* they co-wrote 'You're Not Alone' and 'Chained' (also with guitarist Ernie White.) Sambora has also written and performed with Marolda's two bands: Horizontal Ladies Club and The Toms.

Speaking about his friendship and collaborations with Sambora, Marolda says:

"I owned a recording studio in New Jersey where many future stars were cutting their teeth. Guys from Springsteen's band, Smithereens, Nan Mancini, and that's how I met Richie Sambora at the tender age of 16. He was quite flashy on the guitar and I remember him singing a demo for me called 'One Light Burning' which he later recorded for his solo record. 'Ballad Of Youth' was written at the last minute in the old A&M recording Studio in LA. When Richie is in work mode, he's unstoppable and very creative. This song was pouring out of the both of us at the time. I was pleased to see it hit the charts as well, but I'm not sure who put the brakes on its upward climb. That may have been the demise of Bon Jovi had it become a huge hit. Writing other songs with Richie took place at his Westlake home when he was married to Heather. I lived down the street from him and had a small home studio where we could demo new material.

Working with Richie as I said was very exciting when he was in his creative mode, but as the pressures of stardom and his personal life took a toll on him, I found Richie's creative output suffering and putting a strain on our relationship. I have only fond and warm memories of my friend as he stood in my corner for many years. I just hope that he can put his life on the right track and continue his amazing journey."

Visit *tommymarolda.com*

MARTIN, MAX

Based in Stockholm, Sweden, Max Martin is a Grammy-nominated producer and songwriter. His credits include Backstreet Boys, N'Sync, Pink and Britney Spears. He co-wrote Bon

Jovi's big hit 'It's My Life', and he al-so co-penned 'Complicated' with Jon, Sambora and Billy Falcon, which features on *Have A Nice Day.*

Jon told Philip Wilding at *Classic Rock:*

"He [Max] hadn't worked with a rock band before so he went off to Sweden and put these loops and stuff in and sent them over, and the background arrangement was really fucking great...And now all these teams have picked up on it, that now or never thing in the lyric, it's great."

Visit *maratone.se*

MARTINIQUE HOTEL

A midtown Manhattan house shelter (or as the Americans say, welfare hotel) on Broadway and 32nd Street that partly inspired the song 'Hey

God' on the 1996 album *These Days.* The song is about social inequality, injustice and the breakdown of the American family.

MAY, BRIAN

Brian May achieved global superstardom as the guitarist in Queen; he also holds a Ph.D. in astrophysics and was honoured with a CBE in 2005. His guitar solos and riffs are undoubtedly some of the most recognised in popular music. His heavier riffs (such as the brilliant 'Brighton Rock' and 'Stone Cold Crazy') are just as striking as his more famous melodic ones such as 'Killer Queen' and 'Fat Bottom Girls.' After Freddie Mercury's

death in 1991, May formed the Brian May Band and released *Back To The Light,* a pretty good rock album. The line-up of the band featured a number of musicians through different incarnations; a couple of notable names are ex-Whitesnake guitarist Neil Murray and the late great drummer Cozy Powell. May's second album was 1998's *Another World.* Since 2005, May and Queen drummer Roger Taylor have been busy with their new project Queen + Paul Rodgers, original Queen bassist John Deacon having retired. May's blog 'Soapbox' is excellent reading, often quoted and very popular with fans.

On the first of four dates at London's Wembley Arena in 1989, Brian May (along with Elton John and others) joined Bon Jovi onstage for a version of The Beatles 'Get Back.' It was backstage at this concert that May emphasised to Jon the importance of remembering the good times and to enjoy them while they last, because nothing lasts forever. This is something Jon has reiterated in interviews over the years.

Queen fan Richie Sambora told *Kerrang!* in 1994:

"Backstage at Wembley in '89. He took me and Jon to one side and told us we were workin' too hard. He told us that he wished he could have some of the Queen days back, because he couldn't remember most of them."

Visit *brianmay.com*

MCDONALD, HUGH

Hugh McDonald was born on December 28, 1950 in Philadelphia. He credits his earliest musical influence as Paul McCartney. His friendship with Jon Bon Jovi goes right back to the Power Station Studios years in the early eighties, when he hooked up with Jon to play bass on Jon's demo

'She Don't Know Me.' Following on from that, McDonald and several other musicians (dubbed the All Star Review session band) worked with Jon on the recording of the celebrated 'Runaway' demo. He is credited as an 'Additional Musician' in the sleeve notes to *Bon Jovi*; he is also thanked in the sleeve notes to *Slippery When Wet, New Jersey, Keep The Faith* and *Blaze Of Glory*. He seems to have played bass on all of those albums except *Blaze Of Glory*. It has been suggested that McDonald had to re-work some of the bass parts done by original Bon Jovi bassist Alec John Such.

In addition to his sporadic session work with Bon Jovi in the eighties and early nineties McDonald has also worked with artists of the calibre of Cher, Michael Bolton, Lita Ford, Ringo Star, Willie Nelson and Alice Cooper. More recently, whilst still working for Bon Jovi, he has collaborated with Jaci Velasquez and Ricky Martin, and briefly joined Southside Johnny and The Asbury Jukes at the end of '98.

Although he is not an 'official' member of Bon Jovi he has played bass in the band in the studio and on stage since the latter half of 1994, taking the place of Alec John Such. He does

not appear in any Bon Jovi publicity photos, album covers or take part in interviews with them. The first album that gave him full credit as bassist for Bon Jovi was *These Days* and he has been credited on every new Bon Jovi release thereafter.

McDonald also gave a massive helping hand to Jon during the recording of his solo opus *Destination Anywhere*; he is credited as the bassist on all the tracks except for the demo 'Cold Hard Heart' which doesn't list any musicians. He also toured with Jon to promote the album. Jon's solo band (guitarist Bobby Bandiera and keyboardist Jerry Cohen with Everett Bradley on percussion and Shawn Pelton on drums) was called The Big Dogs.

MCGHEE, DOC

Doc McGhee is a famous manager of rock artists. From 1982 to 1989 he managed Mötley Crüe, and it was in 1983, after the band's terrific *Shout At The Devil* went platinum and they become one of the hottest bands in the States that Bon Jovi signed up with McGhee and his New York based company. McGhee was integral in helping both bands become the most popular and highly-publicised rock bands of the decade.

Mötley Crüe fired him after the Moscow Music Peace Festival (which McGhee organised), allegedly due to the seemingly preferential treatment given to Bon Jovi at the event (full stage set-up, more time on stage, etc.).

In the eighties McGhee found himself in deep trouble for drug smuggling. He had actually committed the offences before he hooked up with Bon Jovi, but it was not until 1988 that he admitted his guilt in court for taking part in shipments of marijuana

(allegedly weighing 40,000 pounds) from Colombia to North Carolina. He was given a five year suspended sentence for his part in criminal activity and fined $15,000. He subsequently set up the Make A Difference Foundation in '88 and organised the aforementioned Moscow Music Peace Festival, starring Bon Jovi, Ozzy Osbourne, Skid Row, Mötley Crüe, Cinderella and others.

In 1991 when relations between the members of Bon Jovi were at a low ebb, being exhausted and fed up with each other's company after the massive *New Jersey Syndicate* tour came to an end, the band and Doc McGhee went their separate ways. McGhee has spoken in interviews about those years with Bon Jovi, and he admits that the disintegration of their professional relationship and personal friendship was mostly his fault.

He has managed KISS since 1996 and the other artists signed to his agency, McGhee Entertainment, include Night Ranger, Ted Nugent, Paul Stanley, Down and Hootie. He has previously worked with Scorpions and Skid Row, and it was actually at Jon and Richie Sambora's behest that McGhee signed Skid Row to his company. Recently, McGhee has been seen in the VH1 show *Super-Group* with Anthrax main man Scott

Ian, Sebastian Bach, Ted Nugent and Jason Bonham.

Visit *mcgheela.com*

MCSQUARE, EDDY

Eddy McSquare is the author of the 46 page book *Bon Jovi: An Illustrated History* which was published in 1990 by Omnibus Press. It is now out of print. McSquare has also authored books on Guns N' Roses, Metallica, Mötley Crüe and Led Zeppelin.

MEADOWLANDS ARENA

A popular venue in East Rutherford, New Jersey, where Bon Jovi played a homecoming gig on March 15, 1989 during the huge *New Jersey Syndicate* tour. They were presented with the keys to the city by the Mayor of Sayreville.

MELODIC ROCK

Of all the sub-genres in rock and heavy metal this is the one that applies the most to Bon Jovi: they make rock music that is melodic, at times almost pop. Melodic rock is a broad spectrum of music that can apply to

bands like The Eagles and Queen, as well as AOR bands like Journey and Toto. Contemporary rock bands like Nickelback and Velvet Revolver also fit the description. Melodic Rock was especially popular during the 1980s. A memorable melody is an obvious trait of the genre, so songs like 'Bad Medicine' and 'You Give Love A Bad Name' most definitely fall into the category.

MELODIYA

A Russian record label, founded in 1964 as the state-owned record company of the Soviet Union. Bon Jovi was the first American rock band to have an album released on a Russian label, when Melodiya issued *New Jersey* on August 11, 1989.

Visit *melody.su/eng*

MEMPHIS

A musical written by classically trained keyboardist David Bryan, together with famed New Jersey playwright and author Joe DiPietro. *Memphis* was performed in 2002 as an "off-Broadway" musical. The story was inspired by the respected Memphis DJ Dewey Phillips, a white man, who played both white and black music in the fifties during racial segregation in the South (Phillips is also famous for playing 'That's All Right', the first record by Elvis Presley on

the famed Sun Records label). The show ran at the La Jolla Playhouse in San Diego during the 2008-09 theatre season. It has been reported that Bryan is endeavouring stage the musical on Broadway in the near future.

MERCY

A metal band that featured Richie Sambora in his pre Bon Jovi days. They were briefly signed to Led Zeppelin's Swan Song label, but little else is known about them other than the fact that they did not achieve much success.

MESSAGE

A New Jersey band that featured Richie Sambora, Alec John Such and Dean Fasano of Phantom's Opera and Prophet. They recorded a mini-album called *Lessons*.

METAL HAMMER

Metal Hammer is the monthly sister magazine of the weekly rock bible *Kerrang!*. First published in 1986, *Metal Hammer* also appears in some foreign language editions, notably

in Germany. Many writers from the *Kerrang!* camp have contributed to *Metal Hammer* over the years, and the magazine frequently featured Bon Jovi during the late eighties and early nineties. Two covers featuring the band spring to mind: No. 14, Vol.4 (1989) and No.18, Vol.5 (1990.)

Visit *metalhammer.co.uk*

MIDNIGHT IN CHELSEA

The first single released from Jon's solo album *Destination Anywhere*. It was issued in the UK on June 14, 1997 and peaked at Number 4. The song was co-written with Dave Stewart, and although the video was shot in New York's Chelsea district it is actually about London's Chelsea which the song references. Jon had spent time in London in '96 whilst filming *The Leading Man* and penned the song in March of that year.

Track Listing:
1. 'Midnight In Chelsea' *(Single edit)*
2. 'Sad Song Night' *(Demo)*
3. 'August 7, 4:15' *(Acoustic version)*
4. 'Midnight In Chelsea' *(Album version)*

MILLS, TONY

The former lead singer of the Birmingham melodic rock band Shy, and since 2006 the frontman in the

Norwegian band TNT. Mills was in Shy when they supported Bon Jovi at the Birmingham NEC and was also briefly involved in the Philadelphia hair metal band Cinderella, whom Bon Jovi recommended to an A&R man at Mercury / Polygram Records after seeing one of their gigs.

Tony Mills:

In the mid/late eighties I was aware of a side project that Jon Bon Jovi had managed or was in the process of nurturing by the name of Cinderella. I was working with a guitarist by the name of Jeff Paris in Los Angeles and Jeff had been asked to session on some backing vocals for the band at the Record Plant.

Jeff had other commitments and asked me if I could cover for him and do the session. I arrived at the studio to find the vocalist Tom Keifer running the session with no sign of the producer Andy Johns. Obviously, Jon had made a wise decision to handle this band, because they well clued up people and Tom operated the SSL desk on his own, which was impressive to say the least. The material had overtones of AC/DC and I delivered background vocals on a track called 'Nothing For Nothing' and it went very smooth. After the session, I was asked if I wanted a percentage or cash in the hand. I thought about this and considered that an AC/DC soundalike band called Cinderella would never go anywhere, so I took $150.00 and left. It was the biggest mistake of my career in retrospect; to what must have been delight to Jon Bon Jovi, as they progressed to sell over seven million albums."

Visit *tnttheband.com*

MILTON KEYNES BOWL

Milton Keynes Bowl is a familiar venue to Bon Jovi fans. They performed there on August 19, 1989 in a big show that served to replace that year's Monsters Of Rock; Europe, Vixen and Skid Row were special guests. Steven Tyler and Joe Perry of Aerosmith joined Bon Jovi onstage to

perform the song 'Walk This Way'. Writing enthusiastically in *Kerrang!* Lyn Guy said:

"...the pinnacle of their career...my sole complaint of the night was that the show was just too damn short!"

In 1993, the band played two gigs (September 18 and 19) there; this time around they were supported by Billy Idol, Little Angels and Manic Street Preachers. On July 6 and 7, 1996 they returned to Milton Keynes during the *These Days* tour, and were back during the 2001 *One Wild Night* tour to play a show on June 16. During the 2006 *Have A Nice Day* tour they played two shows at the venue, on June 10 and 11.

MIRACLE

The second and last single released from Jon Bon Jovi's debut solo album *Blaze Of Glory*. It was issued in the UK on November 10, 1990 and peaked at Number 29 but in America it reached Number 12. It's a mid-paced ballad that features a Jeff Beck guitar solo. The chorus is typical Bon Jovi; anthemic and melodic.

MISTER BIG TIME

Bon Jovi contributed this song to the Bruce Willis and Ben Affleck film

Armageddon, released in 1998. The song was mixed by Kevin Shirley, who had also recorded two previous Bon Jovi tracks, 'Always' and 'Someday I'll Be Saturday Night.' Other contributors to the soundtrack include Aerosmith, Journey and ZZ Top. The film also inspired Jon to write 'Save The World' which features on the album *Crush*.

Shirley remembers:

"I was doing the music for the Armageddon soundtrack and I did a whole bunch of stuff; I produced a Journey track. One of the ones we had to do for the movie was 'Mister Big Time'. I didn't record it; Jon recorded it in their house in New Jersey. And then he brought it into the studio and I mixed it. We mixed it in Avatar Studios [formerly Power Station Studios] in New York City. It was just pretty straight forward. He came in on a Saturday and we just mixed the track. That's all I had to do; I mixed the stereo and the surround sound soundtrack for the movie. There wasn't really anything exceptional about it. I brought some cheesecake

in and I asked Jon if he wanted a slice and he said: 'Oh, I can't do that. I've got to keep my figure'. That's the most exciting thing that happened on that song. There's the story about the hooker that came with me but that's a much longer...

I do remember going into the session in the morning and having a real attitude. I bought a cap on the way in walking down 9th Avenue to the studio...that said 'Fuck Off.'"

MISUNDERSTOOD

The second single taken from the 2002 album *Bounce*. The lyrics were penned by Jon, Sambora, Andreas Carlsson and Desmond Child. It was issued in the UK on December 21, 2002 and made it to Number 21, spending five weeks in the charts. It didn't make it into the American *Billboard* Hot 100 although it peaked at Number 64 on the US Adult Contemporary chart.

Track Listing:
(CD1)
1. 'Misunderstood' *(Single remix)*
2. 'Everyday' *(Acoustic)*
3. 'Undivided' *(Demo)*
4. 'Misunderstood' *(Video)*
(CD2)
1. 'Misunderstood' *(Single remix)*
2. 'Celluloid Heroes' *(Live in London, 2002 – The Kinks 1972 song)*
3. 'Joey' *(Demo)*

MONSTERS OF ROCK

An enormously successful and influential UK rock festival that was first organised in 1980 and finished in 1996 (although no festivals were held in 1989 or 1993). Each festival was held at Castle Donington in the Midlands. Monsters Of Rock festivals were also organised for other

sites around the world (beginning in Germany in 1983) and the festival name continues today in other countries. In 2006, a Monsters Of Rock festival was held at Milton Keynes Bowl in England with Deep Purple headlining, but since then there has been a lack of interest in arranging another one with a big named headlining act.

Bon Jovi played at the UK version of the festival for the first time on August 17 in 1985. Headlined by the Texan band ZZ Top, the other acts included Marillion, Metallica, Ratt and Magnum.

Jason Ritchie, reviews editor at *Get Ready To Rock*, was amongst the headbangers. He recalls:

"I first saw them [Bon Jovi] at Monsters Of Rock at Castle Donington back in 1985... They did seem slightly overawed by the crowd to start with but soon hit their stride and 'Runaway' was a highlight. They certainly blew the more experienced Ratt off the stage! Many in the crowd hadn't really heard much by them although they were getting a decent amount of coverage in Kerrang! *at the time".*

Setlist:
1. 'Tokyo Road'

2. 'Breakout'
3. 'Only Lonely'
4. 'Runaway'
5. 'In And Out of Love'
6. 'I Don't Wanna Go Home'
7. 'Get Ready'

Bon Jovi returned to the festival as the headlining act on August 22, 1987; the other bands that played were Dio, Metallica, Anthrax, W.A.S.P and Cinderella. The band arrived in true style via two helicopters with the band's name printed on their sides. It was a rainy and muddy day and despite a strong crowd of 65,000 crazy rock fans, Jon was in a fatigued state due to the band's relentless touring schedule. Apparently, he does not look back at the festival with positive thoughts, not just because of his health but also due to the technical hitches that plagued parts of their set. He told *Metal Hammer* writer Anders Tengner in 1989:

"...It was the worst time of my life. I need a vacation so badly but I still gave Donington everything I had. But it was steroids, it was shots, it was pills. The steroids took down the swelling on my vocal chords and man I took them because I would do anything to sing".

During their performance (on August 22) Dee Snider of Twisted Sister, Bruce Dickinson of Iron Maiden and Paul Stanley of KISS joined the band to sing 'Travelin' Band' by Creedence Clearwater Revival and the Grand Funk Railroad song 'We're An American Band'. Lars Ulrich and James Hetfield of Metallica allegedly turned Jon down because Bon Jovi flew over the festival grounds in a helicopter *during* Metallica's set.

Setlist
1. 'Pink Flamingos'
2. 'Raise Your Hands'
3. 'I'd Die For You'
4. 'Tokyo Road'
5. 'You Give Love A Bad Name'
6. 'Wild In The Streets'
7. 'Not Fade Away'
8. 'Never Say Goodbye'
9. 'Livin' On A Prayer'
10. 'Let It Rock'
11. 'Get Ready'
12. 'Runaway'
13. 'Wanted Dead Or Alive'
14. 'Drift Away'
15. 'Travelin' Band'
16. 'We're An American Band'

MOONLIGHT AND VALENTINO

Released in 1995 and directed by David Anspaugh, *Moonlight And Valentino* is a comedy-drama starring Whoopi Goldberg, Elizabeth Perkins, Gwyneth Paltrow and Kathleen Turner. Elizabeth Perkins plays a recently widowed teacher who becomes romantically linked with the (much younger) man who is hired to paint her house. The painter is played Jon Bon Jovi in his first major acting role. The film received mixed reviews on its original release; many critics claimed that it is too sentimental. For example, Tom Charity wrote in *Time Out*:

"In his first acting role, Jon Bon Jovi is relegated to the status of sex object and he's every bit as anemic as the rest."

MORELLO, JOE

An American jazz drummer who was in The Dave Brubeck Quartet for almost 13 years. Later in his career Morello became a renowned teacher, and his students included Bon Jovi sticks-man Tico Torres and Max Weinberg of The E Street Band.

MOSCOW MUSIC PEACE FESTIVAL

Organised by the infamous rock manager Doc McGhee, the Moscow Music Peace Festival was a two day anti-drugs charity event held on August 12-13, 1989, a couple of years before the Soviet Union's "official" demise in 1991. McGhee's Make A Difference Foundation was set up in 1988 after he pleaded guilty to struggling drugs into America, the foundation being part of his community service and parole conditions. The Moscow Music Peace Festival was a good way to get his charity some mainstream / global press, as the international media covered the full two day event.

It was time of reflection for the people of Russia who, after a history of communism, were finally witnessing the birth of democracy in their country. Under President Mikhail Gorbachev, Russians were becoming exposed to western pop culture. Unlike U2, Bon Jovi are not a political band so they were perfect mainstream entertainment for the Russian people.

The festival was one of heavy metal's last major events before the full impact of grunge hit home in the nineties. But it also brought on famous clashes of ego, backstage fights and represented the ludicrousness inherent in rock. It was also the first rock concert to be held at the magnificent Lenin Stadium.

On the bill were Cinderella, Scorpions, Skid Row, Mötley Crüe, Ozzy Osbourne and Bon Jovi. Aside from Cinderella and Ozzy, the other acts were part of McGhee Entertainments. The event also included some homegrown Russian talents such as Gorky Park, Nuance, CCP and Brigada S. The event finale was an all-star rendition of Led Zeppelin's 'Rock And Roll' with John Bonham's son Jason on the drum stool.

Arriving in Russia for the festival, 7,000 fans greeted the band at the airport and they had to have a police escort to their hotel. An MTV crew followed the band around during the few days they were in Moscow.

Before the gigs took place Jon Bon Jovi told Mick Wall of *Kerrang!*:

"People are always ready to question the motives behind why a bunch of rock stars would want to get together and do something like this. And, sure, inevitably you get a clash of egos occasionally. It's not exactly the easiest thing to organise in the world..."

Jon made lasting impression during the band's set when, appearing from the crowd with some burly bodyguards, he walked onstage in a Red Army uniform and cap. Yet it was the behind the scenes tantrums that proved of great interest to rock fans.

Each band was supposed to play a six song set without stage lights or theatrics but, of course, it never turned out that way and the other bands were allegedly furious with headliners Bon Jovi (since the *New Jersey* album they were just too big *not* to headline) for having a longer set time and bigger stage show with pyrotechnics.

In fact, it was reported that Mötley Crüe drummer Tommy Lee allegedly punched McGhee backstage because his band couldn't have the same treatment. Upon their return to the States, Mötley Crüe fired McGhee as their manager.

It was reported in *Kerrang!* in November that Mötley Crüe bassist Nikki Sixx said:

"They [Bon Jovi] are like a bunch of babies. It was meant to be equal billing over there, and no-one was meant to be headlining...We felt were here getting second rate treatment from our manager, so we sacked him."

Another issue was when McGhee changed Ozzy's billing from third to fourth, giving Mötley Crüe the third headlining spot. Ozzy was so enraged he threaten to pull out of the gig and fly back home. After some negotiations, the bill stayed as it was originally promoted.

The irony of it all was that it was an anti-drugs campaign yet at the time some of the artists were allegedly hooked on drugs. A case of double standards? Even Nikki Sixx was

annoyed at the bands, as he told *Kerrang!* in 1990:

"If you're over there to talk about not doing drugs, how the f**k can you go over there and get shit-faced? I don' think any of it was done honestly. I don't buy into it."

A compilation album called *Stairway To Heaven / Highway To Hell*, produced by Bruce Fairbairn, was released in November, 1989 via Mercury Records. The album is a collection of cover versions recorded in the studio by the bands that played at the festival. It is interesting that the artists covered for this album had members who had died from alcohol or drug-related illnesses. The profits from the album went to the Make A Difference campaign.

Track Listing:
1. Gorky Park - 'My Generation' *(The Who)*
2. Skid Row – 'Holidays In The Sun' *(The Sex Pistols)*
3. Scorpions – 'I Can't Explain' *(The Who)*
4. Ozzy Osbourne – 'Purple Haze' *(Jimi Hendrix)*
5. Mötley Crüe – 'Teaser' *(Tommy Bolin)*
6. Bon Jovi – 'The Boys Are Back In Town' *(Thin Lizzy)*

7. Cinderella – 'Move Over' *(Janis Joplin)*
8. Drum Madness – 'Moby Dick' *(Led Zeppelin)*
9. Jam
– 'Hound Dog' *(Elvis Presley)*
– 'Long Tall Sally'/ 'Blue Suede Shoes' *(Carl Perkins)*
– 'Rock & Roll' *(Led Zeppelin)*

MTV

Music Television. The New York based station first hit the airwaves on August 1, 1981. Its unparalleled success has provided many rock bands with a perfect platform to promote themselves and their music. As well as using live footage to promote a single, bands started to make mini-films based on the songs lyrics, such as Judas Priest's 'Breaking The Law.'

Bon Jovi was just one band out of dozens that became successful (or *more* successful) through MTV. Others included ZZ Top, Van Halen, Def Leppard and Ratt. Some critics felt that bands like Def Leppard 'sold out' to MTV, and bands of their ilk become known as "MTV bands". After the release of *Slippery When Wet* in '86, Bon Jovi was the most requested band by MTV viewers and the fans kept them in the MTV spotlight well into the following year.

The Internet has unquestionably damaged MTV's once dominant role in promoting new music videos and upcoming artists. Yet MTV still re-

mains hugely popular, although its focus is less on rock and metal and more on pop, rap and hip hop. MTV's sister channel VH1 concentrates on rock and classic metal. Given Bon Jovi's continuing success and popularity, they are still covered on MTV while many of their peers are not.

Visit *mtv.com*

MTV VIDEO MUSIC AWARDS

Like any successful popular music act of the past 25 years Bon Jovi have been featured heavily on MTV. To celebrate the pop music video, MTV launched the annual MTV Video Music Awards in 1984, taking place after the more prestigious and high-brow Grammy Awards.

Bon Jovi have bagged several nominations and awards. In 1987, they won the award for 'Best Stage Performance' for the video to 'Livin' On A Prayer'. At the 1989 awards show the band performed an acoustic set to wide acclaim. This prompted the station to pursue their famous *Unplugged* series. Later, in 1991, the band won the 'MTV Michael Jackson Video Vanguard Award.'

MTV EUROPE MUSIC AWARDS

An alternative to the American MTV Video Music Awards, MTV

Europe Music Awards began in 1994. Bon Jovi won the 'Best Rock' award in 1995 and in 1997 Jon Bon Jovi won the award for 'Best Male.'

MTV UNPLUGGED

Bon Jovi are credited with MTV's decision to make the popular *Unplugged* series after performing an acoustic set at the 1989 MTV Video Music Awards. They recorded a full set for MTV's now legendary *Unplugged* show at the Kaufman Astoria in NYC on October 25, 1992.

Memorable *Unplugged* performances include Eric Clapton, KISS, Alice In Chains and Pearl Jam. By the turn of the millennium the show's popularity had declined.

MTV Unplugged was relaunched in June, 2007 with Bon Jovi performing in front of 400 fans. Amongst other songs, they performed versions of 'Love For Sale', 'Livin' On A Prayer', 'You Give Love A Bad Name', 'Who Say's You Can't Go Home?' and 'It's My Life'.

However all did not go according to plan. A report on *perezhilton.com* said:

"As 'Wanted Dead Or Alive' started, Richie couldn't play along! During the song Jon stops and makes Richie start again and after the sec-

ond take was finished the show was supposed to be over but Jon had the whole band come on stage to re-record the song a third time so Richie couldn't mess it up!"

The media picked up on the fact that at one point Sambora's mic had to be turn off because he was seemingly too drunk to sing. Suffice to say the media referred to the performance as a disaster.

MUSIC VIDEO

A broad term but essentially it is a video/short film or performance intended to promote an artist's latest single/composition. Music videos became hugely important during the eighties, instigated by the rise of MTV. The beginnings of the music video are debatable; many argue that Queen's 'Bohemian Rhapsody' in 1975 kick-started the concept. Similarly to most major rock bands, Bon Jovi have made many videos; amongst the most notable are 'Livin' On A Prayer', 'You Give Love A Bad Name', 'Bad Medicine', 'Bed Of Roses', 'Keep The Faith' and, more recently, 'Have A Nice Day' and 'Who Says You Can't Go Home'. There is a significant difference in production values between the videos of the eighties and the more polished and glossy videos of the post *Keep The Faith* years.

MY CHEMICAL ROMANCE

Known as MCR and My Chem, this band hails from Newark in New Jersey. They formed in 2001 released three albums between 2002 and 2006, and appeal especially to a teenage audience.

Along with several other bands My Chemical Romance supported Bon Jovi for two nights (October 25-26,

2007) during their popular 10 gig stint at the new Prudential Center in New Jersey.

As quoted on the Prudential Center website (*prucenter.com*) frontman Gerard Way enthused:

"Growing up in Jersey isn't like growing up anywhere else; there's an amazing amount of pride involved. To be asked to open up for New Jersey's own Bon Jovi at the grand opening of the Prudential Center is an amazing honour. It's more than anything a group of kids from the Garden State could ever ask for."

Visit *mychemicalromance.com*

MY VH1 MUSIC AWARDS

An awards show arranged by the MTV-owned station VH1. In 2001, Bon Jovi won the 'Video Of The Year' award for the single 'It's My Life', and in 2002 they pocketed the award for 'Hottest Live Band.'

MYSPACE

Launched in 2003, MySpace is a totally free social networking system that is available to anybody who uses the Internet. Many artists and record labels use MySpace to promote their music; fans can download songs and view images and socialise with other fans. Bon Jovi have their own official MySpace page.

Visit *myspace.com/bonjovi*

N

NAILPIN

A Belgian rock band who supported Bon Jovi on June 14, 2008 at the King Baudouin Stadium in Brussels. Nailpin have also supported Avril Lavigne in Japan and have had several hits singles in their native country, including 'Endless Conversations' and 'Worn Out'. Their third album, simply called *III*, was released in 2008.

Visit *nailpin.be*

NANNINI, GIANNA

Italian singer Gianna Nannini released her first album in 1976, but it was with 1979's *California* that she started to make a name for herself in Europe. Her song 'Un'estate Italiana,' with Edoardo Bennato, was the official anthem for the 1990 World Cup.

Nannini supported Bon Jovi on some German dates in 2008 (from

May 22 to May 29) and she returned to support them for one show in Frankfurt on June 3.

Visit *giannanannini.com*

NATIONAL LAMPOON'S PUCKED

A 2006 slapstick comedy, directed by Arthur Hiller. Jon Bon Jovi stars as an ex-lawyer named Frank Hooper who gets himself into debt and ends up in court as he tries to set up the first all-woman hockey team.

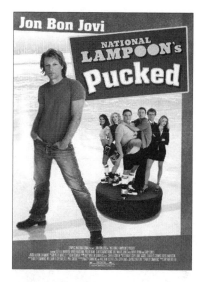

NETHERWORLD

A 1991 horror flick directed by David Schmoeller. The tagline for the film is: *"There is a place between heaven and hell."* David Bryan made a cameo appearance and composed the soundtrack, which was released via Full Moon on February 12, 1992.

Bryan told Dave Reynolds at *Kerrang!* in 1993:

"It was a cool challenge. I just said yes to the project without having a clue how to do it, but I pulled it off... it was scary to do things away from the band...but it helps you grow as a person".

Track Listing:
1. 'Stranger To Love' *(Feat. David Bryan, John Duva, Larry Fast, Bob Gianetti and Edgar Winter)*
2. 'Tonk's Place'
3. 'Birds Of A Feather'
4. 'Black Magic River'
5. 'Open Door Policy' *(Feat. John Duva, Bob Gianetti, Bernie Pershey and Edgar Winter)*
6. 'My Father's Sins'
7. 'Ceremony'
8. 'Into The Netherworld'
9. 'If I Didn't Love You' *(Feat. John Duva, Bob Gianetti, Bernie Pershey and Edgar Winter)*
10. 'Inherit The Dead'
11. 'Mirror Image'
12. What's Your Pleasure?'
13. '100 Reasons' *(Feat. John Duva, Bob Gianetti, Bernie Pershey and Edgar Winter)*
14. 'Netherworld Waltz' *(Live)*

NETTLES, JENNIFER

An American country-folk singer-songwriter from Georgia, USA.

In 2007, Jennifer won a Grammy for 'Best Country Vocal Collaboration' with Bon Jovi for the track 'Who Says You Can't Go Home'. The single reached Number 23 in the *Billboard* Hot 100 and Number 1 on the *Billboard* Hot Country Songs chart.

Visit *jennifernettles.com*

NEVER SAY GOODBYE

The third and final single from *Slippery When Wet* was released in the UK on August 15, 1987. It reached Number 21 in the Top 40 and spent five weeks in the charts. It fared less well in America, hitting Number 28 in the *Billboard* Hot 100. The European release came with a live version of 'Shot Through The Heart' and the American version included the previously unreleased 'Edge Of A Broken Heart'. The song was written by Jon and Sambora and is about a relationship between two lovers who want to stay together.

NEW JERSEY (STATE)

New Jersey (abbreviated to NJ) has been a major source of inspiration to Bon Jovi throughout their entire career. Probably the East Coast State's most famous son is Bruce Springsteen, who has himself written some memorable songs about NJ, including 'Born To Run', 'Spirit In The Night', 'Thunder Road', 'Atlantic City', 'Jungleland' and 'Rosalita (Come Out Tonight.)'. Of course, Bon Jovi have named an album after their native State and one of their most famous songs, 'Livin' On A Prayer', is a reflection of life in NJ. Bon Jovi have remained home birds unlike many bands who, when they make it big, move to New York or LA. Indeed, Bon Jovi are referred to as "New Jerseyans" or "New Jerseyites".

Fellow New Jerseyite Joe Lynn Turner, formerly of Deep Purple and Rainbow says:

"They [Bon Jovi] are pretty honest and forthcoming...not a lot of phoniness. You know the saying, 'Ya gotta problem with that?' - along with the rest of the attitude: it's all Jersey, you don't find it anywhere else really... It's the way people in Jersey are".

NEW JERSEY (ALBUM)

The *Slippery When Wet* tour had been exhausting, but when it was over the time was ripe to make a new album; by Christmas 1987 Bon Jovi already had demos of over 30 original songs available. They hooked up with songwriter Desmond Child and producer Bruce Fairbairn at Little Mountain Sound Studios in Vancouver, British Columbia from May 1 until July 31 1988. There was certainly a lot going on behind the scenes: Jon and Sambora founded the New Jersey Underground Music Company and their manager Doc McGhee had been in court fighting charges of drug smuggling into the United States, but the band's focus remained squarely on their new album.

The bulk of the songwriting was done by Jon, Sambora and Child, although the trio wrote 'Wild Is The Wind' with Diane Warren and 'Stick To Your Guns' was written between

Jon, Sambora and Holly Knight. In fact, the band had written so many songs that they considered releasing a double album. Their record company balked at the idea, however, convinced that the band's fans would be put off by the higher cost. The extra tracks considered for inclusion were:

'Love Is War'
'Let's Make It Baby'
'The Boys Are Back In Town'
'Outlaws Of Love'
'Judgment Day'
'Growing Up The Hard Way'
'Does Anybody Really Fall In Love Anymore?'
'Rosie'
'River Of Love (Come Alive)'
'Backdoor To Heaven'
'Love Hurts'
'Diamond Ring'
'Now And Forever'
'Seven Days'

Several ideas for the album's title had been considered (one of them being *Sons Of Beaches*), but in the end the band named it after their home state of New Jersey. This is something that Jon at least would later regret, as the public would thereafter associate them with Bruce Springsteen.

New Jersey was given a special promotional playback session on August 18, 1988 at the Roseland Ballroom in New York, which was broadcast live by satellite to eleven US cities.

New Jersey was released in the UK on October 1, 1988 and reached Number 1, spending 47 weeks in the charts. It was Bon Jovi's first Number 1 album in the UK, while in the States it was their second to reach that position. To promote the album they committed themselves to 232 gigs during the next two years. The album spawned five global hit singles: 'Bad

Medicine', 'I'll Be There For You', 'Lay Your Hands On Me', 'Born To Be My Baby' and 'Living In Sin'.

Chris Welch reviewed the album in *Metal Hammer*:

"New Jersey is beautifully crafted which shows that for everything from charisma to engineering to sheer musicianship, Bon Jovi are way out in front."

At the time the album quickly sold in its millions, with a reputed seven million sales in the States alone and 18 million worldwide. The album also picked up a fan base in the former Soviet Union after it was released via the home grown Melodiya record label. The latest remastered version of the album includes an enhanced CD video of 'Lay Your Hands On Me.'

Track Listing:
1. 'Lay Your Hands On Me'
2. 'Bad Medicine'
3. 'Born To Be My Baby'
4. 'Living In Sin'
5. 'Blood On Blood'
6. 'Homebound Train'
7. 'Wild Is The Wind'
8. 'Ride Cowboy Ride'
9. 'Stick To Your Guns'
10. 'I'll Be There For You'
11. '99 In The Shade'
12. 'Love For Sale'

Author's Review:

New Jersey *is a fine follow-up to* Slippery When Wet. *The production, as you'd expect from Bruce Fairbairn, is spot on. Whereas the latter album was consistent,* New Jersey *is more varied, with a couple too many ballads but some of the rock songs are certainly memorable: 'Lay Your Hands On Me' and 'Bad Medicine' are great songs to start an album of this kind. Bon Jovi had finally found their sound: good guitars, infectious melodies, harmonic backing vocals and a piano/keys intro. However, it was around this time that they started to become known as a 'ladies band', primarily because of their looks, and surely this had an effect on their music? There are some good ballads here, but also overly-sentimental ones, such as 'Wild In The Wind'. Also, 'Ride Cowboy Ride' is just filler material. In the end, this is a fairly strong melodic rock album that leans a little too much toward the pop side but that doesn't stop it from being a really entertaining release.*

*Rating ****½*

NEW JERSEY SYNDICATE TOUR (1988-1990)

To promote their *New Jersey* album, which landed in the charts at Number 1 in the United States, United Kingdom, Canada, Australia, New Zealand, Sweden, Russia, Brazil, Mexico, Japan and several European territories, Bon Jovi hit the road for their biggest and most exhaustive world, tour notching up 232 live dates beginning on October 30, 1988 and finishing on February 17, 1990. The last shows in Mexico have become famous- a student riot broke out on the very last night of the tour and delayed the band's performance. There is even video footage of it.

In fact, long and tiring touring since '84 had caused Jon such persistent voice problems that he decided to hire a vocal coach; after the tour climaxed in 1990 he vowed to pace himself better. The *New Jersey Syndicate* tour was also fraught with internal squabbling, health issues and personal problems. Despite all this they

managed to put their personal differences aside for some benefit shows at the end of 1990; Doc McGhee was integral in getting the band together and acting as peacemaker. The positives from the tour were that Bon Jovi had become one of the world's biggest touring acts, with two massive selling albums under their belt, and they had learnt how to handle the potential problems of a busy touring schedule.

The tour ran for 10 legs, and kept the band so busy that they had to film live footage for the music videos to 'Lay Your Hands One Me', 'I'll Be There For You' and 'Blood On Blood.' These can be viewed on the VHS releases *New Jersey: The Videos* and *Access All Areas.*

To illustrate the sheer size of the production, Elianne Halbersberg wrote in *Kerrang!*:

"...a massive sound system to drill every note right through your eardrums, pyro blasts, and a cable-suspended 'catwalk' that encircles the arena floor and allows our man of the hour [Jon] and his right-hand man, Richie Sambora to (GASP!) run around the hall right over our very heads!"

NEW JERSEY SYNDICATE TOUR:

EUROPEAN DATES (& VENUES) PART I

October 30, 1988 - RDS Arena, Dublin (Ireland)

October 31, 1988 - RDS Arena, Dublin (Ireland)

November 1, 1988 - RDS Arena, Dublin (Ireland)

November 4, 1988 - Schleyerhalle, Stuttgart (Germany)

November 6, 1988 - Festhalle, Frankfurt (Germany)

November 8, 1988 - Messehalle, Kassel (Germany)

November 10, 1988 - Hallen Stadion, Zurich (Switzerland)

November 11, 1988- Hallen Stadion, Zurich (Switzerland)

November 13, 1988 - Palasport, Florence (Italy)

November 15, 1988 - Palatrussardi, Milan (Italy)

November 16, 1988 - Palatrussardi, Milan (Italy)

November 18, 1988 - Frankenhalle, Nuremberg (Germany)

November 20, 1988 - Le Zenith, Paris (France)

November 21, 1988 - Ahoy, Rotterdam (The Netherlands)

November 24, 1988 - Drammenhallen, Oslo (Norway)

November 25, 1988 - Scandinavium, Gothenburg (Sweden)

November 26, 1988 - Isstadion, Stockholm (Sweden)

November 28, 1988 - Icehallen, Helsinki (Finland)

December 2, 1988 - SECC, Glasgow (Scotland)

December 3, 1988 - SECC, Glasgow (Scotland)

December 5, 1988 - NEC, Birmingham (England)

December 6, 1988 - NEC, Birmingham (England)

December 8, 1988 - Wembley Arena, London (England)

December 9, 1988 - Wembley Arena, London (England)

December 11, 1988 - NEC, Birmingham (England)

December 12, 1988 - Wembley Arena, London (England)

December 13, 1988 - Wembley Arena, London (England)

December 15, 1988 - Forest National, Brussels (Belgium)

December 16, 1988 - Westfalenhalle, Dortmund (Germany)

December 19, 1988 - Olympiahalle, Munich (Germany)

JAPANESE DATES (& VENUES)

December 31, 1988 - Heat Beat Live, Tokyo Dome, Tokyo (Japan)

January 1, 1989 - Heat Beat Live, Tokyo Dome, Tokyo (Japan)

January 5, 1989 - Castle Hall, Osaka (Japan)

January 6, 1989 - Castle Hall, Osaka (Japan)

January 9, 1989 - Castle Hall, Osaka (Japan)

January 10, 1989 - Rainbow Hall, Nagoya (Japan)

January 11, 1989 - Rainbow Hall, Nagoya (Japan)

NORTH AMERICAN DATES (& VENUES) PART I

January 13, 1989 - Neal S. Blaisdell Center, Honolulu, HI (USA)

January 14, 1989 - Neal S. Blaisdell Center, Honolulu, HI (USA)

January 15, 1989 - Neal S. Blaisdell Center, Honolulu, HI (USA)

January 26, 1989 - Reunion Arena, Dallas, TX (USA)

January 27, 1989 - Hemisphere Arena, San Antonio, TX (USA)

January 29, 1989 - Summit, Houston, TX (USA)

January 30, 1989 - Frank Erwin Center, Austin, TX (USA)

February 1, 1989 - Coast Coliseum, Biloxi, MS (USA)

February 2, 1989 - LSU Assembly Center, Baton Rouge, LA (USA)

February 4, 1989 - Civic Center, Pensacola, FL (USA)

February 5, 1989 - Leon County Civic Center, Tallahassee, FL (USA)

February 7, 1989 - Coliseum, Jacksonville, FL (USA)

February 9, 1989 - Miami Arena, Miami, FL (USA)

February 10, 1989 - Orlando Arena, Orlando, FL (USA)

February 11, 1989 - San Juan Stadium, San Juan (Puerto Rico)

February 14, 1989 - Jefferson Coliseum, Birmingham, AL (USA)

February 15, 1989 - Omni, Atlanta, GA (USA)

February 17, 1989 - Coliseum, Charlotte, NC (USA)

February 18, 1989 - University of North Carolina, Chapel Hill, NC (USA)

February 20, 1989 - Murphy Center, Murfreesboro, TN (USA)

February 22, 1989 - Mid-South Coliseum, Memphis, TN (USA)

February 23, 1989 - Thompson-Boling Arena, Knoxville, TN (USA)

February 26, 1989 - Rupp Arena, Lexington, KY (USA)

February 28, 1989 - Coliseum, Hampton, VA (USA)

March 2, 1989 - Civic Center, Providence, RI (USA)

March 3, 1989 - Carrier Dome, Syracuse, NY (USA)

March 6, 1989 - Civic Center, Hartford, CT (USA)

March 7, 1989 - Capitol Center, Largo, MD (USA)

March 8, 1989 - Spectrum, Philadelphia, PA (USA)

March 10, 1989 - Nassau Coliseum, Uniondale, NY (USA)

March 12, 1989 - Centrum, Worcester, MA (USA)

March 13, 1989 - Centrum, Worcester, MA (USA)

March 15, 1989 - Meadowlands Arena, East Rutherford, NJ (USA)

March 21, 1989 - Joe Louis Arena, Detroit, MI (USA)

March 22, 1989 - Roberts Stadium, Evansville, IN (USA)

March 24, 1989 - Rosemont Horizon, Rosemont, IL (USA)

March 25, 1989 - Richfield Coliseum, Richfield, OH (USA)

March 26, 1989 - Market Square Arena, Indianapolis, IN (USA)

March 28, 1989 - University of Iowa, Iowa City, IA (USA)

March 29, 1989 - Assembly Hall, Champaign, IL (USA)

April 1, 1989 - Bradley Center, Milwaukee, WI (USA)

April 2, 1989 - Hilton Coliseum, Ames, IA (USA)

April 4, 1989 - Metro Center, Minneapolis, MN (USA)

April 5, 1989 - Civic Center, Omaha, NE (USA)

April 7, 1989 - Arena, St. Louis, MO (USA)

April 8, 1989 - SIU Arena, Carbondale, IL (USA)

April 10, 1989 - Kansas Coliseum, Wichita, KS (USA)

April 11, 1989 - The Myriad, Oklahoma City, OK (USA)

April 13, 1989 - Kemper Arena, Kansas City, MO (USA)

April 15, 1989 - Municipal Auditorium, Lubbock, TX (USA)

April 16, 1989 - Pan Am Center, Las Cruces, NM (USA)

April 18, 1989 - Tingley Coliseum, Albuquerque, NM (USA)

April 20, 1989 - Compton Terrace, Phoenix, AZ (USA)

April 21, 1989 - Sports Arena, San Diego, CA (USA)

April 22, 1989 - Irvine Meadows, Irvine, CA (USA)

April 24, 1989 - Thomas & Mack Arena, Las Vegas, NV (USA)

April 26, 1989 - Great Western Forum, Los Angeles, CA (USA)

April 27, 1989 - Great Western Forum, Los Angeles, CA (USA)

April 29, 1989 - Shoreline Amphitheater, Mountain View, CA (USA)

April 30, 1989 - Shoreline Amphitheater, Mountain View, CA (USA)

May 2, 1989 - Salt Palace, Salt Lake City, UT (USA)

May 3, 1989 - Salt Palace, Salt Lake City, UT (USA)

May 5, 1989 - B.S.U. Pavilion, Boise, ID (USA)

May 7, 1989 - Washington State, Pullman, WA (USA)

May 8, 1989 - Memorial Coliseum, Portland, OR (USA)

May 10, 1989 - Tacoma Dome, Tacoma, WA, (USA)*

May 11, 1989 - B.C. Place, Vancouver, BC (Canada)

*This was the shoot for the video to 'Lay Your Hands On Me.'

NORTH AMERICAN DATES (& VENUES) PART II

May 27, 1989 - Val du Lakes, Hart, MI (USA)

May 28, 1989 - Joe Louis Arena, Detroit, MI (USA)

May 29, 1989 - Peoria Civic Center, Peoria, IL (USA)

May 31, 1989 - Civic Center, Charleston, WV (USA)

June 2, 1989 - CNE Stadium, Toronto, ON (Canada)

June 3, 1989 - Forum, Montreal, QC (Canada)

June 4, 1989 - Coliseum, Quebec City, QC (Canada)

June 6, 1989 - Seashore Performing Arts Center, Old Orchard Beach, ME (USA)*

June 7, 1989 - Civic Center, Providence, RI (USA)

June 8, 1989 - First Union Center, Wilkes-Barre, PA (USA)

June 11, 1989 - Giants Stadium, East Rutherford, NJ (USA)

June 13, 1989 - Civic Arena, Pittsburgh, PA (USA)

June 14, 1989 - Civic Arena, Pittsburgh, PA (USA)

June 16, 1989 - Point Stadium, Johnstown, PA (USA)

June 17, 1989 - Hershey Stadium, Hershey, PA (USA)

June 19, 1989 - Spectrum, Philadelphia, PA (USA)

June 20, 1989 - Spectrum, Philadelphia, PA (USA)

June 21, 1989 - Spectrum, Philadelphia, PA (USA)

June 23, 1989 - Civic Center, Hartford, CT (USA)

June 24, 1989 - Civic Center, Hartford, CT (USA)

June 25, 1989 - Race Track, Saratoga Springs, NY (USA)

June 28, 1989 - Great Woods, Mansfield, MA (USA)

June 29, 1989 - Great Woods, Mansfield, MA (USA)

July 5, 1989 - Silver Stadium, Rochester, NY (USA)

July 6, 1989 - Convention Center, Niagara Falls, ON (USA)

July 8, 1989 - Riverfront park, Manchester, NH (USA)

July 9, 1989 - Orange County Fairground, Middletown, NY (USA)

July 11, 1989 - Capitol Center, Landover, MD (USA)

July 12, 1989 - Coliseum, Richmond, VA (USA)

July 19, 1989 - Starwood Amphitheatre, Nashville, TN (USA)

July 20, 1989- Lakewood Amphitheatre, Atlanta, GA (USA)

July 28, 1989 - Fiddler's Green, Denver, CO (USA)

July 30, 1989 - Expo Center, Topeka, KS (USA)

July 31, 1989 - Civic Auditorium, Omaha, NE (USA)

August 1, 1989 - Met Center, Bloomington, MN (USA)

August 2, 1989 - Five Seasons Center, Cedar Rapids, IA (USA)

August 4, 1989 - Alpine Valley, East Troy, WI (USA)

* Cancelled – rescheduled later...

FESTIVALS

August 12, 1989 - Moscow Music Peace Festival, Lenin Stadium, Moscow (Russia)

August 13, 1989 - Moscow Music Peace Festival, Lenin Stadium, Moscow, (Russia)

August 19, 1989 - National Bowl, Milton Keynes (England)

NORTH AMERICAN DATES (& VENUES) PART III

August 23, 1989 - The Castle, Charlevoix, MI (USA)

August 25, 1989 - Winnipeg Arena, Winnipeg, MB (Canada)

August 26, 1989 - Agridome, Regina, SK (Canada)

August 28, 1989 - Saddledome, Calgary, AB (Canada)

August 29, 1989 - Coliseum, Edmonton, AB (Canada)

August 30, 1989 - Saskatchewan Place, Saskatoon, SK (Canada)

September 1, 1989 - Event Center, Casper, WY (USA)

September 2, 1989 - Rushmore Plaza, Rapid City, SD (USA)

September 3, 1989 - Arena, Sioux Falls, SD (USA)

September 7, 1989 - Irvine Meadows, Irvine, CA (USA)

September 8, 1989 - Cal Expo, Sacramento, CA (USA)

September 9, 1989 - Cal Expo, Sacramento, CA (USA)

September 10, 1989 - Irvine Meadows, Irvine, CA (USA)

September 12, 1989 - Compton Terrace, Phoenix, AZ (USA)

September 14, 1989 - Convention Center, Tulsa, OK (USA)

September 15, 1989 - Hirsch Memorial Coliseum, Shreveport, LA (USA)

September 16, 1989 - Barton Coliseum, Little Rock, AR (USA)

September 17, 1989 - Coliseum, Jackson, MS (USA)

September 19, 1989 - Von Braun Center, Huntsville, AL (USA)

September 21, 1989 - Civic Center, Augusta, GA (USA)

September 23, 1989 - Civic Center, Lakeland, FL (USA)

AUSTRALIAN & NEW ZEALAND DATES (& VENUES)

October 30, 1989 - Brisbane Entertainment Center, Brisbane (Australia)
October 31, 1989 - Brisbane Entertainment Center, Brisbane (Australia)
November 3, 1989 - Sydney Entertainment Center, Sydney (Australia)
November 4, 1989 - Sydney Entertainment Center, Sydney (Australia)
November 13, 1989 - Melbourne Entertainment Center, Melbourne (Australia)
November 14, 1989 - Melbourne Entertainment Center, Melbourne (Australia)
November 18, 1989 - Western Springs Stadium, Auckland (New Zealand)

EUROPEAN DATES (& VENUES) PART II

November 29, 1989 – Cascais (Portugal)
December 1, 1989 - Palacio de Desportes, Madrid (Spain)
December 2, 1989 – Barcelona (Spain)
December 3, 1989 - Velodromo de Anoeta, San Sebastian (Spain)
December 4, 1989 - Virgin Megastore, Paris (France)
December 5, 1989 - Palais des Sports, Paris (France)
December 6, 1989 - Ahoy, Rotterdam (Netherlands)
December 7, 1989 - Sporthalle, Cologne (Germany)
December 8, 1989 - Alsterdorfer Sporthalle, Hamburg (Germany)
December 9, 1989 - Weser-Ems-Halle, Oldenburg (Germany)
December 11, 1989 – Copenhagen (Denmark)

December 13, 1989 - Ice Hall, Helsinki (Finland)
December 15, 1989 - Globen Arena, Stockholm (Sweden)
December 16, 1989 - Scandinavium, Gothenburg (Sweden)
December 18, 1989 - Oslo (Norway)
December 21, 1989 - Olympiahalle, Munich (Germany)
December 22, 1989 – Zurich (Switzerland)
December 23, 1989 - Festhalle, Frankfurt (Germany)
* This was a free acoustic set
January 2, 1990 - Wembley Arena, London (England)
January 3, 1990 - Wembley Arena, London (England)
January 4, 1990 - Wembley Arena, London (England)
January 6, 1990 - Kings Hall, Belfast (Northern Ireland)
January 7, 1990 - Point Depot, Dublin (Ireland)
January 8, 1990 - Point Depot, Dublin (Ireland)
January 10, 1990 - Hammersmith Odeon, London (England)
January 11, 1990 - Hammersmith Odeon, London (England)
January 12, 1990 - Hammersmith Odeon, London (England)
January 13, 1990 - Hammersmith Odeon, London (England)
January 14, 1990 - Hammersmith Odeon, London (England)
January 15, 1990 - Hammersmith Odeon, London (England)
January 16, 1990 - Hammersmith Odeon, London (England)

SOUTH AMERICAN DATES (& VENUES)

January 18, 1990 - Maracanã Stadium, Rio de Janeiro (Brazil)
January 19, 1990 - São Paulo (Brazil)

January 27, 1990 - Praça da Apoteose, Rio de Janeiro (Brazil)
January 28, 1990 - Rio de Janeiro (Brazil)
February 1, 1990 - Buenos Aires (Argentina)
February 6, 1990 - Estadio Nacional, Santiago (Chile)
February 9, 1990 – Monterrey (Mexico)
February 10, 1990 – Monterrey (Mexico)
February 16, 1990 – Guadalajara (Mexico)
February 17, 1990 – Guadalajara (Mexico)

As already mentioned, the band regrouped to play some benefit shows in 1990/91 mostly at the behest of their then manager Doc McGhee. Those shows were:

December 23, 1990 - Christmas Benefit, Count Basie Theater, Red Bank, NJ (USA)
December 31, 1990 - Tokyo Dome, Tokyo (Japan)
January 3, 1991 - Yokohama Arena, Yokohama (Japan)
January 5, 1991 - Rainbow Hall, Nagoya (Japan)
January 6, 1991 - Osaka Castle Hall, Osaka (Japan)
January 9, 1991 - Osaka Castle Hall, Osaka (Japan)
December 21, 1991 - Christmas Benefit, Count Basie Theater, Red Bank, NJ (USA)

NEW JERSEY: THE VIDEOS

Running for 45 minutes and released in 1989, *New Jersey: The Videos* features all the music videos from the album of the same name and has since been deleted. The single VHS release also featured interviews and backstage footage. Even better was

the double VHS version (released in 1990) which featured the acclaimed behind the scenes documentary *Access All Areas: A Rock & Roll Odyssey.* Fans are eager to see a DVD version of this compilation.

Dave Shack reviewed the collection in *Metal Forces*:

"All in all a great stocking filler that might tide you over until the next album."

Track Listing:
1. 'Bad Medicine' *(First version)*
2. 'Born To Be My Baby'
3. 'I'll Be There For You'
4. 'Lay Your Hands On Me'
5. 'Living In Sin'
6. 'Blood On Blood' *(Live)*
7. 'Bad Medicine' *(Second version)*

NEW JERSEY UNDERGROUND MUSIC COMPANY

New Jersey Underground Music Company was a publishing company formed by Jon Bon Jovi and Richie Sambora in 1987. Its primary purpose was to monitor their royalties from the band and from their collaborations with other artists. Skid Row's self-titled debut album was released via NJUMC in 1989; it was a massive hit in the States reaching Number 6 in the *Billboard* Hot 100. Controversially, in return for Jon's help in getting them a record deal, all of Skid Row's publishing royalties from the album allegedly went to NJUMC (i.e. Jon and Sambora). That's 100% royalties. Skid Row went public over this and a nasty public argument ensued between Jon Bon Jovi and Skid Row singer Sebastian Bach. Sambora gave his share (allegedly 50%) of the royalties back to Skid Row.

Sebastian Bach told *Kerrang!* in October, 1990:

"Richie gave the money back. He was too embarrassed about people like Slash coming up to him and going, 'You know what, man, it's a really shitty thing you did to the kids'. He f**kin' gave it all back. So you can see what kind of person he is – rock solid."

The legal case between Bach and Jon was reportedly resolved in the mid-1990s. NJUMC also signed Aldo Nova, but the company is no longer in operation, having been dissolved not long after the release of Skid Row's debut album.

NEW YORK GIANTS

An American football team from East Rutherford, New Jersey. Jon Bon Jovi is a big fan of the team and regularly attends games when he's not on tour. Their home ground is the Giants Stadium at the Meadowlands Sports Complex in East Rutherford, New Jersey. Since their foundation in 1925, the New York Giants have featured a total of 15 Hall Of Fame play-

ers and have succeeded in winning seven NFL titles. They won Super Bowl XLII on February 3, 2008.

Visit *giants.com*

NEW YORK ROCKS 1983

A compilation of unsigned bands that was made courtesy of the Long Island radio station WAPP FM 103.5, whose parent company was Doubleday. The record included Jon Bon Jovi's 'Runaway', and other offerings such as 'Jaded Heart' by Humans From Earth, 'She Got Free' by Mike Corbin and 'Outlaw (Josie Wales)' by the Southern Cross Band. Fortunately for Bon Jovi, the album was circulated for free on other stations owned by Doubleday across the country and consequently the song picked up quite a fan base. Later in the same year Jon was signed to PolyGram, one of America's major record labels.

NICKELBACK

A popular Canadian rock band formed in 1995. The current line-up of the band is singer Chad Kroeger, lead guitarist Ryan Peake, bassist Mike Kroeger and drummer Daniel Adair. Previous members include Ryan Vikedal, Mitch Guindon and Brandon Kroeger. *Silver Side Up*, their third album, was a huge hit when it was released in 2003 and gave the band a smash-hit single with 'How You Remind Me'. 2003's *The Long Road* and 2005's *For All The Right Reasons* also sold millions of copies each. Nickelback's hit singles include 'Photograph', 'Far Away', 'Someday' and 'Rock Star'.

Similarly to Bon Jovi, Nickelback have been criticised for being too simplistic and chart-friendly. They supported Bon Jovi on a European tour in 2006. The UK and Ireland dates were:

May 20 – Croke Park, Dublin
June 3 – Hampden Park, Glasgow
June 4 – City of Manchester Stadium, Manchester

June 7 – Ricoh Arena, Coventry
June 9 – St. Marys Stadium, Southampton
June 10 – National Bowl, Milton Keynes
June 11 – National Bowl, Milton Keynes

Visit *nickelback.com*

NICKS, STEVIE

An American singer-songwriter who, in addition to enjoying a suc-

cessful solo career, also achieved world-wide fame as a member of the legendary Fleetwood Mac, which she joined in 1975. She released her first solo album in 1981. Tico Torres drummed for Nicks prior to joining Bon Jovi, and is credited on the 1991 CD release *Timespace - The Best of Stevie Nicks.* Also, Jon co-wrote (with Billy Falcon) and produced the track 'Sometimes It's A Bitch', the opening track on the album.

Visit *nicksfix.com*

NO LOOKING BACK

A 1998 romantic comedy written and directed by the actor Edward Burns. Essentially, *No Looking Back* explores the relationship between Jon Bon Jovi's character Michael and his girlfriend Claudia, played by Lauren Holly.

NOLL, SHANNON

An Australian singer-songwriter who made his name as a runner-up on the first series of *Australian Idol*, which is essentially the same format as the popular *American Idol*. His soft rock style has been compared to the likes of Bryan Adams and Bon Jovi. Noll sang 'Livin' On A Prayer' during the eighties-themed episode in the series. Richie Sambora co-wrote the track 'Sorry Is Just Too Late' which features on Noll's third album *Turn It Up*, released in September, 2007. This album was produced by Luke Ebbin, who co-produced the Grammy nominated Bon Jovi album *Crush*.

Visit *shannonnoll.com.au*

NOTORIOUS

A song written by Jon Bon Jovi and Richie Sambora for the Canadian melodic rock band Loverboy. It is the first track on their 1987 album *Wildside*, which was produced by Bruce Fairbairn.

NOVA, ALDO

Born in Montreal in 1956, Aldo Nova is a Canadian guitarist, singer-songwriter and producer, known for his guitar solos and entertaining music videos. His only hit album in the States is his self-titled 1981 opus, which peaked at Number 8. His popular singles are: 'Fantasy' (1982), 'Foolin' Yourself (1982), 'Monkey

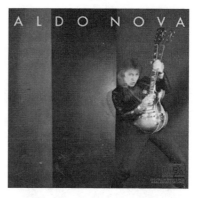

On Your Back' (1983) and 'Blood On The Bricks' (1991).

Nova played on Jon Bon Jovi's 'Runaway' demo, recorded in June, 1982 at Power Station Studios in NYC. The pair kept in touch and wrote songs together throughout the decade. Nova played guitars, keyboards and tambourine on Jon's debut album *Blaze Of Glory*, but their most notable collaboration was Nova's "comeback" album *Blood On The Bricks*, which was the first release on Jon's label Jambco in 1991. However, despite good reviews, the album failed to gain any commercial success, reaching Number 124 in the US album chart. Of the 12 tracks on the album, only 'Bright Lights' was written solely by Nova.

'Blood On The Bricks' *(Bon Jovi, Nova)*
'Medicine Man' *(Bon Jovi, Nova)*
'Bang Bang' *(Bon Jovi, Nova)*
'Someday' *(Bon Jovi, Hughes, Nova)*
'Young Love' *(Bon Jovi, Nova, Vallance)*
'Modern World' *(Bon Jovi, Nova)*
'This Ain't Love' *(Bon Jovi, Nova)*
'Hey Ronnie (Veronica's Song)' *(Bon Jovi, Nova)*
'Touch Of Madness' *(Bon Jovi, Nova)*

'Naked', from Jon's 1997 album *Destination Anywhere,* also credits Nova as guitarist.

11. 'Hear Our Prayer'
12. 'Summer Of Dreams'
13. 'Up The River'
14. 'Netherworld Waltz'

ON A FULL MOON

David Bryan's debut solo album is a 14-track instrumental recording that was released in 1995 via Ignition Records. Not entirely instrumental, however, as the second track, 'In These Arms,' which was originally included on Bon Jovi's *Keep The Faith* album, features Bryan on vocals. Fans were pleased that the classically trained keyboard player had finally started to display his talents outside the Bon Jovi camp, and have his name on a CD cover. The album has now become something of a rarity – a second-hand copy was offered for sale on Amazon.co.uk for no less then £45.00.

Track Listing:
1. 'Awakening'
2. 'In These Arms'
3. 'It's a Long Road'
4. 'April'
5. 'Kissed By An Angel'
6. 'Endless Horizon'
7. 'Lullaby For Two Moons'
8. 'Interlude'
9. 'Midnight Voodoo'
10. 'Room Full Of Blues'

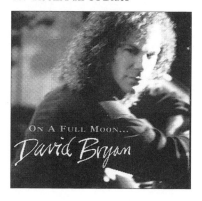

ON THE LINE

A comedy film released in 2001 and directed by Eric Bross. The plot concerns a man who meets a woman on a train, falls in love with her at first sight, and spends the rest of the film trying to find her again. Richie Sambora plays a peripheral character called Mick Silver, and also contributed the song 'Take Me On' to the movie's soundtrack.

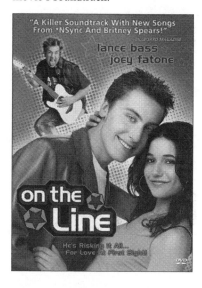

100,000,000 BON JOVI FANS CAN'T BE WRONG

The cover of this four CD / one DVD box set famously mimics the Elvis Presley collection *50,000,000 Elvis Fans Can't Be Wrong*. *100,000,000 Bon Jovi Fans Can't Be Wrong* was released through Island Records on November 16, 2004. Its purpose was to celebrate the band's twentieth anniversary and the title referred to the fact that the band had sold over 100 million albums during their career to date. Discs one to three are collections of previously unreleased tracks, B-sides, demos, soundtrack compositions and obscurities. The fourth disc is a DVD of interviews and archive footage. The Japanese release featured a bonus fifth disc.

Jon told *Classic Rock* (January, 2005):

"Gives us a chance to see where we came from, appreciate where we are...And then time to move on and look to the next chapter in the band's history."

Track listing:
(Disc 1)
1. 'Aren't You Dead?'
2. 'The Radio Saved My Life Tonight'
3. 'Taking It Back'
4. 'Someday I'll Be Saturday Night' *(Demo)*
5. 'Miss Fourth Of July'
6. 'Open All Night'
7. 'These Arms Are Open All Night'
8. 'I Get A Rush'
9. 'Someday Just Might Be Tonight'
10. 'Thief Of Hearts'
11. 'Last Man Standing'
12. 'I Just Want To Be Your Man'

(Disc 2)
1. 'Garageland'
2. 'Starting All Over Again'
3. 'Maybe Someday'
4. 'Last Chance Train'
5. 'The Fire Inside'
6. 'Every Beat Of My Heart'
7. 'Rich Man Living In A Poor Man's House'
8. 'The One That Got Away'
9. 'You Can Sleep While I Dream'
10. 'Outlaws Of Love'
11. 'Good Guys Don't Always Wear White'
12. 'We Rule The Night'

(Disc 3)
1. 'Edge Of A Broken Heart'
2. 'Sympathy'
3. 'Only In My Dreams (*Feat. Tico Torres on vocals*)
4. 'Shut Up And Kiss Me'
5. 'Crazy Love'
6. 'Lonely At The Top'
7. 'Ordinary People'
8. 'Flesh And Bone'
9. 'Satellite'
10. 'If I Can't Have Your Love' (*Feat. Richie Sambora on vocals*)
11. 'Real Life'
12. 'Memphis Lives In Me' *(Feat. David Bryan on vocals, from the musical Memphis)*
13. 'Too Much Of A Good Thing'

(Disc 4)
1. 'Love Ain't Nothing But A Four Letter Word'
2. 'Love Ain't Nothing But A Four Letter Word' *(Demo)*
3. 'River Runs Dry'
4. 'Always' *(Demo)*
5. 'Kidnap An Angel'

6. 'Breathe'
7. 'Out Of Bounds'
8. 'Letter To A Friend'
9. 'Temptation'
10. 'Gotta Have A Reason'
11. 'All I Wanna Do Is You'
12. 'Billy'
13. 'Nobody's Hero *(Demo)*
14. 'Livin' On A Prayer' *(Previously unreleased; hidden track)*

ONE WILD NIGHT 2001 (SINGLE)

The only single taken from the live album *One Wild Night Live 1985-2001.*

'One Wild Night 2001' is actually a re-recording of 'One Wild Night', which first appeared on the 2000 album *Crush.* It was issued in the UK on May 19, 2001 and reached Number 10, spending seven weeks in the singles chart. The lyrics were penned by Jon and Richie Sambora.

Track Listing:
1. 'One Wild Night'
2. 'Lay Your Hands On Me' *(Live)*
3. 'I Believe' *(Live)*
4. 'Hey God' *(Live)*
5. 'Tokyo Road' *(Live)*

ONE WILD NIGHT LIVE 1985-2001

Released in the UK on May 26, 2001, *One Wild Night Live 1985-2001* is Bon Jovi's only live album, which is surprising given that they have been together for over 25 years. It hit Number 2 in the UK Top 40 and spent nine weeks in the charts, while in the States it only made it to Number 20. The track listing includes cover versions of Neil Young's anthem 'Rockin' In The Free World'

and the Boomtown Rats' hit single 'I Don't Like Mondays,' featuring vocals from Bob Geldof, which was recorded at Wembley Stadium on June 25, 1995. The album was produced by a collective of Obie O'Brien, Bon Jovi, Richie Sambora, Luke Ebbin and Desmond Child. It features Jon Bon Jovi, Richie Sambora, David Bryan, Tico Torres and bassists Alec John Such and Hugh McDonald.

Track Listing:

1. 'It's My Life' *(Recorded: November 27, 2000 in Toronto, Ontario, Canada)*
2. 'Livin' On A Prayer' *(Recorded: August 30, 2000 in Zurich, Switzerland)*
3. 'You Give Love A Bad Name' *(Recorded: August 30, 2000 in Zurich, Switzerland)*
4. 'Keep The Faith' *(Recorded: September 20, 2000 in New York City, USA)*
5. 'Someday I'll Be Saturday Night' *(Recorded: November 10, 1995 in Melbourne, Australia)*
6. 'Rockin' In The Free World' *(Recorded: December 1, 1995 in Johannesburg, South Africa)*
7. 'Something To Believe In' *(Recorded: May 19, 1996 in Yokohama, Japan)*
8. 'Wanted Dead Or Alive' *(Recorded: September 20, 2000 in New York City, USA)*
9. 'Runaway' *(Recorded: April 28, 1985 in Tokyo, Japan)*
10. 'In And Out Of Love' *(Recorded: April 28, 1985 in Tokyo, Japan)*
11. 'I Don't Like Mondays' *(Feat. Bob Geldof) (Recorded: June 25, 1995 at Wembley Stadium, London, England)*
12. 'Just Older' *(Recorded: November 27, 2000 in Toronto, Ontario, Canada)*
13. 'Something For The Pain' *(Recorded: November 10, 1995 in Melbourne, Australia)*
14. 'Bad Medicine' *(Recorded: August 30, 2000 in Zurich, Switzerland)*
15. 'One Wild Night 2001' *(Remix)*

Author's Review:

One Wild Night Live *is the worst kind of live album: a cut and paste job featuring 13 live tracks from various concerts between 1985 and 2001. After each track the sound fades and a new song begins which ruins the consistency; also, because these songs are culled from various phases of the band's career, the difference in the band's playing and sound is all too obvious.*

It also doesn't represent the best of the band's onstage ability; many of the songs are sung in a lower register than the studio versions so instead of enhancing the songs (which all great live albums do) it actually degrades them. Give me the live version of, say, 'Livin' On A Prayer' any day. The cover of 'Rockin' In The Free World' is actually a good attempt. It seems as though it was a 'let's release this now or don't bother' idea. They're got a much better live album in them.

*Rating **

ONE WILD NIGHT TOUR (2001)

This was just an extension of the 2000 *Crush* tour. The band had released their first live album *One Wild Night Live 1985-2001* and chose to stay on the road to promote it. They succeeded in playing to over one million people during 54 concerts.

ONE WILD NIGHT TOUR:

AUSTRALIAN & JAPANESE DATES

March 24, 2001 – Melbourne (Australia)

March 28, 2001 – Yokohama (Japan)
March 29, 2001 – Yokohama (Japan)
March 31, 2001 – Osaka (Japan)
April 3, 2001 – Nagoya (Japan)
April 5, 2001 – Tokyo (Japan)

NORTH AMERICAN AND SOUTH AMERICAN DATES PART I

April 18, 2001 - Phoenix, AZ (USA)
April 20, 2001 - Anaheim, CA (USA)
April 21, 2001 - Las Vegas, NV (USA)
April 23, 2001 - San Jose, CA (USA)
April 25, 2001 - Mexico City (Mexico)
April 28, 2001 - Salt Lake City, UT (USA)
April 30, 2001 - Denver, CO (USA)
May 2, 2001 - Dallas, TX (USA)
May 4, 2001 - Columbus, OH (USA)
May 5, 2001 - Cleveland, OH (USA)
May 8, 2001 - Grand Rapids, MI (USA)
May 10, 2001 - Raleigh, NC (USA)
May 11, 2001 - Atlanta, GA (USA)

May 13, 2001 - Washington, D.C. (USA)
May 15, 2001 - Greenville, SC (USA)
May 17, 2001 - Ottawa, ON (USA)
May 19, 2001 - Quebec City (USA)
May 20, 2001 - Albany, NY (USA)

EUROPEAN DATES

May 31, 2001 – Stockholm (Sweden)
June 3, 2001 – Werchter (Belgium)
June 5, 2001 – Amsterdam (Netherlands)
June 6, 2001 – Amsterdam (Netherlands)
June 8, 2001 – Glasgow (Scotland)
June 10, 2001 – Dublin (Ireland)
June 13, 2001 – Huddersfield (England)
June 16, 2001 - Milton Keynes (England)
June 17, 2001 – Cardiff (Wales)
June 19, 2001 – Paris (France)
June 20, 2001 – Cologne (Germany)
June 22, 2001 – Stuttgart (Germany)
June 24, 2001 – Hamburg (Germany)
June 26, 2001 – Zurich (Switzerland)
June 27, 2001 – Padova (Italy)
June 29, 2001 – Vienna (Austria)
June 30, 2001 – Munich (Germany)

NORTH AMERICAN DATES PART II

July 8, 2001 - Milwaukee, WI (USA)
July 9, 2001 - Minneapolis, MN (USA)
July 13, 2001 - Chicago, IL (USA)
July 15, 2001 - Detroit, MI (USA)
July 16, 2001 - Detroit, MI (USA)
July 17, 2001 - Toronto, ON (Canada)
July 19, 2001 - Montreal, Quebec (Canada)
July 21, 2001 - Pittsburgh, PA (USA)
July 22, 2001 - Hershey, PA (USA)
July 24, 2001 - Camden, NJ (USA)
July 25, 2001 - Boston, MA (USA)
July 27, 2001 - E. Rutherford, NJ (USA)
July 28, 2001 - E. Rutherford, NJ (USA)

ONLY LONELY

The third single taken from the band's second album *7800° Fahrenheit*. Not issued in the UK, it was released in America in April, 1985 and peaked at Number 54 in the *Billboard* Hot 100. It features on the soundtrack to the Michael J. Fox film *Light Of Day*.

OPEN AIR THEATRE

Bon Jovi kicked off the American leg of their 1993-94 *Keep The Faith* world tour at the Open Air Theater in San Diego, where they were supported by Extreme.

OPEN ALL NIGHT

'Open All Night' is the last track on the 2002 hit album *Bounce*. It was written by Jon Bon Jovi and Richie Sambora. The song reflects the relationship between Jon's character Victor Morrison and Ally in the hit TV show *Ally McBeal*, in which he starred in for 10 episodes in 2002. He was allegedly asked to stay for another few shows but had to leave because his wife was pregnant. Jon was reported to be unhappy about the way his character was written out of the show.

Jon told Philip Wilding at *Classic Rock* in 2001:

"We wrote the song, and I gave Calista Flockhart [Ally McBeal] the lyrics as a gift, and we cut the track. Had David [Kelley, the producer and show's creator] worked with me, we would have jived, I would have given him an unreleased song....Victor would have had a backbone. Basically, the guy turned into this spineless non-entity."

OPERACION TRIUNFO

A Spanish reality TV show from 2001. One episode featured Bon Jovi's 'Livin' On A Prayer', resulting in the show often being listed in the soundtracks section of Bon Jovi filmographies.

O2 ARENA, LONDON

Previously known as the Millennium Dome, London's O2 Arena (situated close to the River Thames) has become one of Britain's most successful venues.

Bon Jovi was the first band to play a concert there when the Arena was opened to the public on June 24, 2007. There was considerable hype around the concert, which resulted in the 20,000 tickets selling out within 30 minutes of going on sale. The O2 Arena also famously played host to the Led Zeppelin reunion in 2007.

OXFORD UNIVERSITY

Over the years many high-profile names have been invited to address the Oxford Union, the celebrated debating society of Oxford University. On June 15, 2001 Jon spoke to the Oxford Union about music, the charities he has aided and life in general.

Author Michael Heatley recalls:

"I interviewed Jon at Oxford University where he addressed the Union in 2001, having swept in with a Clinton-sized retinue of minders and drivers. Never took his shades off once during our encounter, so the quotes I had already gleaned [for my book Bon Jovi: In Their Own Words*] revealed more than he did on the day!"*

P

PAHIRAM KAHIT SANDALI

A 1998 film made in the Philippines, directed by Maryo J. De los Reyes. The soundtrack features Bon Jovi's 'Bed Of Roses'.

PALMER, TIM

Based in California, Tim Palmer is an English songwriter-producer who has worked with some of the biggest names in the business, including Robert Plant and David Bowie. Originally a punk fan, Palmer moved into the alternative rock area in the eighties before turning his attention to metal acts such as Ozzy Osbourne and H.I.M. He has also worked with the famed grunge outfit Pearl Jam. Palmer mixed some tracks on the mega-selling U2 opus *All That You Can't Leave Behind*, and re- mixed 'Misunderstood' from Bon Jovi's album *Bounce*.

Palmer:

"I was asked by their record label to remix a song called 'Misunderstood' from the Bounce *album. I thought the track had strong potential, but I did not like the transition to the chorus. I felt it didn't kick in with any impact, so I wanted to make a few changes to the arrangement. I started mixing it in LA at Record Plant, the band at that time were in NY. I began by changing the drums around so that the chorus groove kicked off with full throttle, right at the head of the chorus, rather than about two beats later on in the original arrangement! I was happy with the change, but of course, in these situations, it is always a gamble. Often, when you change around a bands recording, they can hate it! Luckily when they heard my first draft, the band understood what I was trying to do, and liked it.*

The band wanted to make a few small changes to the arrangement themselves, so they flew me to New York to finish the mix at Right Track Studios. I love to get an offer like that, two nights in New York, a stay in a nice hotel, a bit of mixing, a couple of dinners, it is always a pleasure!

When I got to the studio, Richie Sambora was replaying a few parts. When that was all completed, I went upstairs and started to re-build the mix. Overall, my goal was just to make a powerful compact rock single. I treated the high vocal lines in the chorus and added some filtering to the drums at the top. Jon came by the studio and gave the approval to the final mix. I enjoyed my time with the guys, even though it was very brief. I had a long chat with Jon and he seemed like a really good guy. Overall it was a fun experience".

Visit *timpalmer.com*

PARASHAR, RICK

An American music producer famous for his work with two of grunge music's biggest bands: Alice In Chains (*Sap*) and Pearl Jam (*Ten*).

He co-produced several tracks on Bon Jovi's album *Have A Nice Day*: 'Wildflower', 'Last Cigarette', 'Novocaine' and 'Story'.

PARINELLO, AL

One of Jon Bon Jovi's neighbours in Sayreville, Parinello was not a professional guitar teacher per se but he did help Jon learn to play his first tunes on the instrument, beginning with a version of The Animals' 'House Of The Rising Sun'. Parinello is thanked in the sleeve notes to the band's self-titled debut album.

PAY IT FORWARD

Directed by Mimi Leder, *Pay It Forward* is a romantic comedy starring Kevin Spacey, Helen Hunt, Hayley Joel Osment, Angie Dickinson, James Caviezel and Jon Bon Jovi, who stars as the alcoholic father of a young boy. The boy, played by Osment, believes that if he can perform three well-meaning deeds in a day

he can "pay it forward" so others can similarly do good deeds; but those three deeds turn out to be a lot harder to instigate than he initially thought. The film was released in America on October 20, 2000.

PELLINGTON, MARK

An American film director from Baltimore who directed the 1997 45-minute film *Destination Anywhere* with Jon Bon Jovi (budget $2million). His other films include *The Mothman Prophecies* and *Arlington Road*. Pellington has also worked on the TV series *Homicide: Life On The Streets* and *Cold Case*, and has directed music videos for Pearl Jam, Foo Fighters, Alice In Chains and U2, amongst many others.

PEOPLE'S CHOICE AWARDS

An American awards show, held annually since 1975, that recognises the best work in popular culture. Although not as prestigious as the Grammys or the Golden Globes, the People's Choice Awards are highly respected in the United States.

In 1987, when Bon Jovi were on the verge of world domination, they picked up the award for 'Band Of The Year', and 20 years later their success continued when they picked up the

'Best Rock Song' for the single 'Who Says You Can't Go Home'.

Visit *pcavote.com*

PERTH AMBOY

A city in Middlesex County, New Jersey, Perth Amboy was the birthplace of Richie Sambora in 1959, and of Jon Bon Jovi and David Bryan three years later.

PHANTOM'S OPERA

From New Jersey, Phantom's Opera was a popular "theatrical metal band" that featured drummer Tico Torres and original Bon Jovi bassist Alec John Such, along with Dean Fasano,

later of Message and Prophet. Founder member John Peter "Jack" Yanoso (stage name Jack Young) passed away on August 12, 2008.

PHILADELPHIA SOUL

An Arena Football League team formed in 2004, which is partly owned by Jon Bon Jovi and Richie Sambora. Bon Jovi's official title is "Founder, Majority Owner and Co-Chairman of the Board" while Sambora's is "Member of the Ownership Group". The team plays in the Eastern Division.

Visit *philadelphiasoul.com*

PIERCE, TIM

Tim Pierce is a highly sought after session guitarist who has worked with everybody from Bruce Springsteen to Meat Loaf and John Waite to Phil Collins, and even pop stars like Faith Hill and Christina Aguilera.

Pierce played the guitar on Jon's four-track demo 'Runaway', recorded at New York's Power Station Studios with Billy Squier, Roy Bittan, Hugh McDonald and Frank LaRoca in June, 1982. It was this demo which secured Jon's record deal with PolyGram in '83. The session band was named The All Star Review, and they are thanked in the sleeve notes to Bon Jovi's self-titled debut album, released in 1984.

PINK

A Grammy award winning American singer, whose second album *M!ssundaztood*, released in 2001, remains her biggest selling and best-known release. The track 'Misery' features contributions from Richie Sambora and Steve Tyler of Aerosmith.

Visit *pinkspage.com*

PLAGIARISM

In August 2008 Bon Jovi were hit with two accusations of plagiarism. It was reported in *Boston* magazine that Bart Steele, a Boston native, had penned a song called 'Man, I Love This Team' about his favourite baseball team, the Boston Red Sox. Steele alleged that the song 'I Love This Town' from *Lost Highway* was similar to his original composition, and threatened legal action.

It was then reported on *Sleaze Roxx* (*sleazeroxx.com*) that singer Joel Ellis, formerly of Cats In Boots (*catsinboots.com*) and Heavy Bones, had emailed a little story of his own.

The email reads:

"It was back in the 1980's when Denny Holan and I were recording our pre-production demos for At-lantic Records with Merri Hoaxx. We had just finished tracking a studio session that included our original song 'I'll Be There For You.' We left Paramount Studios in Hollywood with a cassette tape of rough mixes and headed straight for The Rainbow Bar & Grill on Sunset. When we got there we gave the tape to Michael to put on the Bar's sound system, it was the classic 'Is It Worthy' test for demos and mixes that a lot of bands used to gauge their night's work. We'd always pop on the song and listen for the sounds then we would watch to see if people were digging the songs. The place was definitely digging the songs that night. I ran into Sam Kinison who asked me to come back to his table and hang out. So while our tape was playing, we sat at the table in the back with Sam, Jon Bon Jovi, Peter Aykroyd (Dan's brother) and Doc McGhee, etc...Johnny gave us this line of BS that if we gave him this tape he would take it to his uncle at Polydor Records and try to get us out on tour with him. I somehow felt like I was going to regret that, but we agreed to take a chance and trust him, so we gave Jon Bon Jovi the cassette that night and we never heard back from him. A short time later we heard the chorus for our song 'I'll be theeerrre for youuuu' as JBJs next big hit. My manager at the time wanted to sue his ass but we were doing well and were very busy with all the Atlantic developments going on that I didn't want to cause problems for our momentum that we had going at the time. I hated when people would note the resemblance between Jon Bon Jovi and me at the time and I didn't want to give the world any other reasons to compare me to the Golden Boy Johnny. We were in no way similar to each other and strongly resented any com-

parison...I wasn't a pop singer, I was a rock singer and I wasn't a self-righteous frosted hair perm boy with relatives who paved my way so I could steal songs from real artists and get rich off of ripping them off. I was a self made true rocker from the streets to the stage to the studio to the stores, with no help from daddy's friends & relatives and we rocked without the posing. Whatever successes or shortcomings I had were of my own making, but it was real. So I didn't care about that song. Later on during the Heavy Bones days, I was dating a girl named Lehua Reid, who was previously engaged to Richie Sambora. While she lived at Richie's house, she told me about how she remembered the nights that Jon Bon Jovi and Richie Sambora would sit at Richie's piano with boxes full of tapes they had collected from trusting aspiring musicians who trusted them with their creations for a shot at success, how they would play through tape after tape looking for catchy songs to rip off all the while laughing at the suckers who gave them their tapes. When she heard my demo recording of 'I'll Be There For You' she sat back, eyes wide open, saying 'NO WAY!!! This is YOU??', and went on to tell me about the night that they were so excited to be ripping off this song and how Johnny had always wanted an excuse to rip off John Lennon for his vocal in the verse of 'Don't Let Me Down' by The Beatles. They worked on that song for hours playing my demo over and over again and it stuck in her head. Of course I had already known where their recent huge hit single had come from but hearing her tell that story was like salt in the wound...I've always felt that people should know about this and I still have the original demo. If anyone in the world wants

to hear it I'll be happy to put an Mpeg up on my website so they can hear it too. I wonder how many other guys are out there right now feeling the same burn from the Golden Boy Jon Bon Jovi and his trusty side kick Richie Rich."

PLATINUM DISC

Platinum status in the UK is awarded by the British Phonographic Industry for album sales of 300,000+ copies, the artist(s) receiving a Platinum Disc by way of recognition.

The following Bon Jovi albums have gone Platinum:

Slippery When Wet (Triple Platinum. Released in 1986)
New Jersey (Double Platinum. Released in 1988)
Keep The Faith (Platinum. Released in 1992)
Cross Roads: Greatest Hits (5 x Platinum. Released in 1994)
These Days (Double Platinum. Released in 1995)
Crush (Platinum. Released in 2000)

PLEASE COME HOME FOR CHRISTMAS

Bon Jovi covered this famous yuletide classic in the mid-nineties as a three track single with 'I Wish Everybody Could Be Like Christmas' and 'Back Door Santa'. Cindy Crawford

appeared both in the song's music video and on the CD cover. Released on December 17, '94, it reached Number 7 in the UK charts but failed to chart in America. The song was recorded for the 1992 compilation album *A Very Special Christmas* in aid of the Special Olympics for people with learning disabilities, a cause which Jon has supported since the eighties. Other artists who have covered 'Please Come Home For Christmas' include The Eagles, Charles Brown, B.B. King and Luther Vandross.

POLYGRAM

After shunning Atlantic Records, Jon signed to PolyGram on July 1, 1983 on the advice of senior record executive Derek Shulman. Both PolyGram and Atlantic had been keen to sign him after hearing the single 'Runaway'. Jon initially signed to the label as a solo artist, and it was arranged for his records to be released through their music division Mercury Records.

In 1998, PolyGram merged with the Universal Music Group, and Bon Jovi are still effectively signed to UMG. Mercury is operated through Island Def Jam Music Group in the USA, and runs as a stand-alone company in the UK. Both entities are subsidiaries of UMG.

Visit *universalmusic.com*

POWER STATION

A recording studio based in downtown Manhattan. In 1980 Jon Bon Jovi (then known as John Bongiovi) secured a $50-a-week job at Power Station Studios, working as a janitor. At that time was co-owned by his father's cousin Tony Bongiovi (he sold it in 1996). It had previously been a Cod Edison power plant and then a TV studio (used for the game shows

Let's Make A Deal) before Tony and some colleagues rebuilt it. Since '96 the facility has been known as Avatar.

It was not uncommon for Jon to see the likes of David Bowie or Mick Jagger at the studio - like the typical studio runner, he would make coffee and run errands for them. Working at Power Station also gave him the much needed opportunity to cut his own demo recordings. The 1999 CD release *The Power Station Sessions* is a collection of 14 songs recorded during Jon's time there between 1980 and 1983. The CD was compiled by Tony and was not authorised by Jon, hence he is credited as John Bongiovi.

Visit *avatarstudios.net*

POWER STATION SESSIONS, THE (ALBUM)

This is a collection of 14 previously unreleased tracks which were written and recorded by Jon at the famed Power Station Studios in NYC between 1980 and 1983. Jon did the rounds of the record labels, using many of these songs to try and get a recording deal. Suffice to say, these approaches did not yield much success at the time, but Jon gained some useful experience.

This controversially released CD was not authorised by Jon, and allegedly furthered the rift between Jon and his father's cousin, the producer and former co-owner of Power Station, Tony Bongiovi. As a producer of the band's self-titled debut album, he always felt he should have received more credit and financial recompense from Jon once Bon Jovi made it big. The collection was released via Masquerade Records in 1997, the same year Jon released his solo opus *Destination Anywhere*. Presumably to avoid copyright infringement the CD

Track Listing:
1. 'Who Said It Would Last Forever'
2. 'Open Your Heart'
3. 'Stringin' A Line'
4. 'Don't Leave Me Tonight'
5. 'More Than We Bargained For'
6. 'For You'
7. 'Hollywood Dreams'
8. 'All Talk, No Action'
9. 'Don't Keep Me Wondering'
10. 'Head Over Heels'
11. 'No One Does It Like You'

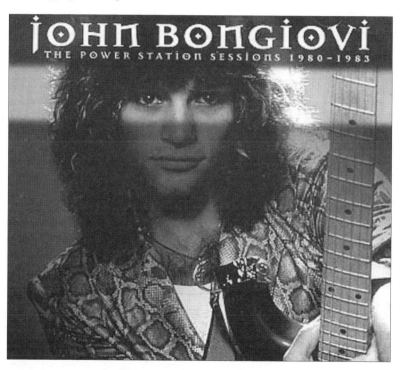

was released under Jon's real name, John Bongiovi. It remains something of a treasure chest for serious fans and a document of Jon's struggle to achieve fame and fortune. In 2001, an expanded version of the collection was released with an extra six tracks, including 'Runaway'. Revered rock scribe and Bon Jovi author Malcolm Dome provided the liner notes.

12. 'What You Want'
13. 'Don't You Believe Him'
14. 'Talkin' In Your Sleep'
15. 'Bobby's Girl'*
16. 'Gimme Some Lovin' Charlene'*
17. 'Don't Do That To Me Anymore'*
18. 'This Woman Is Dangerous'
19. 'Maybe Tomorrow'*
20. 'Runaway'*

* Extra tracks on the extended 2001 version

Author's Review:

This is an interesting set that will surprise many Bon Jovi fans simply because of the type of songs that are on offer here; for example, the opening track, which is pretty good, is basically Jon copying Bruce Springsteen and The E Street Band. There are other songs of this nature with lots of piano. After 'Who Said It Would Last Forever,' there's the sax-led 'Open Your Heart' which is a bit rough and Jon is not vocally at his best; and you can tell Born To Run had been on his playlist at the time. 'Stringin' A Line' is a surprisingly strong ballad, quite tender and emotional. 'Don't Leave Me Tonight' has a progressive guitar riff that is quite catchy and saves what is essentially an underdeveloped song from further embarrassment. 'More Than We Bargained For' is probably the most Springsteen-esque song here; even the lyrics sound like Springsteen. 'For You' is an odd one with a Spanish flavoured sound to the guitars. 'Hollywood Dreams' is a weak mid-paced ballad. 'All Talk, No Action' is nothing but an unmemorable repetitive soft rocker. The Buddy Holly-style vocal sounds that Jon makes sporadically throughout 'Don't Keep Me Wondering' are a bit irritating but 'Head Over Heels' is a slightly better (and faster) track that gives a slight glimpse of what Jon would sound like on the first two Bon Jovi albums. 'No One Does It Like You' sounds a bit rough but it's a fairly well-composed song considering his constraints at the time. 'What You Want' is another mid-paced rocker which would not sound entirely out of place on Bon Jovi and 7800° Fahrenheit. 'Don't You Believe Him' has some nifty guitar work; ditto the closing track 'Talkin' In Your Sleep' which gets heavier as the song progresses.

The extra songs on the later edition follow a similar pattern of underdevelopment but still showing promise; obviously 'Runaway' is now a classic. The Power Stations Years *is an interesting collection whose appeal to Bon Jovi collectors might, however, be lost on others.*

Rating ***

PRAYER '94

Bon Jovi's own "remake" of 'Livin' On A Prayer' originally appeared on the US edition of *Cross Road* but was also released in the UK as a B-side to the single 'Always'.

PRESLEY, ELVIS

The King - the most famous rock and roll singer of all time. There are few stars who are known to millions by their first name alone. That's pretty much it really. His iconic songs include 'That's All Right', 'Heartbreak Hotel', 'Don't Be Cruel', 'Hound Dog', 'Blue Suede Shoes', 'Love Me Tender' and 'All Shook Up'. Like most rock stars, Jon's looks, stage persona and charismatic attitude owe a certain debt to Elvis. It has also been suggested that he has, at various points

in his career, adorned his dressing room walls with Elvis posters. During the recording of his *Young Guns II* soundtrack at A&M Studios in LA, he reportedly nicknamed his residence 'Disgraceland' (a pun of Elvis' home Graceland) and also covered the walls in his rented mansion with Elvis posters. And apparently Richie Sambora came up with the idea of calling the *Cross Road* compilation *Elvis Is Dead But We're Not*.

Visit *elvis.com*

PRUDENTIAL CENTER

Between October 25 and November 10, 2007, Bon Jovi played 10 consecutive dates at Newark's Prudential Center. For two nights each, the band was supported by My Chemical Romance, Big & Rich, Gretchen Wilson, Daughtry and The All-American Rejects. The Prudential Center was the first new entertainment venue to open in the tri-state area for over 25 years, and approximately 150,000 fans attended the 10 Bon Jovi concerts to celebrate its opening.

Amongst these many thousands of fans was *Black Velvet* editor Shari Black. She recalls: *"In 2007, I enjoyed the shows in Newark, NJ where My Chemical Romance, The All-American Rejects and others opened for Bon Jovi at the brand new Prudential Center. Bon Jovi were the first band to headline the new venue and were playing 10 nights. I've been a fan of My Chemical Romance for the last few years and The All-American Rejects also – in fact, I'd been hinting to various people that Bon Jovi should actually have The All-American Rejects as a support – and then they did - so I had to make the trip over. It was great to see two of my fave bands sharing the same stage. The My Chemical Romance support shows were especially awesome and it made my day seeing Jon come onstage wearing an MCR T-shirt at one point. Although the bands are a little different musically they both share the same Jersey attitude, the same conviction to rock and roll and create awesome music and live shows. And to see them getting together for some shows was bliss".*

Visit *prucenter.com*

195

QUEEN OF NEW ORLEANS

The second single from Jon's solo album *Destination Anywhere* was released in the UK on August 30, 1997, peaking at Number 10 in the Top 40 singles chart. The song was co-written with Dave Stewart of the pop duo The Eurythmics and features Bon Jovi bassist Hugh McDonald.

QUEENSRŸCHE

Formed in 1981, Queensrÿche are a progressive heavy metal band from Seattle, Washington. Lead singer Geoff Tate is recognised as one of the genre's finest singers, alongside Judas Priest's Rob Halford and Iron maiden's Bruce Dickinson. Their most successful album is the highly revered 1988 concept piece *Operation Mindcrime*.

Queensrÿche supported Bon Jovi on some UK and European dates during the start of the *Slippery When Wet* tour in late 1986. Reviewing one of the four Hammersmith Odeon shows in November for the monthly magazine *Metal Hammer*, Harry Doherty said Queensrÿche *"proved that they are made of the Right Stuff"*. Speaking about Bon Jovi he said: *"Overall,*

the set was a wham-bam-thank-you-mam affair".

Visit *queensryche.com*

QUINN, LANCE

A successful rock producer who had collaborated with Talking Heads, Lita Ford and Aerosmith before working with Bon Jovi.

Quinn co-produced Bon Jovi's 1984 self-titled debut album with Tony Bongiovi at Power Station Studios in NYC. He also produced the band's second album, *7800° Fahrenheit*, recorded at The Warehouse in Philadelphia. The band were not entirely happy with the resulting record, so turned to producer Bruce Fairbairn for their next two albums. Jon teamed up with Quinn once more for his 1997 solo album *Destination Anywhere*. Quinn contributed guitars to the tracks 'Staring At Your Window With A Suitcase In My Hand', 'Destination Anywhere' and 'Little City'.

QUIREBOYS, THE

Led by Newcastle-born singer Spike, The Quireboys formed in London in 1984. Despite some success in the early 1990s with the albums *A Bit Of What You Fancy* and *Bitter Sweet & Twisted*, and with management from Sharon Osbourne during that period, they never made it as a major rock band.

The Quireboys are a support band rather than a headlining act, although that's not to say they are a weak band. They've made some good songs over the years and are a good live act. They split up in '93 but reformed later in the decade and in 2002, with a new line-up, Spike and his cohorts released *This Is Rock N' Roll*. They have been active ever since.

On New Years Eve, 1990 The Quireboys and Skid Row supported Bon Jovi at the Tokyo Dome in Japan in front of 50,000 rock fans. It was the first night of a short Japanese tour by Bon Jovi. The tour dates were:

31 December, 1990 - Tokyo Dome, Tokyo (Japan)
3 January, 1991 - Yokohama Arena, Yokohama (Japan)
5 January, 1991 - Rainbow hall, Nagoya (Japan)
6 January, 1991 - Osaka Castle Hall, Osaka (Japan)
9 January, 1991 - Osaka Castle Hall, Osaka (Japan)

Visit *quireboys.com*

R

RATT

During the eighties there was a whole movement of glam/hair metal bands in southern California, of which Ratt was one of the most popular. Between 1984 and 1990 they released five albums: *Out Of The Cellar* (1984), *Invasion Of Your Privacy* (1985), *Dancing Undercover* (1986), *Reach For The Sky* (1988) and *Detonator* (1990). Their most famous singles include, 'Round And Round,' 'You're In Love,' 'Lay It Down' and 'Way Cool Jr.' Ratt lost much of their allure in the 1990s, due to the huge popularity of grunge and alt-rock bands, who were basically the antithesis of bands like themselves and Poison, In 1992, the band pretty much dissolved although a break-up was never made official.

In '96 there was a brief reunion with and in 1999 they released their sixth album *Ratt*, which was not a hit. The definitive line-up still remains: Stephen Pearcy (vocals), Warren DeMartini (lead and rhythm guitar), Robbin Crosby (rhythm and lead gui-

tar), Juan Croucier (bass) and Bobby Blotzer (drums).

Crosby had suffered from AIDS, but it is alleged that it was his addiction to heroin that killed him on June 6, 2002. He was 42 years old, and because of his health issues he had lost much of his wealth from Ratt's glory days. In 2007, the remaining members went back on tour and began working on their seventh album. The 2008 line-up is: Bobby Blotzer, Warren DeMartini, Stephen Pearcy, bassist Robbie Crane and guitarist Carlos Cavazo who replaced John Corabi.

Bon Jovi supported Ratt on a six month tour of North America in 1985, only weeks after their debut headlining UK tour. The tour came to an end on New Year's Eve, 1985 in San Diego at the Sports Arena.

Guitarist Steve Blaze of the rock band Lillian Axe says:

"I saw them open for Ratt on their first tour. I recall between them and Ratt there was an immense volume to the crowd reaction. The fans were incredibly loud! I have seen them on TV and they always sound great, raw and polished at the same time".

During that tour Bon Jovi and Ratt flew to England to appear at the Monsters Of Rock festival in Donington on August 17.

Jon told Mick Wall at *Kerrang!* in 1988:

"... they [Ratt] really do live that whole LA kind of thing. And they were doing such big business with their second album and we're still nowhere. And we're saying to ourselves – we're better than this, we're a better band, you know. What the f**k's going on? Maybe we need mascara, you know..."

In 1998, however, the tables were turned when Ratt supported Bon Jovi (with Kingdom Come) for some Japanese concerts during the *New Jersey Syndicate* tour.

Visit *therattpack.com*

RAW

A bi-weekly heavy metal magazine that was first published in 1988 and viewed as a rival to *Kerrang!*. Before its demise in the mid-nineties the magazine gave good coverage to Bon Jovi, including a cover interview in the January 1992 issue.

RAZE

Jon Bon Jovi's first band, put together in '74 whilst he was a pupil at Sayreville Memorial High School in New Jersey. Their first appearance on stage was at the school's talent contest, where each band was allowed to perform three songs. Raze played a version of Bachman Turner Overdrive's 'Takin' Care Of Business', a predictable cover of Chuck Berry's 1958 classic 'Johnny B. Goode' and a version of 'Strutter' by glam rockers. *"I was about 12 or 13, I came in last place,"* Jon told *Kerrang!* in 1991.

RAZORLIGHT

A British indie band that formed in 2002. Their first two albums, *Up All Night* (2004) and *Razorlight* (2006), were big chart hits. Their best-known singles include 'America,' 'Somewhere Else' and 'In The Morning.' They supported Bon Jovi with Kid Rock at the Punchestown Racecourse in Kildare, Ireland on June 7, 2008.

Visit *razorlight.co.uk*

RDS HALL

Bon Jovi's *New Jersey Syndicate* tour kicked off at the RDS Hall in Dublin on October 31, 1988. Support came from Lita Ford.

Visit *rds.ie*

REAL LIFE

'Real Life' is an original Bon Jovi song that was released in the UK on April 10, 1999 as a CD single, and as part of the soundtrack to the Ron Howard film *EdTV*. It reached Number 21 in the UK Top 40 singles chart. The song is also included in the box-set *100,000,000 Bon Jovi Fans Can't Be Wrong*.

RECORDING INDUSTRY ASSOCIATION OF AMERICA (RIAA)

A trade organisation that represents the American music industry and its artists. Amongst its many functions the Association conducts research on the music industry and distributes royalties and licences. They also award commemorative discs for certified record sales:

Silver: 100,000
Gold: 500,000
Platinum: 1,000,000
Multi-Platinum: 2,000,000
Diamond: 10,000,000 *(Since its 1986 release,* Slippery When Wet *has sold approximately 28 million copies around the globe.)*

Visit *riaa.com*

RED SHOE DIARIES: THE MOVIE

A 1992 film based on the erotic TV series. The movie stars David Duchovny as a man who discovers that his wife (who had committed suicide) had been having an affair. He finds out that her lover was the salesman who sold her the red shoes of the title.

Richie Sambora contributed 'You Never Really Know' to the movie soundtrack.

REHAB

A treatment programme intended to help addicts break their drug and alcohol dependencies. In 2007, during his divorce from Heather Locklear, Richie Sambora spent two separate stints in rehab.

REST, THE

A New Jersey band in which Jon Bon Jovi spent six months as singer and guitarist after leaving the 10-piece outfit Atlantic City Expressway. The Rest also featured lead guitarist Jack Ponti, who would later find success of his own as a songwriter for Michael Bolton and other artists. With the help of Southside Johnny and Billy Squier, The Rest made

some demos and Columbia Records were briefly enthused by them. They played mostly small pubs and clubs: Jon's father's cousin, Tony Bongiovi, saw The Rest playing at a club in NYC and was impressed by Jon's on-stage charisma. The pair would work together for the next few years until a legal dispute over money and royalties allegedly set them apart. When The Rest split up Jon moved to NYC and a job at Power Station Studios.

RICHARDS, DENISE

An American actress TV and film actress. Her most popular films include *Starship Troopers*, *Wild Things*, *Scary Movie 3* and the James Bond film *The World Is Not Enough*. She dated Richie Sambora after she spilt

up from her husband actor Charlie Sheen and after Sambora separated from Heather Locklear. Their relationship in 2006-07 was high-profile and short-lived.

ROCK, BOB

A distinguished producer, engineer/mixer, Bob Rock has worked on some of the biggest selling albums in rock history. His credits include Metallica, Mötley Crüe, David Lee Roth, Skid Row and Aerosmith.

Amongst many others, he has produced the following albums:

Bryan Adams – *On A Day Like Today* (1998)
The Cult – *Sonic Temple* (1989)
Lostprophets – *Liberation Transmission* (2006)
Metallica – *Metallica* (1991)
Mötley Crüe - *Dr. Feelgood* (1989)
Skid Row – *Subhuman Race* (1995)

As a sound engineer/mixer he worked on albums by Aerosmith, Black N' Blue, Kingdom Come, Krokus, Loverboy and Survivor. As a musician he played bass on Metallica's critically mauled album *St. Anger* (2003) as well as albums by Mötley Crüe and Strange Advance.

A protégé of Bruce Fairbairn, Bob Rock was the sound engineer on the massive selling albums *Slippery*

When Wet and *New Jersey*. In 1992 he produced *Keep The Faith*, which marked a turn in musical direction for the New Jersey lads.

ROCK, KID

A controversial American musician and singer. His biggest selling album is 1998's *Devil Without A Cause*, and his debut album *Grits Sandwiches For Breakfast* was released in 1990. He is also known for his five month marriage to actress Pamela Anderson in 2006. He supported Bon Jovi at the Punchestown Racecourse in Kildare, Ireland on June 7, 2008.

Visit *kidrock.com*

ROCK IN RIO LISBOA

The 2004 Rock In Rio festival was the first to be held in Lisbon, a controversial move by organiser Roberto Medina. Bon Jovi performed at Rock

In Rio in Lisbon on May 31, 2007, along with Skank, Alanis Morissette and Alejandro Sanz.

ROCK STAR

Loosely based on the famed Judas Priest-Tim Owens story, *Rock Star* is a film about a singer in a tribute band who becomes the singer of the real band. The film stars Jennifer Aniston and Mark Wahlberg. The soundtrack features Bon Jovi's 'Livin' On A Prayer'.

ROCK STAR BABY

A company set up and owned by Tico Torres to sell baby clothing, soft toys, prams and suchlike. Torres started the company when members of the band became parents. He felt that there weren't enough "hip kids" even though their parents dressed in designer clothes. The website says, *"Initially using the true colours of Rock - black & white with shades of grey in between - designs were created for these cool kids"*.

Visit *rockstarbaby.com*

ROLLING STONE

An internationally known American music magazine, founded by Jann Wenner and Ralph J. Gleason in San Francisco in 1967. Aside from music the magazine also covers politics and pop culture in general, including films and television.

Bon Jovi have never been *Rolling Stone* darlings. Before appearing on the cover, *Rolling Stone* said of the band: *"...a third generation smudgy xerox of Quiet Riot"*. However in May, 1989 Bon Jovi featured on the cover of *Rolling Stone*'s 500th issue: 'Hot Throb: Bon Jovi'. In February, 1989 Jon appeared on the cover yet again with the headline: 'Bon Jovi: Rock's Young Gun'.

Visit *rollingstone.com*

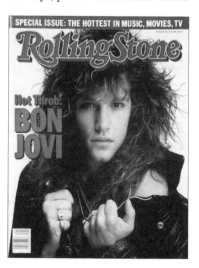

ROLLING STONES, THE

Undoubtedly one of the most important and popular rock and roll bands of all time. The current core members of the band are Mick Jagger, Keith Richards, Charlie Watts and Ronnie Wood. Hailing from the London area, The Stones became popular in the sixties with their steamy covers of classic American blues songs. They most revered albums are *Beggars Banquet, Let It Bleed, Exile On Main Street* and *Goat's Head Soup.* Bon Jovi supported them at Longchamps (Paris) on June 30 and July 1, 1995. during the Stones' huge *Voodoo Lounge* tour,

ROMEO IS BLEEDING

A 1993 black comedy starring Gary Oldman and directed by Peter Medak.

Jon wrote the power ballad 'Always' for inclusion in the soundtrack but after watching a preview of the film, he allegedly chose to pull it from the final version as he didn't like the film. *Romeo Is Bleeding* was not well received by critics.

ROW YOUR BOAT

A dramatic film that was released in 2000 and directed by Sollace Mitchell. Jon Bon Jovi stars in the lead role as a Jamey Meadows, who attempts to begin a new life in New York after being released from prison. He meets a fellow lonely soul, a Chinese immigrant, and they begin a relationship.

ROYAL VARIETY PERFORMANCE

The very famous annual concert held in the UK, which dates back to 1912 and is attended by members of the British Royal Family. The concert encompasses a variety of artists, entertainers, comedians and TV presenters. Bon Jovi played at the 2007 Royal Variety Performance, which was held in Liverpool and attended by Her Majesty the Queen.

RUNAWAY

This is the song that started it all really. Written by Jon and George Karak, it was originally part of a four track demo that Jon had recorded with a bunch of session musicians working as The All Star Review at Power Station Studios in Manhattan in June, 1982.

As quoted in *Metal Hammer* (No. 8, Vol. 5) Jon said:

"When I was living in New York, 53rd Street...I'd drive out to Jersey to see my parents, I'd pass by the Greyhound bus station, and all the hookers would hang out there. I'd see these girls who would come out to New York, much the same way they'd come out to Los Angeles, looking for dreams".

The song was picked up by several radio stations, notably Long Island's WAPP FM 103.5, and it featured on the compilation *New York Rocks 1983*, released by Doubleday, the parent company of the aforementioned station. The song was noticed by Derek Shulman at PolyGram who enticed the company's bosses to sign Jon to their label. A deal was done - Jon got himself a band and called it Bon Jovi.

'Runaway' was re-recorded by the band when they recorded their debut album in June, '83 at Power Station Studios with Lance Quinn and Tony Bongiovi. The really cool keyboard intro was penned by Mick Seeley, later of Southside Johnny and The Asbury Dukes. When the single was released in the States in February, '84 it reached Number 39 in the *Billboard* Hot 100. The accompanying video was filmed over a three day period at a Silver City Studios in Queens and was made for approximately $60,000. The band were purportedly not happy with their first ever music video but had no option but to go along with it as it had been instigated by their record company.

A live version of the song (recorded on April 28, 1985 in Tokyo, Japan) appears on the 2001 set *One Wild Night Live 1985-2001*. It also features on the 1994 collection *Cross Road*.

RUSH

A Canadian progressive rock band that formed in 1968. Famous for their science-fiction and fantasy themes, their most famous albums include *2112*, *Moving Pictures* and *Grace Under Pressure*. The critically acclaimed *Snakes & Arrows* was released in 2007 and to support it the band embarked on a massive world tour.

Jon Bon Jovi took the train from Sayreville, NJ to see Rush live in New York City in 1975, the year Rush released two albums: *Fly By Night* and *Caress Of Steel*. Suffice to say the gig inspired the young wannabe rock star to pursue his dreams of forming a band.

Visit *rush.com*

RUTGERS UNIVERSITY

David Bryan briefly attended this New Jersey University, before quitting to enrol at The Juilliard School.

Visit *rutgers.edu*

S

SABO, DAVE

Born in Perth Amboy and raised in Sayreville, New Jersey, Dave "Snake" Sabo was a childhood friend of Jon Bon Jovi.

As normal teenagers in a working class neighbourhood the pair would drink, listen to rock and roll and do the usual things feisty young kids do. They were in a band, The Wild Ones, with David Bryan Rashbaum, and they even supported local legends Southside Johnny and The Asbury Jukes on a few dates. During the days of the 'Runaway' demo, when Jon was gathering musicians for the band that would become Bon Jovi, Dave Sabo would help him out by playing guitar on a temporary basis. They played some small, local gigs together until Richie Sambora came into the picture. Sabo is credited in the sleeve notes to *Slippery When Wet* as Davey "the Snake".

In 1986, when Sabo co-founded Skid Row with Rachel Bolan, Jon was instrumental in getting the band a record deal. Sabo was as important to Jon's musical plans during those early years as Jon was to Sabo once Bon Jovi hit the big time. In 2007, Sabo contributed music to the Joel Miller directed film *The Still Life* with a stream of other rock stars, including Dizzy Reed, Bad Religion and Guns N' Roses.

Visit *skidrow.com*

SAMBORA, RICHIE

Probably just as iconic as Jon Bon Jovi, guitarist Richie Sambora was born on July 11, 1959 to mixed Polish and Italian parentage. He was raised in Woodbridge Township, New Jersey and was educated at Woodbridge High School.

Like many guitarists of his age he was influenced by the guitar wizardry of Jimi Hendrix and the great guitarists of the sixties, who gave Sambora the inspiration he needed to head for a life in rock and roll. Guitar players like Jimmy Page, Eric Clapton and Jeff Beck, and later talents like Joe Perry of Aerosmith, the Texan blues master Johnny Winter and Stevie Ray Vaughn empowered his confidence and vigour. In fact, as can be seen from those names, most of his inspirations were guitarists rooted

in the blues tradition, an influence which is evident in Sambora's interesting solo material.

His pre-Bon Jovi years were eventful. The most notable band he was in was Shark Frenzy with Bruce Foster (Sambora fans would be interested in the two collections, *Shark Frenzy Volumes One and Two*). He was also in a little-known metal outfit called Mercy, who were briefly signed to Led Zeppelin's label Swan Song, and he played with the musical group Duke Williams And The Extremes.

An often quoted anecdote is that at some point Sambora even auditioned for KISS. Bruce Foster (Shark Frenzy):

"I don't remember if it was I or Hugh McDonald who set Richie up for the audition...or someone else! I can only imagine that Richie scared the living shit out of Paul [Stanley] and Gene [Simmons] with his amazing playing - and they passed on him!".

But in a way it was the band Message that set Richie on the road to future success and fame. Message also featured bassist Alec John Such and singer Dean Fasano, and together they made a mini-album called *Lessons*. He also co-owned a bar called Poor Willies and fronted his own indie label, Dreamdisc Records.

In 1983, when Jon was recruiting musicians for the band that would become Bon Jovi, Such recommended his one-time colleague Richie Sambora, who was then playing in Joe Cocker's backing band. Impressed with his guitar talents, Jon hired Sambora to replace temporary guitarist Dave Sabo. Another story is that Sambora saw The Wild Ones (featuring Jon, David Bryan, Alec John Such and Dave Sabo) perform at some New Jersey club and told Jon that was he was going to be the guitarist in the band. Whichever story is true it was at this point in mid-1983 that Sambora and Jon formed a professional relationship that would last to this day.

Sambora and Jon became the core of Bon Jovi, co-writing most of the songs and quickly becoming two very recognisable characters. They may not reach the level of such incredible talents as Jagger and Richards or Lennon and McCartney, but they do know how to compose a well-crafted commercial rock song. One of Sambora's early innovations was to introduce the musical device known as a

talk-box, which certainly helped Bon Jovi songs stand out from similar FM rock records being made at the time, 'Livin' On A Prayer' being a prime example. As time progressed Sambora carved an easily recognisable image for himself, with cowboy hat and long leather jacket, whereas Jon was constantly changing his image with the times. Like all famous songwriting duos of rock music Sambora and Jon have had their ups and downs. It is common knowledge amongst fans that the two had their fair share of arguments after the *New Jersey Syndicate* tour came to an end in February,

1990, disagreements which resulted in a lengthy break in the Bon Jovi schedule.

Speaking about the divide between the singer and guitarist, Jon told *Metal Hammer* in 1990:

"I think if Richie left the band he'd be stupid. But if he leaves, it's no big deal. The band will still continue".

Sambora's solo work is something of a surprise, being bluesier and far more personal than anything Bon Jovi have put out.

In 1991, when the various members of Bon Jovi were on a 17 month sabbatical, Sambora released his debut solo album, the excellent and underrated *Stranger In This Town*. His idol Eric Clapton played on the track 'Mr. Bluesman'; Richie later got the chance to play Eric Clapton in an episode of the 2003 US comedy show *American Dreams*. Sadly, the album was not a commercial success, although it was well received by music critics. Richie undertook a hasty tour of the USA in support on the album, taking a group of respected musicians on the road with him: bassist Tony Levin, guitarist Dave Amato, percussionist Crystal Taliefero and his Bon Jovi pals, Messrs. Tico Torres and Dave Bryan.

His second solo album, the Don Was produced *Undiscovered Soul*, was issued in 1998 via Mercury. He embarked on a much longer tour this time around, hitting Japan, Australia and Europe in the summer of '98. His touring band for this jaunt consisted of guitarist Richie Supa, drummer Ron Wikso, bassist Kasim Sulton and keyboardist Tommy Mandel. Percussionist Everett Bradley joined the band for the Japanese leg of the tour, while Gioia Bruno performed

with them in Australia and Crystal Taliefero in Europe.

To keep himself busy outside of Bon Jovi and to follow his love of classic American blues Sambora has made various contributions to other artists work over the years. He contributed guitars to the songs 'Can I Walk You Home' and 'Oops! Bo Diddley' on the Bo Diddley album *A Man Amongst Men,* released in 1996. A couple of years later he sang the Deep Purple song 'When A Blind Man Cries,' which features on the album *Stuart Smith's Heaven & Earth.*

Other musical bits and pieces from throughout his career include some songwriting with Jon for other artists such as Loverboy, Cher, Ted Nugent, Gorky Park, Alice Cooper, Paul Young and Witness. 'Trail Of Broken Hearts,' which he co-wrote with Bruce Foster, was sung by his then girlfriend Cher, and can be heard on the soundtrack to the 1990 blockbuster movie *Days Of Thunder.* He worked with the Japanese actor and musician Takashi Sorimachi on the song 'Forever,' which features on the 1997 Japanese drama *Beach Boys.* Another tune of his, 'Long Way Around', features on the soundtrack to the 1997 Steven Segal action mov-

ie *Fire Down Below,* and he has done further soundtrack work for the films *Red Shoe Diaries, On The Line, The Adventures Of Ford Fairlane* and *The Banger Sisters.*

Sambora played guitar on the song 'Misery' - also featuring Aerosmith singer Steve Tyler – on Pink's 2001 album *M!ssundaztood.* He has also worked with the Australian pop star Shannon Noll on his third album *Turn It Up.* In 2005, he hooked up with *American Idol* singer Bo Bice for his take on the song 'Vehicle,' originally a 1970 hit single by the rock band Ides Of March.

Sambora has also developed plenty of non-musical interests over the years: together with Jon he is co-owner of the Arena Football Philadelphia Soul, and like his Bon Jovi colleagues he has committed himself to various charities, including Michael J. Fox's Parkinson's Charity. In addition, he has made cameo appearances in two films: 1983's *Staying Alive* and 2001's *On The Line.*

Lately, events in his personal life have caught the attention of the press, including his highly-publicised divorce from Heather Locklear, a failed relationship with actress Denise Ri-

chards, drinking problems and a DUI arrest in California.

Visit *bonjovi.com*

SAY IT ISN'T SO

The second single taken from the hit album *Crush* was issued in the UK on September 9, 2000. It peaked at Number 10 in the Top 40 and spent seven weeks in the chart. The music video stars some big names: Claudia Schiffer, Arnold Schwarzenegger, Emilio Estevez and Matt LeBlanc. The solo is handled by pianist/keyboard player David Bryan rather than Richie Sambora who sings the lead vocal with Jon.

SAYREVILLE

A borough of New Jersey that was the childhood home of Jon Bon Jovi after his family moved from Perth Amboy. Skid Row guitarist Dave

Sabo was also born there. Inevitably the blue collar neighbourhood in which Jon was raised inspired him to write the lyrics for such songs as 'Livin' On A Prayer,' which reflects the ideals of a working class East Coast American.

SAYREVILLE WAR MEMORIAL HIGH SCHOOL

Jon Bon Jovi attended this high school in Parlin, New Jersey. It was during those years that he "discovered" rock and roll and formed his first band, Raze.

Visit *sayrevillehigh.net*

SCOOBY DOO 2: MONSTERS UNLEASHED

A 2004 film, adapted from the Hanna-Barbara cartoon series, starring Freddie Prinze Jr., Sarah Michelle Gellar, Matthew Lillard and Linda Cardellini. The soundtrack features Bon Jovi's classic eighties rock anthem 'Wanted Dead Or Alive'.

SCORPIONS

A German heavy rock band that formed way back in 1965. Given the length of their career and the different directions they have taken there have been many line-up changes over the years. The nucleus of the band is the duo of guitarist and founder Rudolf Schenker and singer Klaus Meine (who joined in 1969). They made some classic albums during, including *Lonesome Crow* (1972), *Fly To The Rainbow* (1974), *In Trance* (1975), *Virgin Killer* (1976) and *Taken By Force* (1978). Their 1978 live album *Tokyo Tapes* is also a cherished album amongst fans.

It was in the eighties, however, when they hit the international market in a big way with *Love At First Sting* (1984) which gave birth to the hard rock stomper 'Rock You Like A Hurricane'. The 1990 album *Crazy World* gave them a hit single with the dreadfully sentimental 'Wind Of Change', which reflected on the end of the Cold War and the destruction of the Berlin Wall.

Scorpions had a rough ride in the 1990s and early 2000s, with albums like *Eye II Eye* doing nothing to please their hard rock fan base. More recently, however, they have released two robust rock albums: *Unbreakable* (2004) and *Humanity - Hour 1*

(2007). They toured extensively behind both albums and proved that they are still a dominating and energetic live band.

Bon Jovi and the Scorpions have crossed paths on two major occasions. The New Jersey rockers supported Scorpions on a 28-date tour of America in 1984. The tour started in Philadelphia and continued through 15 states, including a visit to New York's legendary Madison Square Garden. The tour ended in July at the Charlotte Coliseum in North Carolina. Both bands also performed at the Moscow Music Peace Festival on August 12-13, 1989.

Herman Rarebell was the drummer in the Scorpions from 1977 to 1995.

Interview:

What do you remember about the Bon Jovi / Scorps US tour?

I watched some of their shows and I knew that this guy [Jon] was gonna make it! You could see it on the reaction of the girls in the audience.

Why did Bon Jovi support the Scorps? Whose idea was it for that to happen?

The idea came from Doc McGhee, their manager. He came up to us and played us the single 'Runaway.' After that we took Jon out to open up for us.

What did you think of Bon Jovi back then? Did they make much of an impression on you and the others in the Scorps?

Yes, as I said, we all watched some of the shows and we were quite impressed with just how good the band was.

Did you have any inkling that Bon Jovi would become such a popular stadium rock band?

Oh yeah, for sure! We all had the feeling that they were gonna make it!

Did you have much/any interaction with members of Bon Jovi on that tour?

I went out a couple of times with Tico on tour and we had a good time together. I also talked to everybody else in the band when I was hanging out with them.

What do you remember about the Moscow Music Peace Festival held on August 12-13, 1989?

Well, it was mind blowing. Imagine: this was the first time the Russians saw something like this!

Bon Jovi had a longer set than the other bands (Cinderella, Ozzy, Skid Row and Mötley Crüe *et al*); do you recall any conflict between them and the other bands on the bill?

Not that I know of...

Did you have chance to speak to any of the guys in Bon Jovi in Moscow?

Yes, we were hanging out together backstage!

Have you meet any of the band members since then?

I met Jon a few years back at the Monte Carlo World Music Awards; Jon, his wife Dorothea and myself had dinner together.

What is your favourite Bon Jovi album?

I like Slippery When Wet *because you can feel the urge and energy to make it. The vibe on the record is really good from beginning to end.*

Visit *the-scorpions.com* and *hermanrarebell.com*

7TH HEAVEN

Formed in 1985, 7th Heaven is a band based in Chicago, Illinois. From 1997 to 1998 they were managed by ex-Bon Jovi bass player Alec John Such *and* James Young of the melodic rock

band Styx. At the time this was one of Such's main activities after being dismissed from Bon Jovi in 1994.

Richard Hofherr of 7th Heaven says,

"Both [Alec and James] were really great to us... I learned a lot about the deep roots of the actual business from them, more from Alec as we were around Alec more than James. We stayed at his house a few times and he came to Chicago to see us as well. He is a great guy. I still send him our CDs as they come out".

Visit *7thheavenband.com*

7800° FAHRENHEIT

By the time they came to make their second album, Bon Jovi had severed their ties with Tony Bongiovi and Power Stations Studios, so *7800° Fahrenheit* was recorded during January and February of 1985 at The Warehouse in Philadelphia with producer Lance Quinn. The title of the album is code for 'American Hot Rock', 7800° Fahrenheit being the temperature at which stone liquefies. The songwriting was handled by Jon, David Bryan and Richie Sambora, although 'Secret Dreams' was penned by Jon, Sambora, drummer Tico Torres and Bill Grabowski.

7800° Fahrenheit hit the record shops in the UK on May 11, 1985 and peaked at Number 28 in the Top 40, spending a total of 12 weeks in the charts. In America, it reached Number 37. The sales of the album

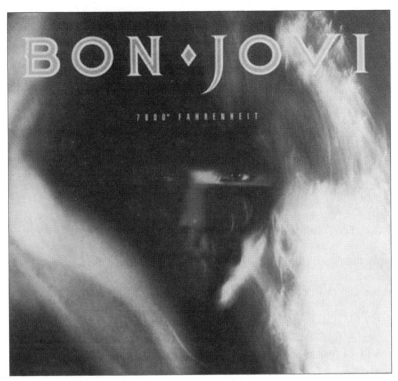

were not that great by Bon Jovi's standards (one million copies) and the reviews were somewhat mixed.

Howard Johnson wrote in the British heavy metal bible *Kerrang!* :

"I can only say that this is a pale imitation of the Bon Jovi we have got to know and learnt to love".

Sounds scribe Mary Anne Hobbs penned a review saying:

"...the sad new opus barely bubbles at ten degrees, let alone erupting in the dangerous fashion that its moniker would have us believe...".

The critics were not alone in their criticism of the album. The band themselves have often told the press that they dislike it, blaming a number of factors such as the production and the tight schedule in which they had to record it. Songs from the album are not performed during their tours (although they did play 'Tokyo Road' in Osaka, Japan during the *One Wild Night Live* tour in 2001).

The cover artwork shows a single shot of Jon's face, again giving some music fans the idea that it could possibly be a solo album. There is a full band shot on the back cover, which shows that their fashion sense (even for the time) left a lot to be desired. The remastered version of the album comes with an enhanced CD video of 'In And Out Of Love'.

Track Listing:
1. 'In And Out Of Love'
2. 'The Price Of Love'
3. 'Only Lonely'
4. 'King Of The Mountain'
5. 'Silent Night'

6. 'Tokyo Road'
7. 'The Hardest Part Is The Night'
8. 'Always Run To You'
9. '(I Don't Wanna Fall) To The Fire'
10. 'Secret Dreams'

Author's Review:

7800° Fahrenheit *is not the poor album the band have made out; in fact it is far from being their weakest full length studio composition. The melodies and riffs give us an idea of better things to come and even though the lyrics are still pretty adolescent (two songs titles have the word 'love' in them) this is one of their grittiest and heaviest albums to date. Jon actually sings like a grown man; there is power and anxiety to his voice that makes songs like 'The Hardest Part Is The Night' work really well. Without question 'Tokyo Road' is the stand out rock track and one that the band should still play live on every tour. 'King Of The Mountain' would be the joint stand out song; the harmonies work brilliantly and Sambora delivers a surprisingly progressive riff. Actually, Sambora churns out some nifty riffs throughout the album, including 'In And Out Of Love' and David Bryan's keys show progression since the band's first album. One of the weaker tracks is the mundane 'The Price Of Love' but to say this album is naff misses the point. It's a good example of entertaining eighties melodic rock.*

Rating ***½

7800° FAHRENHEIT TOUR (1985)

To promote their second album, Bon Jovi embarked on their first tour as headliners, after playing a single show in Munich, Germany in April, '85. They flew to the Far East for some dates in Tokyo, Nagoya, Osaka and Sapporo. In Europe, they played France, Sweden, Finland, Germany and Holland. In the UK, they played Manchester, Birmingham, London, Newcastle and Edinburgh, with Lee Aaron as support. In the States, however, they were the support act for Ratt, having achieved headline status earlier in other countries than they managed in their homeland. During the tour with Ratt both bands flew to England to perform at the famed Monsters Of Rock festival on August 17, 1985.

SEX AND THE CITY

The hugely successful HBO television series which ran from 1998 until 2004. The series chronicled the lives of four very different New York women. Jon Bon Jovi appeared in an episode called 'Games People Play' as Seth, a therapist, a role which gave him considerable exposure as an actor. His scenes were filmed in a restaurant in NYC and at Silvercup Studios in Queens, where the video for 'Runaway' had been filmed way back in 1984. The episode was first aired in the States on August 29, 1999.

SHANKS, JOHN

John Shanks is a Los Angeles based record producer and songwriter, who co-produced 2005's *Have A Nice Day* with Jon and Sambora and 2007's *Lost Highway*. He has also worked with Sheryl Crow, Celine Dion, Take That, Kelly Clarkson, Fleetwood Mac, Santana and Keith Urban, amongst others.

Shanks has co-written the following songs with Bon Jovi:

'Have A Nice Day' (with JBJ/RS – *Have A Nice Day*)
'I Want To Be Loved' (with JBJ/RS – *Have A Nice Day*)
'Welcome To Wherever You Are' (with JBJ/RS – *Have A Nice Day*)
'I Am' (with JBJ/RS – *Have A Nice Day*)
'Dirty Little Secret' (with JBJ/RS and Desmond Child – *Have A Nice Day*)
'Lost Highway' (with JBJ/RS – *Lost Highway*)

'Summertime (with JBJ/RS – *Lost Highway*)
'Whole Lot Of Leavin'' (with JBJ – *Lost Highway*)
'The Last Night' (with JBJ/RS – *Lost Highway*)

Visit *johnnshanks.net*

SHARK FRENZY

A pre-Bon Jovi rock band featuring Richie Sambora, Bruce Foster, Steve Mosley and Jody Giambelluca. A collection of their unreleased material was issued in 2004 as *Volume One: 1978* and *Volume Two: 1980-1981 – (Citizen Invisible) Confessions Of A Teenage Lycanthrope*, both of which were fully endorsed by Sambora and Foster.

Foster recalls:

"We were supposed to be a group that performed our own songs, however, there were only so many concert gigs we could find to do at our meagre level of fame so we also started doing clubs playing cover material that we liked. We enjoyed each others company so much that we played more and more nights. After a four hour gig ending at 2am we would hang out in the parking lot or a late night eatery 'til 4 or 5am and then drive home for an hour. I never laughed so much in my life as I did with those guys! The beauty of it is we're all still the best of friends!

Musically, Steve 'Mose' Mosley, Bill Ring or Sam Masiello played drums and percussion. Sometimes our dear roadie Tim Rudolph played congas and tambourine; Jody 'Monster Magnet' Giambelucca or Harvey 'X Mbutu' Lame played bass. Richie 'Sambo' Sambora played lead guitar and I ('Fang Face') played piano, keyboard, rhythm guitar and alter-

nate lead (usually slide) guitar. We all shared a talent for being able to brilliantly fake any song we all mutually knew without having to rehearse, so every night was a little different than the previous. We also took great liberties with improvising on cover songs to make them our own warped style! The nucleus of the group, Richie, Mose, Jody and I, also shared one other important trait: we were all out of our freakin' minds! For instance, after our fanbase knew that we played several of the same clubs every week, we thought it was moot to have our name Shark Frenzy over and over again in the ads, so we changed our name every week. Some that I can remember were: Renfrew Zetz & The A&P Gypsies, Ignatz Papnik & The Baritone Dwarves, Gringo Pachiki & The Terrified Farm Animals and more. We all were prolific writers so once or twice a month we'd put our pennies together and go to Joe's Sound and Salami recording studio or my buddy Tom Marolda's basement studio, both in Trenton, New Jersey (and both long gone), and record a new song or two. An eight track tape was 120 dollars a reel at the time so we used to 'borrow' the last four minutes of tape on one of Tom Marolda's personal reels. (He was multi tracking himself playing all instruments and vocals with his amazing songs and called it 'The Toms.') He's still doing it!

We played pretty much 'live' in the studio to capture the spirit of our sound. We all agreed that rock and roll should never be too slick, so we rarely did more than three takes. Many of the songs are only one take! We would then do a mix onto a seven inch reel and Tom Marolda would erase the eight track master after we left and record one of his own songs over our 'borrowed' four minutes of tape therefore there are NO Shark Frenzy master reels that could be remixed for some future purpose - only the seven inch mixes! We never got to shop the tapes to labels at the time because Richie by now had one foot in Bon Jovi. The rapid success of Bon Jovi swept Richie away from us and we somewhat disassembled as a singular unit. I was spending more time in LA and working as a solo act.

In 1992 all of my copies of the mixes went under salt water and river silt in a major flood (The Perfect Storm movie was about the Halloween Nor'easter that put my entire life work and memorabilia under three feet of nasty water.) Ten years later, new computer formats were invented that made me realize I could restore the soggy tapes. Thank God I never threw them out! I had them cleaned and baked to reaffix the magnetic particles and had all the music transferred to computer. After six months of splicing and dicing I had a product that SURPASSED the original reels!

Shark Frenzy Volumes One and Two *are now released [in the States] on the Sonic Past label. Richie wrote some of the liner notes and* Volume Two [US edition] *includes a live recording of 'Golden Slumbers,' an eight minute version of The Beatles classic recorded at our 2004 Shark Frenzy reunion. I'm sure there will be more ... Shark Frenzy lives!"*

Visit *brucefoster.com*

SHARK FRENZY:
VOLUME ONE - 1978

The first collection of Shark Frenzy archive material was released in the UK on March 22, 2004 by Castle/Sanctuary. The album is an essential purchase for fans of Richie Sambora and illustrates the guitarist's expertise even at a young age. The CD is still available to buy although it can be quite difficult to track down. Second hand copies have been selling for £22.00+ on Amazon.co.uk.

Track Listing:
1. 'Come Saturday Night'
2. 'Live Fast, Love Hard, Die Young'
3. 'Law Of The Jungle'
4. 'Nobody'
5. 'The One With Angel Eyes'
6. 'The Power'
7. 'I'll Play The Fool'
8. 'Laura's Birthday'

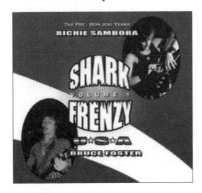

9. 'Southern Belle'
10. 'Don't Stop Loving Me Now'

Author's Review:

Jon Bon Jovi may not be enthusiastic about having his early solo material and demos heard by the band's countless fans, but Richie Sambora doesn't seem too bothered by the release of this collection and its sibling, Volume Two. *On this collection you get the chance to listen to an expert guitarist play brilliantly even at an early age; and he's a pretty good lead singer too. The delicate remastering job gives a thoroughly enjoyable song like 'Laura's Birthday' a chance to flourish once again. Sambora's guitar playing on 'Southern Belle' is superb. Obviously releases like this tend to be only for serious enthusiasts while others may be less interested. If you're a keen Sambora fan, both* Volumes *are essential. Here's you chance to listen to a serious musical talent in the making.*

Rating ***

SHARK FRENZY:
VOLUME TWO - 1980-1981

The second set of Shark Frenzy archive material has the sub-title *(Citizen Invisible) Confessions Of A Teenage Lycanthrope.* Volume Two was issued in the UK on October 18, 2004 via Cherry Red/Lemon Recordings. It includes a brief but interesting interview with Richie Sambora and Bruce Foster conducted by *Classic Rock*'s Sian Llewellyn. The collection is still easily available on many Internet retailers, including the label's website *cherryred.co.uk.*

Track Listing:
1. 'Goodbye To Me'

2. 'Crashing Kites'
3. 'Devil On The Run'
4. 'Till The Walls Come Down'
5. 'Any Woman Like You'
6. 'I Need Your Love'
7. 'Cruising Lines'
8. 'I Haven't Changed'
9. 'Out In The Heat'
10. 'A Good Life'
11. 'Man With A Dragon'
12. 'Confessions Of A Teenage Lycanthrope'

Author's Review:

It's pretty obvious these guys had been raised on a diet of British rock; there's some Clapton, Beatles and prog sounds in this interesting mix of ideas. It's often been said by Sambora and Foster that Shark Frenzy was pretty much a live band and that rawness, energy and spontaneity that occurs on stage comes through in these recordings. 'Devil On The Run' is one of the memorable tracks and there are some worthwhile riffs ('A Good Life') and guitar solos ('Out In The Heat'). The sound quality is not that great compared to Volume One *but this collection tells an interesting story. What if Sambora had not joined Bon Jovi and had continued with bands similar to Shark Frenzy?*

Rating ***

SHE DON'T KNOW ME

The second and final single released in the States from the band's 1984 debut album. Written by keyboardist Marc Avsec, it was initially intended for Fair Warning's debut album but was given by their label to Bon Jovi.

It was recorded in June, 1983 at Power Station Studios in Manhattan and produced by Lance Quinn and Tony Bongiovi. It peaked at Number 48 in the *Billboard* Hot 100 when it was issued as a single in May '84. The band refuses to play this song now because it is contains the *only* set of lyrics in their entire back catalogue that was *not* written by at least one member of Bon Jovi.

SHEEDY, ALLY

An American actress who was part of the famed 'Brat Pack,' a group of actors (Sean Penn, Demi Moore, Emilio Estevez, Anthony Michael Hall *et al*) who starred in the same or similarly themed films during the early-mid eighties. Sheedy's most popular films remain *War Games, The Breakfast Club, St. Elmo's Fire, Short Circuit* and *Maid to Order*. Since the 1990s she has worked mostly on TV and on stage. Richie Sambora famously dat-

ed Sheedy between 1988 and '89; he has had many high-profile relationships with women and his love life is often covered in the celebrity press.

SHEPHERDS BUSH EMPIRE

Tickets for Bon Jovi's gig at London's intimate Shepherds Bush Empire (1,200 capacity) on September 18, 2002 sold out in eight minutes. Touts were selling tickets for £500 on the night. The band's first indoor gig in the UK in over a decade, it was part of a publicity drive before the release of their new album *Bounce* two weeks later. Ray Davies of The Kinks joined the band on stage for an acoustic version of the Kinks classic 'Celluloid Heroes'. The entire gig was available to download live on a global webcast to 60 countries.

Setlist:
1. 'Celluloid Heroes'
2. 'Livin' On A Prayer'
3. 'You Give Love A Bad Name'
4. 'Everyday'
5. 'Born To Be My Baby'
6. 'Just Older'
7. 'Bounce'
8. 'Undivided'
9. 'Wanted Dead Or Alive'
10. 'It's My Life'
11. 'Misunderstood'
12. 'The Distance'
13. 'Captain Crash & The Beauty Queen From Mars'

14. 'I'll Sleep When I'm Dead'
15. 'Bad Medicine' / 'Shout'
16. 'Joey'
17. 'Blood On Blood'
18. 'Keep The Faith'

SHIRLEY, KEVIN

Otherwise known as "The Caveman", Kevin Shirley is a successful South African born producer/engineer who is notable for his work with Iron Maiden, Journey, HIM, Slayer and Aerosmith. He recorded the Bon Jovi tracks 'Always' and 'Someday I'll Be Saturday Night' for *Cross Road* with producer Peter Collins and mixer Bob Clearmountain. Shirley also mixed 'Mister Big Time,' which was a soundtrack contribution for the film *Armageddon*.

Speaking about the first two tracks, which feature on the collection *Cross Road* and were recorded in July, 94, Shirley remembers:

"We set up Tico Torres' drum kit in the big room [in Emerald Studios, Nashville]; David Bryan had his piles of plastic keyboards set up along with a grand piano in one of the bigger isolation booths; Richie Sambora had his racks of guitars in another, and his amplifiers and cabinets, including an old wooden Leslie organ cabinet, set up in another. Jon Bon Jovi had a microphone, an old tube Neumann U47, set up in a smaller booth from where he sang his vocals; and session bass guitarist Hugh McDonald, while not the touring bass player, had been enlisted to play on the record, which he did through a direct box from his station in the big studio alongside Tico. The first day of recording was very productive, and the session went very quickly. The song was called 'Always,' and it sounded like a conglomeration of many other

rock hits to me, from the first time I heard it: Bryan Adams meets Whitney Houston with a big Def Leppard middle section. I was an enormous fan of the Slippery When Wet album, [but] the ballad was quite disappointing to me. Once again, Peter Collins as producer showed remarkable restraint in adjudicating the recording proceedings...So after the first day, we had the basic track 'Always' in the bag, and we hit the town.

By ten o'clock the following sweltering morning, I was back at the studio, masticating a bagel and nursing a cup or three of strong, muddy studio coffee, and setting up for another day of basic tracking. By noon, the last of the band had staggered in, and we cut the basic track for a song called 'Someday I'll Be Saturday Night' Weaker than the previous day's ballad, in my opinion, it was an acoustic guitar driven song and there was a notion that it should be quite sloppy, in a sort of early Rolling Stones 'Sweet Virgina' style, but when I had the rough mixes sounding all full of attitude, with all the raw edges on display, Jon pulled out a copy of the Soul Asylum track, 'Runaway Train' as a reference point, and I realised that it was sonically wide of the intended mark...In the early afternoon, long time Bon Jovi collaborator and genius songsmith Desmond Child came mincing into the studio - resplendent in some gaudy cowboy outfit that was definitely way more 'Village People' than it was 'The Good, The Bad And The Ugly'. Actually, it was just plain 'ugly,' and when I politely asked him what he was doing there, he joyously lisped gayly and preened, 'Just protecting my investment!', and smiled - and then he took us all to a wonderful restaurant.

As the sessions came to an end, we all went to see Mötley Crüe (the ugly stepsister version with John Corabi singing), at the Starwood Amphitheatre in Nashville. The show was just okay, and afterwards we went backstage to meet the guys in the band. They were towelling down after the sweaty gig, and offered us a beer each, which we were happy to knock back with them. There was a knock on the door, and a security guard came and whispered something to the made-up and pasty-faced Mötley Crüe guitarist, Mick Mars, who nodded, and the security guard brought in a very pretty young blonde, about 18 or 19 years old, who in turn whispered something to Mick, who said, 'Sure!', got up off the vanity counter he'd been sitting on and disappeared into the toilet with her for five or six minutes, after which she headed out the dressing room wiping her mouth, and Mick exited pulling up his fly. I said, incredulously, 'Who was that?' and he said swigging his beer, 'I dunno, she just wanted to give me a blow job!', and turned back to talk to Richie. I realized that us studio guys have seen nothing of the rock 'n roll world.

After about a week, or ten days, we'd finished the tracks and after safety copies were made, the masters of 'Always' were sent off to have strings scored for them. Michael Kamen scored and recorded an entire orchestra first, but when A&R guru John Kalodner, who Jon Bon Jovi really trusts, heard them, he was insistent that they be redone, and David Campbell scored a new orchestration of strings for the final version, which Bob Clearmountain mixed. The single eventually became one of Bon Jovi's biggest hits, spending some 32 weeks on the charts, and selling almost three million copies - and the Greatest Hits compilation [Cross Road] exceeded everyone's expectations, sales-wise".

Visit *cavemanproductions.com*

SHULMAN, DEREK

Scottish-born musician, singer and A&R guru, Shulman was a formerly a member of the rock outfit Gentle Giant, a six-piece band who released 12 albums in just a decade (1970-1980). Shulman subsequently turned his hand to rock promotion and became an A&R man for PolyGram. It was Shulman who persuaded Jon Bon Jovi to sign to PolyGram after the label bosses heard 'Runaway'. Jon turned down another offer from Atlantic and signed with PolyGram on July 1, 1983.

Whilst working for PolyGram, Shulman signed Cinderella and Kingdome Come, and he has also worked with Pantera and Nickelback. Shulman is currently running DRT Entertainment, based in New York City.

Interview:

When did you first hear Jon Bon Jovi's demo 'Runaway?'

I had heard the demo through two routes virtually in the same week.

The radio station in NYC WAPP was featuring local bands and their songs and I heard Jon Bongiovi's 'Runaway' on it; I was very impressed.

The next day an attorney, Arthur Mann from Philadelphia, came to my office with a three track demo of "a kid from NJ". He played 'Runaway' for me. I was amazed that only the day before I had heard and loved this song. We then set up a meeting with Jon and the band.

Do you remember when you first met Jon?

I was invited to a showcase at the old Copacabana club in midtown New York by the attorney. Jon had put a band together and he played about five or six songs at this showcase. After the showcase we sat down and I started getting to know 'kid from NJ' John Bongiovi.

What attracted you to want to represent him?

Perhaps the most vivid memory I had as I started getting to know Jon was his undeniable star quality and his incredible drive to succeed and be the 'biggest and the best' whether as live musician, as a songwriter or in any other goal that he had set for himself. Even then I knew that NOTHING would hold him back. He wanted to be 'bigger than Elvis' and he probably is on his way to accomplishing that.

What did the label bosses at Poly Gram think of him and his song 'Runaway?'

The song was undeniable. The staff at the label were very supportive. Jon and the band did a private showcase for me and several others of my co-

horts at the company. To be honest it wasn't the best scenario to be seen at and it was a little ragged. However, again Jon (and Richie) showed how they could become HUGE stars... ragged or not.

Why did Jon sign to PolyGram and not Atlantic who also made an offer?

I think and I hope that I had something to do with this. I was totally taken with Jon and the band. I could feel this incredible drive and potential from him and the band and I promised them I would give it MY ALL to make it happen at the company. Poly-Gram at the time was going through a major re-organisation. He would have me as a champion inside the company. I promised him they would have priority. Two European owners (Philips and Siemens) had combined two years prior to make this a North American record label. It was all slightly haphazard. My background as a musician and my commitment to the band to be a major priority at a company just getting on its feet con-

vinced Jon and his parents that Poly-Gram was the place to be.

Was it Ted Green at PolyGram who negotiated the deal? What was stated in the contract?

Ted Green was head of business affairs and it probably was him who negotiated the deal. I'm sure the deal was fair although probably slightly lopsided to PolyGram at the time. Jon and the band were brand new. There was certainly a great deal of commitment and expenditure made available to develop the band until they finally broke through in a huge way on their third album Slippery When Wet.

Did Jon sign initially as a solo artist?

Jon did in fact want to be signed as a solo artist with his band in tow.

PolyGram ultimately signed all the players of the band but initially it was Jon's deal. Rightly so as it was him who put everything together for the deal to happen.

Was he keen to get a band together?

100%. He absolutely knew he wanted this to be a rock band. He had already put this showcase band together and we both wanted the band to be a band NOT a solo rocker. He ultimately stuck with the group of musicians who performed at the Copacabana.

Once Jon got a band together; what was your initial impression of Bon Jovi?

To be honest, Jon and myself would confer regularly about how and in what market he should be developed in. We discussed at length whether he might be construed as the new Rex Smith or the new Van Halen.

Obviously Jon and the band ultimately wanted the latter as did I.

In so doing to get the 'rock audience' behind him and the band, they started touring incessantly with the biggest and heaviest rock bands of the day. Not just in the USA but all over the world. I was amazed and loved the band's work ethic. Nothing was too small, too far, too anything for them to go out and win fans. This has been the secret to their longevity.

Whose idea was it to name the band 'Bon Jovi?'

Okay, for good or for bad: it was me who thought of this idea. It wasn't original but I knew it would work. Jon was such a star in his own right but we knew he needed to have the band be a star rock band also. Names were bandied around for the band, some good some laughable. I thought about Jon's name and said let's shorten it. Jon Bongiovi was too 'ethnic'.

Jon Bon Jovi was WAY better and I said: 'Let's do what Van Halen did... call the band Bon Jovi. That way Jon Bon Jovi the singer and Bon Jovi the band can be marketed in duplicate'. It worked.

Of the bands that were very popular in the early-mid eighties (Def Leppard, Mötley Crüe, etc.), were exactly did Bon Jovi fit in?

Bon Jovi fitted into the mainstream rock marketplace in virtually the same way as Mötley Crüe and Def Leppard did. Most of these bands appealed to both a male and female audience. This was NOT metal; it was rock with great songs and not just attitude. The hair, clothes, and the advent of MTV helped make this genre enormous. The key thing about Bon Jovi was that he/they did appeal to a female audience without alienating their male audience. On tour, they would rock as hard as the Scorpions, KISS, Van Halen, etc., while still making the females in the crowd want to take him/them home.

Do you have any memorable anecdotes/stories from that period?

There are so many anecdotes and stories that have been told, written and re-written that there is NOT one but thousands. My personal anecdote is that when I met and sat down with Jon from the very beginning I KNEW he was destined for greatness. I remember saying to him in 1983: 'Someday you'll be President of the United States of America'. He laughed but with a glint in his eye. I still stand by that statement.

How long did you work with Jon?

I worked with Jon for the first four albums. I left PolyGram in 1988 as New Jersey *was being launched to become President and CEO of Warner Music Group's newly activated ATCO Records in late 1988.*

What was the best Bon Jovi concert you attended in the eighties?

I attended so many shows they become blurred. However, I think that some of the earliest UK and European shows were the best ones. Mainly because I saw how the band were able to hit a new audience and foreign city and be totally unafraid of working and building their following city by city, country by country. Slippery When Wet *was a culmination of incredible hard work from the management, the company, but most importantly the band over four-five of development and ultimately major record sales, finally.*

Finally, what else is there that you'd like to say about Bon Jovi?

Only that Bon Jovi the band and Jon Bon Jovi the man have withstood the tests of time and musical shifts and fads for over 25 years in a business that spits out stars that shine and fizzle in a space of a year these days.

This band is the essence of what artists and their representatives should and can be for the future. Develop your skills and your chops over a period of time. Become GREAT performers live, write GREAT songs and believe in yourself whether the record company is there or not. Jon Bon Jovi did and still does 25 years later.

Visit *drt-entertainment.com*

SHY

A British melodic rock band from Birmingham. Although they came close to becoming a major rock act in the 1980s, Shy never really achieved the acclaim or popularity that they deserved, although they remain a favourite band in the melodic rock community. As well as supporting Bon Jovi, Shy also supported Meat Loaf, UFO, Twisted Sister and Gary Moore during their most productive period.

Former lead singer Tony Mills, says,

"The show was packed with 11,000 people in the auditorium and the stage was magnificent. State of the art monitoring built beneath the stage which was constructed of enormous aluminium grills was one of the most hi-tech set-ups that I ever walked across. I spoke to Jon briefly backstage to wish him a great show, but he was pre-occupied, as we all are before performances of such magnitude, and due to other commitments I never got the chance to see him again...".

An interview with Shy bassist Roy Davis:

How did the support slot to Bon Jovi come about?

If I remember correctly Lita Ford was doing the whole Bon Jovi UK tour, but for some reason, due to her voice, couldn't do that particular night [in December, 1988]. Doc McGhee knew our manager and asked him if there were any local bands who could step in. Hence we got the call. What was hilarious though was that it very nearly didn't happen. I had gone to a local garden centre with the missus and we had a blazing row. Luckily enough as it happens, this was in the days before mobile phones, because of the row we had gone home early and there had been a note stuck through the letter box saying I had to get to the NEC to support Bon Jovi. I thought it was a wind-up and threw the note in the bin. Then the phone calls started. I still thought it was a

wind up and because of my extremely bad mood, told everyone to fuck off! Eventually I got the message from the NEC that the crew were already there. Now I believed!

What do you remember about the gig?

An awesome night, of course. Bon Jovi did their soundcheck and then there was an almighty bomb scare (still in the days of the IRA troubles etc.), so the building had to be evacuated. So there we were outside the backstage area, all crews, all bands, drivers, everyone. Turns out, if I remember correctly...The Pogues had played the night before and it was something to do with that.

Did you meet any of the guys in Bon Jovi?

The guys were great. They came into the dressing room and introduced themselves to us. They were really cool and friendly. Unfortunately, because of the bomb scare time was really short and we didn't have too long to chat.

What was Bon Jovi's road crew like with you and the others in Shy?

The crew were fine. We actually knew quite a lot of the crew anyway, it was only the 'personals' that we didn't know and because we were of a 'certain level' at the time, we were given a certain amount of respect.

How did the audience treat you?

The audience were great. Because of the delay, due to the bomb scare, we had no chance for a sound check, etc. We literally wheeled the gear on stage and played! It was really funny because obviously no one knew that we were playing, but because it was Bon Jovi, most of our friends and family were in the audience any-

way! To say they were shocked to see us is an understatement, but we certainly had our five minutes of fame in Birmingham.

How long did Bon Jovi give you to play?

I think we did about 40 minutes, which was pretty much our normal support slot anyway.

Did you watch Bon Jovi perform that night?

I watched most of the set from on stage standing by their bass player... very interesting because this was the era of sampling and all that kind of stuff. To watch the 'big boys' doing it close up was great.

Have you met them since then?

We met the drummer about 18 months later. We were in LA recording Misspent Youth *(without doubt, the biggest budget, pile of shit ever recorded) and most of rock's finest gentry had landed in LA for Jon Bon Jovi's wedding. I'd gone for a beer at The Rainbow with Alan [Kelly, ex-Shy drummer] and had what turned out to be an awesome night. Had a beer with Steve Clarke [of Def Leppard] and met Dave Lee Roth, which was brilliant because all and sundry were trying to meet him, and his security guys were letting no one through. We just sauntered through them all, as if we already knew Dave, he was flabbergasted and acted as if he knew us and couldn't quite remember why... great fun! Tico Torres was there so we went over and said hello. He remembered us from the gig, which was incredibly flattering considering all the bands they would have played with since us. He thought we were a great band and wished us all the best...didn't invite us to the wedding though (laughs).*

Have you seen Bon Jovi live before or since Shy supported them?

Have never seen them since and unfortunately never had the chance to play with again.

Anything else?

Did play with a Bon Jovi tribute band not too long ago...their ego and attitude was worse than the real thing. I must admit I threw my dolly out of the pram and reminded them of who I thought I was!

Visit *shyonline.co.uk*

SIDNEY MYER MUSIC BOWL

A concert venue in Melbourne,

Australia. Bon Jovi played here on January 19, 2008 and tickets for the show sold out within record time. They were on the road to promote their greatest hits package and the *Lost Highway* album.

SILENT NIGHT

The fourth and final single released in America from Bon Jovi's second album *7800° Fahrenheit.* It was released in December, 1985 and failed to chart in the *Billboard* Hot 100, although it managed to make it to Number 24 in the *Billboard* Mainstream Rock Tracks. It was not released in the UK.

SILVER DISC

Album sales of 60,000 units in the UK are given Silver status by the British Phonographic Industry, and a Silver Disc is presented to the artist(s). Every Bon Jovi studio album has sold over one million copies worldwide and with the exception of *Bon Jovi* and *7800° Fahrenheit,* the band's first two albums, all other Bon Jovi albums have entered the UK Top 10. Only *7800° Fahrenheit* didn't make it into the Top 20.

SIMS SUPERSTAR, THE

An interactive computer game that is part of the famed series, *The Sims.* The game features computer-generated versions of real-life celebrities, including Richie Sambora. Like many modern rock bands, Bon Jovi have embraced the multimedia age.

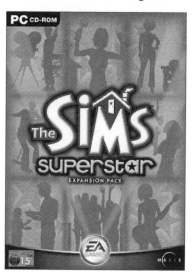

SKID ROW

There are several notable connections between Bon Jovi and Skid Row so it is worth giving a detailed biography of this once important New Jersey hard rock band.

Skid Row was formed in 1986 in Toms River, New Jersey. They share their name with the Irish rock band that featured Gray Moore and Phil Lynott. Skid Row was brought together by Jon Bon Jovi's childhood friend Dave "Snake" Sabo and bassist Rachel Bolan after Sabo met Bolan at a music store where he worked. The pair hit it off immediately.

Slowly but surely new members where added. On the back of a demo recording called 'Saved By Love Again' made by the Canadian band Sebastian, Skid Row hired Sebastian Bach as their new frontman; they were also impressed with a performance he gave at a wedding they attended. It has been suggested that Jon Bon Jovi came up with the $200,000 required to buy Bach out of the contract he had with his ex-manager. Bach's pre-Skid Row bands included Madam X, Kid Wikkid, Hope and the aforementioned Sebastian. In early 1987, the classic line-up of Skid Row was cemented: Sebastian Bach (lead vocals), Dave Sabo (lead and rhythm guitars), Scotti Hill (second lead and rhythm guitars), Rachel Bolan (bass) Rob Affuso (drums).

They were initially turned down by both Atlantic and PolyGram, but with some help from Jon and a contract with his and Sambora's newly founded publishing company New Jersey Underground Music Company (NJUMC) Skid Row were eventually signed to Atlantic Records in 1988. Jon even enticed rock managers Doc and Scott McGhee to sign the band to their company McGhee Entertainment, joining a roster that included Mötley Crüe and Bon Jovi. Scott McGhee became their personal manager.

Skid Row's self-titled debut album was released in 1989. *Skid Row* was recorded at the Royal Recorders near Lake Geneva, Wisconsin, and was produced by the renowned Michael Wagener, who had previously mixed Metallica's classic 1986 opus *Master Of Puppets*.

Michael Wagener: *"The only time I ran into Jon (related to Skid Row) was when he came up to listen to the album right before the mix. He is a very nice guy and I feel he helped the band a lot by taking them on tour"*.

Skid Row is a classic heavy metal album that represents some of the best HM to come out of the States in the eighties. It peaked at an impressive Number 6 in the US *Billboard Hot 100* and has been certified Plati-

num five times. It produced three hit singles: '18 And Life', 'I Remember You' and 'Youth Gone Wild'. With Bach's good looks and sense of humour and the band's heaviness, they appealed to a glam audience as well as the hardcore heavy metal fans.

The band supported Bon Jovi on a North American leg of their exhaustive *New Jersey Syndicate* tour.

Speaking about the last night of the US Skid Row/Bon Jovi tour, Jon told *Metal Hammer* (No. 1, Vol.5) in 1989:

"This particular night the crew decided to razz him [Sebastian] before the band went on stage and tipped a load of cold milk all over Sebastian.

The next thing is he's on stage whilst I'm in the dressing room and I hear him up there calling me a wimp and all this shit. On my own stage! ...When he came off stage, instead of laughing it off...he said 'Man you fucked with me, you can't fuck with me!' So I punched him in the face and said 'How's that for fucking with you?'".

Jon went on to say that they made friends again, and both bands played at the Moscow Music Peace Festival on August 12/13, 1989 and at a summer rock festival at Milton Keynes Bowl in England on August 19, with Europe and Vixen.

Besides the petty squabbles of two ego-driven rock and roll bands, a

more serious issue divided Skid Row and Bon Jovi when Bach sued for Skid Row's share of the publishing royalties from the first album. The terms of the contract allegedly stipulated that 100% of Skid Row's royalties went to Jon and his NJUMC partner Richie Sambora, because they had got Skid Row a record deal with Atlantic and helped kick-start their career.

Sebastian Bach informed *Kerrang!* in October, 1990:

"I stuck up for Jon Bon Jovi all f**king year while he took 100 per cent of our [Skid Row's] publishing... We are getting out of that deal with Jon now because Doc [McGhee] un-

derstands that I'm not the naïve 19 year old that I was three years ago when I signed a piece of paper that says 'Jon Bon Jovi gets 100 percent of the publishing from Skid Row'".

Sambora gave his supposed 50% share of the royalties back to Skid Row but it has been said that the case between Jon and Bach was not resolved until the mid-nineties. It seems there is still some bad blood between them, and Bach now refuses to speak about the issue. Incidentally, NJUMC was shut down after the release of Skid Row's debut album in 1989.

As quoted in Mick Wall's feature in *Classic Rock* (March/April, 1999), Jon was adamant that he deserved payment for his help with Skid Row:

"We were writing songs with them, paying for studio time, paying their rent and every single thing that came with them..."

Perhaps the most infamous incident in Skid Row's career was at a gig in Springfield, Massachusetts when they supported Aerosmith. A bottle was thrown at Bach onstage, he threw it back at the "fan" but missed, and hit a girl who sustained some nasty facial injuries. He was given a suspended sentence and a fine of $15,000. Bach was also banned from his home country, Canada, and still lives in his adopted state of New Jersey.

Skid Row's second album *Slave To The Grind* was a worthy, if not better follow up to their debut. Again, it was produced by Wagener.

It reached the top spot in the US *Billboard* Hot 100 and on the back of that they supported Guns N' Roses on an American tour in 1991 and returned to support the Gunners in Europe later in the year. Bach and Axl Rose have had a topsy-turvy friendship but it is now apparent from their live performances together, and studio work on the new Gunners album *Chinese Democracy* and on Bach's 2007 opus *Angel Down* that they are now good friends again.

However, from 1992 onwards Skid Row's career would not be quite so interesting. They released *B-Side Themselves* in 1992, featuring a selection of covers of songs by songs by other bands, including Judas Priest and Rush. 1995's *Subhuman Race*, produced by Bob Rock, was nowhere near as popular as its predecessors, largely due to the damage grunge had done to heavy metal. They received little play on MTV and sales suffered as a consequence. After the accompanying tour, Skid Row's career went on a downhill slide, even as Bon Jovi's career continued to prosper. After internal conflicts between Bach and bassist Rachel Bolan, Bach was fired in late '96. It didn't help Bach's cause that he was allegedly late for an opening slot of a big KISS show.

Bach pursed other musical projects, including solo work and some musical theatre, while Bolan formed Prunella Scales. Sabo, Bolan and Hill went on to form the short-lived Ozone Monday with Shawn Mars and Charlie Mills from Dee Snider and Strength.

Skid Row was reignited in 1999 with a new line-up: Dave Sabo, Rachel Bolan, Scotti Hill, drummer Charlie Mills and frontman Johnny Solinger. In 2000, they supported Bon Jovi on a selection on American dates with new drummer Phil Varone. In 2006, with yet another new drummer, Dave Gara, Skid Row released the Wagener-produced album *Revolutions Per Minute* to mixed reviews.

Despite a small creative output the band have had an interesting history and continue to provide the goods for their fans.

As for a reunion between Bach and Skid Row, well, both parties consistently change their mind but if the money is right and the timing is good…

Visit *skidrow.com* and *sebastian-bach.com*

SLIPPERY WHEN WET

For Bon Jovi's third album they hooked up in early '86 with the then relatively unknown songwriter and producer Desmond Child, who had been recommended to Sambora by KISS guitarist Paul Stanley. Jon, Richie and Desmond wrote 'You Give Love A Bad Name' in the basement of Sambora's parent's house in New Jersey, and they also penned songs and made demos together New Jersey Century Productions studio in Sayreville, NJ. In all, they had around 40 songs to play with. They hired the talents of Bruce Fairbairn to produce the album at Little Mountain Sound Studios in Vancouver, Canada during the Spring of '86. Fairbairn's protégé Bob Rock was the album's studio engineer. Fairbairn worked the band hard for two months, with early mornings and late nights, in pursuit of the perfect record. One of the album's best-known known songs is 'Livin' On A Prayer'. Jon was originally not keen on the song but the band re-recorded it at Sambora's behest (the first version is a hidden track on the box-set *100,000,000 Bon Jovi Fans Can't Be Wrong*). Sambora, a fan of classic rock, added the musical device called a talk-box to the song which gives it its distinctiveness. In all, the album took nine weeks to record.

Suggested titles for the album included *Wanted Dead Or Alive* (which would have included include a photograph of the band dressed as cowboys). Doc McGhee was reportedly not impressed by this idea, so it was scrapped. They even considered the name *Guns N' Roses,* as a sort of homage to the burgeoning fame of the notorious LA rock band. *Slippery When Wet* is said to have been inspired by Vancouver's red light district, and by one bar in particular, called *No. 5,* in which had dancers would strip off and take showers in front of the customers. *"We lived in those [strip] joints!"* Jon told *Kerrang!* in 1994. Also, during one disastrous photo session in the mountains near Vancouver there was a street sign which read 'Slippery When Wet'. The name just stuck.

For the album's cover various ideas had been tried; the initial concept was a photograph of a woman in a wet yellow t-shirt with *Slippery*

When Wet written across her chest as a sort of cheesy homage to the Vancouver strip clubs. The sleeve also had a dreadful pink border around the cover. Jon was not a fan of this design, but it several hundred thousands copies had already been made and sent to Japan before the rest were destroyed.

Another version of the story relates that the record company's American office did not want the original cover, thinking that stores would be more likely to stock an album with a less controversial cover, but that the Japanese office were quite happy to go ahead with it.

Richie Sambora told *Kerrang!* in July, 1993:

"I'm not ashamed of the original Slippery When Wet *cover – it's just some chick with big tits!"*

It was at Weiss' New Jersey studio that Jon laid out a black refuse bag, splashed water on it with a spray bottle and wrote *Slippery When Wet* with his finger. Weiss photographed it and that image was used for the finished cover. A piece of classic rock history had been made.

Slippery When Wet was released in the UK on September 20, 1986 and peaked at Number 6, spending an exhaustive 123 weeks in the charts. In the States it reached the top spot in the *Billboard* 200, although it actually entered the chart at Number 45. The album's success went global and it went on to sell 16.9 million copies in the States alone and 26 million worldwide. In the USA it occupied the Number 1 spot for 15 weeks and was the most commercially successful album of 1987.

Slippery When Wet also gave birth to two Number 1 American singles, 'Livin' On A Prayer' and 'You Give Love A Bad Name'. 'Wanted Dead Or Alive' was also a Top 10 hit. The album is frequently voted as one of the best rock albums of all time, and it remains Bon Jovi's most popular and biggest selling album. They had finally made it.

A special edition remastered version of the album was issued on September 20, 2005 to celebrate (somewhat prematurely) 20 years since its original release. The CD was accompanied by a DVD that contains an expanded version of the album and five promo videos: 'You Give Love A Bad Name', 'Livin' On A Prayer', 'Wanted Dead Or Alive', 'Never Say Goodbye' and 'Wild In The Streets.' The standard remastered release comes with an enhanced CD video of 'Wanted Dead Or Alive'.

Track Listing:
1. 'Let It Rock'
2. 'You Give Love A Bad Name'
3. 'Livin' On A Prayer'
4. 'Social Disease'
5. 'Wanted Dead Or Alive'
6. 'Raise Your Hands'
7. 'Without Love'
8. 'I'd Die For You'

9. 'Never Say Goodbye'

10. 'Wild In The Streets'

Author's Review:

What can be said about Slippery When Wet *that hasn't been said a million times before? It is without question one of the best rock albums ever. The production is first rate, there is a good mix of rock songs and ballads and the melodies are just spot on. Obviously it was a major coup for the band to team up with Desmond Child for the lyrics and Bruce Fairbairn for the production, so credit for the album's success must go to them first and foremost. The harmonies on songs like 'Let It Rock' work superbly and Sambora adds a nice touch with the talk-box on 'Livin' On A Prayer.' Jon hits the higher notes with ease and he sounds much more confident with his voice. It is also surprisingly heavier at times which is why it is often called a pop metal album with songs like 'Raise Your Hands' and 'Social Disease' being the heaviest tracks. It remains one of rock's best albums for a reason...*

Rating *****

SLIPPERY WHEN WET: THE VIDEOS

This VHS collection from 1986 features six videos from the massively popular *Slippery When Wet* album. Also included is a live performance of 'Livin' On A Prayer' from the 1987 MTV Awards. It was released via Mercury and runs for 40 minutes.

Track Listing:

1. 'Wild In The Streets'
2. 'Livin' On A Prayer' *(Live)*
3. 'You Give Love A Bad Name'
4. 'Never Say Goodbye'

5. 'Livin' On A Prayer'

6. 'Wanted Dead Or Alive'

SLIPPERY WHEN WET TOUR (1986-1987)

Bon Jovi's first *major* headlining tour began in November, 1986 in the UK and Europe, and hit America in December. *Slippery When Wet* had been selling at around one million copies per month so the band had the confidence to headline major venues themselves. They were no longer the support act. The tour rolled into early '87 and the band realised it was their longest time on the road up to that point. During this tour they headlined shows at New York's Madison Square Garden, the 15,000 capacity stadium in San Diego, Meadowlands in East Rutherford and at the British Monsters Of Rock festival on August 22, 1987. The toured started to wind down in Britain, Australia and Japan. The final night of the tour was actually on American soil in Honolulu, Hawaii on October 16.

SMITH, STUART

Born in York, England, Smith is one of the most respected blues/classic rock guitarists around. He is classically trained and at one point was taught by Richie Blackmore of Deep Purple. He has played with Joe Lynn Turner (ex-Deep Purple and Rainbow) and Keith Emerson (ex-The Nice and E.L.P.), and is currently taking part in a reformed version of The Sweet.

In 1999, Smith released his debut album *Stuart Smith's Heaven & Earth*, which was produced by Pat Regan and Howard Leese. The album featured a host of top artists, including Richie Sambora (who contributed to a cover of Deep Purple's 'When A Blind Man Cries' – a B-side to the 1972 single 'Never Before'), Joe Lynn Turner, Glenn Hughes, Kelly Hansen, Steve Priest and Carmine Appice. The album was licensed and distributed in Europe by Frontiers Records and by Pony Canyon in Japan.

Smith says:

"At the time of recording my Heaven & Earth album I was married to Colleen Locklear, Heather's sister, so Richie was my brother-in-law. I've always loved Richie's voice as much as his guitar playing; to my mind he's one of the most soulful singers there is. When I first got the record deal to do a solo album I put together a 'wish list' of who I'd like on it and Richie was one of my first calls. I said to Richie: 'Listen, I don't want you to do this just because you're my brother-in-law but I'd really like you to sing a track on my album'. And he said: 'Great, no one ever asks me to sing'. I sent him the tracks of 'When A Blind Man Cries' and 'Do You Ever Think Of Me.' When Richie turned up at the studio

he had his guitars with him and I when I asked why he'd brought them he said he liked the tracks so much he'd like to play on them, which was just fine by me. He sang 'When A Blind Man Cries' first and did an amazing job. There were about 20 people in the studio that night and everyone was just blown away. When it came to singing 'Do You Ever Think Of Me' it was really the wrong key for him so he ended up just playing the amazing solo on the end and then added the second solo to 'When A Blind Man Cries'. The session went on from 12.00 noon on the Thursday and I drove Richie home at 9.30am the following day. I've always felt that if Richie went out on his own he'd be our next Clapton".

Visit *heavenandearthband.com* and *thesweetband.com*

SOMEDAY I'LL BE SATURDAY NIGHT

The second of two original songs recorded for the 1994 collection *Cross Road: The Best Of Bon Jovi*. It was recorded on July 6, 1994 at Emerald Studios in Nashville with producer Peter Collins and Kevin Shirley, who recorded it. Issued in the UK as a single on February 25, 1995 it hit Number 7, spending the same amount of weeks in the chart.

SOMETHING FOR THE PAIN

Written by Jon, Richie Sambora and Desmond Child, 'Something For The Pain' was the second single off *These Days*. It was issued in the UK September 30, 1995 and peaked at Number 8, spending seven weeks in the charts. In the States it only made it to Number 76.

SONGS & VISIONS

A concert to celebrate 40 years of popular music, held at Wembley Stadium in London on August 16, 1997. Jon Bon Jovi played a solo set that included covers of 'Heartbreak Hotel' and 'Like A Rolling Stone' and joined the other performers, amongst whom were Toni Braxton, Rod Stewart, K.D. Lang and Steve Winwood.

SOPRANOS, THE

One of the most revered American television dramas of all time. The series chronicles the life of New Jersey mobster Tony Soprano and his family. The series ran from 1999 to 2007. The episode 'A Hit Is A Hit' featured the popular Bon Jovi rocker 'You Give Love A Bad Name'.

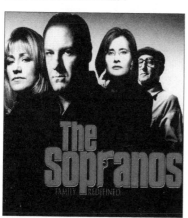

SOUTHSIDE JOHNNY

A New Jersey singer-songwriter (real name John Lyon) whose backing band is The Asbury Jukes. Especially prominent in the 1970s, Southside Johnny was part of the 'Jersey Shore Sound' which also included Bruce Springsteen. Jon Bon Jovi was in awe of The Asbury Jukes and even admitted that he wanted to be one. Southside Johnny got to know Jon when he was in Atlantic City Expressway and the pair became friends. In the early eighties, whilst singing in a band called The Wild Ones, (also featuring Dave Sabo and David Bryan) Jon supported Southside Johnny and The Asbury Jukes on a series of dates on the East Coast.

Southside Johnny's career suffered a slump during the eighties, but it was relaunched 1991 with the release of *Better Days*, an album that featured Jon Bon Jovi and Bruce Springsteen.

Visit *southsidejohnny.com*

SPACEBALLS

Spaceballs is a 1987 Mel Brooks spoof of the popular space saga *Star Wars*. Bon Jovi's 'Lay Your Hands On Me' features on the soundtrack.

SPRINGSTEEN, BRUCE

An incredibly influential singer-songwriter from New Jersey. It has been said that if you come from New Jersey and don't like 'The Boss' you are committing a sin. His work with The E Street Band is especially popular. Signed to Columbia Records, his first two albums were slow sellers, despite strong critical reviews, but his third release, *Born To Run* flung Springsteen into the American consciousness onwards to global success. Akin to what punk bands like The Clash were doing in the UK, Springsteen was writing about everyday people in America; the politics and the places. 'Born In The USA', one of his most famous songs, is often misconstrued as a pro-American flag waver when it is, in fact, highly critical of how the American government treated their Vietnam veterans.

There are numerous connections between Bon Jovi and Springsteen, the most obvious being their home state of New Jersey. As a Springsteen obsessed kid Jon even got himself in trouble with the police for selling bootleg posters of The Boss.

Jon told *Kerrang!* in 1991:

"I did that at Madison Square Garden in 1978. I didn't have money to

buy a ticket and the only way to get in was by selling these posters. I got arrested and went to jail for it...I didn't do it for a living so they let me out in time to get back to the show. But we still didn't have enough money for a ticket..."

Jon, the band and Springsteen have shared the stage together many times over the years. It all began in the late seventies, when Springsteen first saw Jon Bon Jovi and David Bryan's band Atlantic City Expressway onstage at various clubs around NJ, including the famous Fastlane. Roy Bittan of The E Street Band contributed keys to the original demo recording of 'Runaway' in June, 1982 alongside several other musicians who were known as The All Star Review.

In 1998, in memory of a policeman who was killed on duty, Jon Bon Jovi arranged a charity concert at Count Basie Theater in Red Bank, NJ, called 'Jon Bon Jovi & Friends Benefit Concert'. Bruce Springsteen was one of the guest performers.

In 2001, Bon Jovi and Springsteen took part in the 'America: A Tribute To Heroes' charity concert, which raised money for the 9/11 victims and their families. They also took part in a series of benefit gigs in NJ called 'Alliance Of Neighbors'.

In December, 2003 at Ashbury Park in NJ, Jon joined Springsteen onstage to sing the Bon Jovi hit 'It's My Life' and a version of the yuletide classic 'Santa Claus Is Coming To Town'.

Visit *brucespringsteen.net*

SQUIER, BILLY

Squier's debut album *Tale Of The Tape* was released in 1980 but it wasn't until his second album, 1981's *Don't Say No* that he would become a well-known figure in the rock world. His next couple of albums, *Emotions In Motion* and *Signs Of Life* were Top 10 hits in the States. His most successful singles include 'The Stroke', 'Rock Me Tonite', 'My Kinda Lover' and 'Everybody Wants You'. Squier is still active in the music scene although his last album, *Happy Blue,* was released back in 1998. He often plays in his hometown, New York. In 2008 he toured with Ringo Starr's All-Star Band.

Squier was enticed by Jon to produce his four track 'Runaway' demo with the session band The All Star Review, featuring Hugh McDonald, Roy Bittan, Frank LaRocca and Tim Pierce. The demo was recorded at Manhattan's Power Station Studios in June, 1982. Squier:

"I first met Jon when he was more than likely still 'John'. This would have been late '70s, when he was in a band from Toms River called The Rest. Jack Ponti, the lead guitarist, came to me and asked if I'd help them out with some demos. Jon hadn't found himself at this point - heck, he was barely street-legal, and the days of big hair and MTV were still a ways off. But he knew where he wanted to be...and this is what stuck in my mind: HE KNEW WHERE HE WANTED TO BE...and was prepared to do

whatever it took to get there. Having talent is one thing - having the perseverance to stick it out when talent doesn't get you through is a whole other trip. Jon took that trip...which is why he's where he is today".

In 1989 during the *New Jersey Syndicate* tour, Billy Squier (along with Skid Row) supported Bon Jovi at New Jersey's Giants Stadium in a gig dubbed 'The Homecoming'. Squier:

"In 1989, Bon Jovi was on top of the world. Jon rang me up and asked me if I wanted to do a string of dates to kick off his New Jersey Syndicate *tour. This made sense, as I'd been off the road and out of the public eye for a few years, and as the saying goes, 'Out of sight, out of mind'. I had a new record coming out and the timing seemed perfect. Only hitch was, Jon was offering me a paltry sum of money to do most of the shows. He reasoned that my playing with him would resuscitate my career and therefore, I should be happy to do the dates regardless of the lack of financial consideration. He said that if I wasn't interested, he'd give the dates to Bad English, who'd be happy to have them. We ultimately settled on*

one gig at Giants Stadium, at terms we both agreed upon."

Visit *billysquier.com*

SR-71

Baltimore alternative rock band that formed in 1998. They have released just three albums: *Now You See Inside* (2000,) *Tomorrow* (2002) and *Here We Go Again* (2004.) Their most popular singles are 'Right Now' and 'Tomorrow.'

The band supported Bon Jovi on the North American leg of the 2001 *Crush* tour, which kicked off in Phoenix, Arizona at the Desert Sky Pavilion. They performed all over the USA and Canada, including shows in California, Mexico City, Nevada, Colorado, Carolina, Quebec City and Ontario, and obviously New Jersey and New York. The tour finished on May 20 at the Pepsi Arena in Albany, New York.

Visit *sr-71.net*

ST. JOSEPH HIGH SCHOOL

Jon Bon Jovi attended this all-boys Catholic preparatory school in Metuchen and Edison, New Jersey.

ST. MARY'S, SOUTHAMPTON

As part of their *Lost Highway* world trek, Bon Jovi stopped at St. Mary's

stadium in Southampton, England on June 11. 2008. Writing in *The Times*, critic David Sinclair gave the concert 3/5 and said:

"Very few bands have been able to function at this gargantuan level of activity over an extended period. But Bon Jovi have managed it for so long with so little fuss or pretension that it's spooky. Of course, the huge lighting rig and screen projections were expertly managed, while the band's playing and presentation were faultless throughout. But you would look in vain for any garish lasers, inflatables, hydraulic stunts or pyrotechnic displays."

STADIUM ROCK

Similar to arena rock but much grander in scale, stadium rock is the height of rock's vanity. The stages are bigger, there is room for more video screens, the lighting is more extravagant and, of course, the crowd is bigger and louder. Archetypal stadium rock bands include Queen, The Rolling Stones, U2 and Bon Jovi. Stadium rock is not as popular as it once was, but bands such as KISS, Aerosmith and Bon Jovi manage to pack stadiums during every tour. In 2008, while promoting *Lost Highway*, Bon Jovi sold out a series of stadium dates in the UK while the rest of their world tour was equally successful.

STAND UP FOR A CURE

A non-profit making American organisation that helps to raise funds for and global awareness of lung cancer research at Memorial Sloan-Kettering Cancer Center in New York. In 2008, the organisation held a series of benefit concerts.

Bon Jovi played at the opening concert on February 12, 2008 at the New York Hammerstein Ballroom. The concert was dedicated to Richie Sambora's father, Adam Sambora, who had died from cancer in 2007.

Visit *sufac.org*

STATION WAGON TOUR

With no album to their name, only the 'Runaway' demo, Bon Jovi toured around the East Coast of America in 1983 supporting Eddie Money on a road jaunt dubbed *Station Wagon Tour.*

STEWART, DAVE

Born in Sunderland, England in 1952, Dave Stewart is probably best known as one half of the pop duo Eurythmics. He is also a highly successful solo artist, record producer and songwriter. In 1991 he released an excellent collaborative documentary called *Deep Blues: A Musical Pilgrimage To The Crossroads,* and in 2000 he directed his first film, *Honest.*

Stewart made significant production and songwriting contributions to Jon Bon Jovi's second solo album *Destination Anywhere.* He worked with Jon on the following tracks:

'Queen Of New Orleans'
Recorded at Chapel Studios, California; December, 1996.
(Co-writer, producer and guitar)
'Midnight In Chelsea'
Recorded at Right Track Studios, New York; December, 1996.
(Co-writer, co-producer and guitar)
'It's Just Me'
Recorded at Chapel Studios, California; December, 1996.
(Producer and guitar)
'August'
Recorded at Sanctuary II Studios, New Jersey and Chapel Studios, California; December, 1996.
(Co-producer)

Visit *davestewart.com*

STILL STANDING

An American TV series that ran from 2002 until 2006. The show was about the marriage of high school sweethearts Bill and Judy Miller as they grew older and coped with having three kids. Richie Sambora starred in one episode ('Still Getting Married') as the character Roach.

STONE PONY, THE

The Stone Pony is a popular club in Asbury Park, New Jersey, which the young Jon Bon Jovi used to frequent. Atlantic City Expressway also played there, as did many other local bands. It is often referred to in articles about Jon's pre-Bon Jovi years.

Visit *stoneponyonline.com*

STORYTELLERS

A television show produced by the VH1 network. The first broadcast was in 1996 and featured Ray Davies, formerly of The Kinks. At the time Davies was on his *Storyteller* tour, and VH1 used the same title for the show. *VH1 Storytellers* has since seen over 60 artists deliver performances. The venues tend to be small with an intimate audience and the artists take questions from various members of the audience. The shows are taped, broadcast and often released on CD and/or DVD. The series has included famous performances by artists such as Meat Loaf, Billy Joel, Elton John and Bruce Springsteen. Bon Jovi's performance aired on September 22, 2000.

Visit *vh1.com*

STRANGER IN THIS TOWN

After the sheer size, length and spectacle of the *New Jersey Syndicate* tour Bon Jovi took a break

– from each other. During that period Richie Sambora recorded his excellent debut solo album, a personal composition that showed his love of the blues whilst also giving him the chance to sing, something he is very good at. Even now some of the material is so strong that Sambora sang the title track on Bon Jovi's *Lost Highway Tour* in 2007-08.

Produced by Sambora and Neil Dorfsman, the album was recorded at A&M Recording Studios in Los Angeles and mixed and mastered at Skyline Studios and Masterdisk in New York, respectively. His session band for the album was his Bon Jovi mates David Bryan and Tico Torres, with Tony Levin on bass.

Sambora hooked up with some notable talents, including legendary guitarist Eric Clapton, one of Sambora's idols. Clapton played the guitar solo on 'Mr. Bluesman'. Another collaborator was Randy Jackson (known these days as a judge on *American Idol*) who played bass on 'One Light Burning'.

Sambora roped in some of his friends to help with songwriting: he co-wrote 'Rest In Peace' and 'Stranger In This Town' with David Bryan; 'Ballad Of Youth' with Tommy Marolda; 'One Light Burning' with Marolda and his former Shark Frenzy band mate Bruce Foster; 'Father Time' with Desmond Child and 'The Answer' with Foster.

In particular, Bruce Foster recalls the songwriting sessions for 'The Answer':

"'The Answer' started at my house across the river from Richie's and was finished on the beach in Bay Head, New Jersey. It was a deserted beach in the off season of early October and we sat in a gazebo just beyond the waves.

The sky above us was full of dark clouds that were tumbling and boiling like the scene in The Ten Commandments *as Moses parts the sea...There was a symbiotic bond between us and some serious elemental forces".*

'Rosie' was initially a Bon Jovi song written by Sambora, Jon and Diane Warren for the *New Jersey* album; some bootlegs of this version do exist.

Released via Mercury on September 14, 1991 in the UK, the album was not a commercial success, despite the glowing reviews. It peaked at Number 39 in the *Billboard* 200 but in Britain Sambora fans showed their support and helped the album make it to Number 20, spending a total of three weeks in the charts. 'Ballad Of Youth' was released as a single (with a cover of Jimi Hendrix's 'The Wind

Cries Mary' as the B-side) on September 7 but only made it to Number 59. It peaked at a lowly Number 63 in the *Billboard* Hot 100 Singles.

A special edition box-set of the album was released with 'The Wind Cries Mary' included as a bonus track. The box-set also included a Richie Sambora dog tag and a bonus interview disc which makes for quite interesting listening; Sambora not only talks about the actual album but the things and people that inspired him to pick up a guitar in the first place.

Sambora put forward his reflections on the album to *Kerrang!* writer Steffan Chirazi in 1993:

"I got to the point where I personally was losing the guy I used to be. My solo record was a direct reflection of all that – dark, dingy, but also

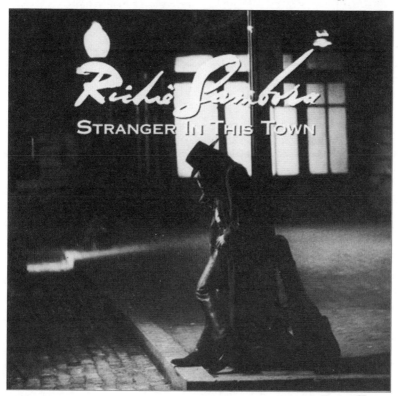

hopeful, because I had to come out of that a little bit. That record was finding myself".

Track Listing:

1. 'Rest In Peace'
2. 'Church Of Desire'
3. 'Stranger In This Town'
4. 'Ballad Of Youth'
5. 'One Light Burning'
6. 'Mr. Bluesman'
7. 'Rosie'
8. 'River Of Love'
9. 'Father Time'
10. 'The Answer'
11. 'The Wind Cries Mary' *(Bonus track on the Special Edition version)*

Author's Review:

Stranger In This Town *is an entirely different beast to any album released by Bon Jovi. If you want stadium anthems or huge power ballads, go somewhere else because this is not that kind of album.* Stranger In This Town *is mostly a mid-tempo and bluesy affair with some wonderful harmonics and memorable choruses. Sambora sings with plenty of soul and even angst. It's certainly more personal than anything he had committed himself to before; and even though it did not match the heights of success achieved by Jon Bon Jovi's debut solo album Blaze Of Glory, it sounds fresh and inspiring.*

*The first track 'Rest In Peace' is a low-key song, short and broody; it's almost an instrumental. It gives you a small taster of what is in store. 'Church Of Desire' is a great track that shows just how good a vocalist Sambora is; there's a blues vibe but there's a soulful yearning with some harmonic backing vocals that work to great effect. 'Stranger In This Town' is one of the album's strong-*est tracks; like some of Clapton's solo stuff, it's mellow but the guitars suck you in and make you happy to stay for the short journey. 'Ballad Of Youth' brightens things up as Sambora shouts "Oh yeah!" There's nothing wrong with this track; it's got a bit more substance than the other songs. There are some neat production effects and arrangements on 'One Light Burning' which give it some distinction and 'Mr. Blues Man' is a solid tune with a nifty solo from Mr. Eric Clapton. At this point the blues shifts away. 'Rosie' stands out for the wrong reasons; it sounds just like a Bon Jovi song and doesn't fit on this particular album. Next up is the groovy 'River Of Love' and 'Father Time', which is a decent ballad. The closing track 'The Answer' is a bit too sentimental but as it is mostly acoustic it's well handled.

Overall, despite a quiet production, Stranger In This Town *is a robust album that has some strengths but fewer weaknesses. Recommended.*

Rating: ****

STRANGER IN THIS TOWN TOUR (1991)

To promote his first solo album *Stranger In This Town*, Richie Sambora made a brief tour of the United States in 1991. His backing band was: Tony Levin on bass, Dave Amato on guitars and percussionist Crystal Taliefero, with fellow Bon Jovi band mates Tico Torres and Dave Bryan.

SUCH, ALEC JOHN

The original bass player in Bon Jovi, Alec John Such has not been seen in the press in recent years, preferring to remain low key at his home in New York.

He was born in Yonkers, New York, on November 14, 1952. Having cut his teeth as an experienced session musician, Alec played bass in two notable New Jersey outfits: he was in Message with Richie Sambora on guitar but once that band folded he joined Phantom's Opera, with Ticco Torres on drums. Soon the lives of all three musicians were about to change dramatically. In 1983, after Jon had signed a record deal with PolyGram, he was eager to get a band together and make an album. Having already hooked up with his childhood buddy David Bryan, through word of mouth Jon hired Alec John Such, who in turn recommended his previous band mate Ticco Torres. Dave Sabo was the temporary guitarist, but one story goes that Such jumped in and suggested a talented young player by the name of Richie Sambora. And so in the summer of 1983 the band that would become Bon Jovi was complete. There is no doubting that in those early years Such was a strong bass player and the triumvirate of Such, Torres and Bryan made one hell of a rhythm section

behind Jon and Sambora's great guitar-singer duo.

Throughout his years in the band, Such was *the bass player*; not really a famous figure in the manner of, say, The Who's John Entwistle. Onstage, he was a fairly unspectacular bassist, although he did contribute some backing vocals and he occasionally sang the lead part on the track 'Blood On Blood' (from *New Jersey*). He also sang backing vocals on some of the session work and is credited as such on *Bon Jovi, 7800° Fahrenheit* and *New Jersey*.

It was alleged that Such had been threatened with dismissal from the band after the *New Jersey Syndicate* tour because of his drink problem.

When the band was interviewed by Dave Reynolds for *Kerrang!* in the summer of 1993, Such said:

"I was the mystery guy! I always seemed to be in the background in the past, cos that's just how it was when we put the band together...Hey, I was lazy! But I feel now that I do want to contribute more."

Fast forward to 1994 and long after the tension between Jon and Sambora had faded there was allegedly growing resentment between Such and Jon. Such was interviewed for *RAW* magazine and said that *"Jon tells me I suck all the time"*. It has been sug-

gested that a lot of his bass work had been redone by session bassist Hugh McDonald, who is credited on all Bon Jovi albums pre-*Keep The Faith* except for *7800° Fahrenheit.*

As the bassist and drummer are often the less familiar figures in a rock band, Such felt his talents were always overlooked. He told noted journalist Dave Ling at *RAW*:

"I was told that nobody wanted to talk to me, and that came right from Jon's mouth".

Word got back to the main man that Such had been making some slightly bitter remarks about him to the British music press. This went against Jon's notion that *"what happens in the family, stays in the family",* and by the end of 1994, Such was no longer the bass player in Bon Jovi.

He was still in the band for the promotional duties for the 1994 greatest hits collection *Cross Road,* including a spot on *Top Of The Pops* playing the hit single 'Always', but that was it. Jon had allegedly asked Such to leave for the sake of the band's credibility although at the time the band said the split was amicable. The press, on the other hand, obviously thought otherwise, claiming he was fired. Many allegations and claims were thrown but nothing was confirmed.

Jon told *Kerrang!* (December, '94):

"Alec was not pushed! I don't want to speak on behalf of him, but there just comes a time when you don't feel like your lives are going the same way. Bon Jovi's not a life sentence, for any of us, and I'm still friends with Alec".

In recent years, however, it has been claimed that Such was making mistakes during some of their live shows on the 1993 *Keep The Faith* tour and the session work that had been done for the *Cross Road* collection was not up to scratch. This is discussed on the VH1 documentary *Behind The Music,* with Jon and Sambora shedding some light on the situation; Such declined to take part in the programme so it is really a one-sided argument.

Jon told *Classic Rock* (March, 2001) years after Such was fired or quit:

"Jumped or pushed? A little bit of both. He was burned, he couldn't do it any more, he was 10 years older than us, remember".

Such was not officially replaced; the band stayed as a four piece with Hugh McDonald, a familiar face to Bon Jovi fans, handling the bass duties in the studio and onstage. *Cross Road* was the *last* release to feature Such on the cover and *These Days* was the *first* album *not* to feature the original bass player: the photography for *These Days* shows the four remaining members – Jon, Sambora, Bryan and Torres – for the first time.

Unbelievably, despite all that had gone on between them, Such joined Bon Jovi on stage at Giants Stadium, New Jersey in July, 2001 during the *One Wild Night* tour.

To keep himself busy, Such has worked on variety of projects: with James Young of Styx he managed the Chicago band 7th Heaven. He also managed some New Jersey bands and even bought a motorbike store in the Big Apple. However, recent years he has disappeared from view. During the band's promotional work for *Crush* in 2000 Jon told *Classic Rock* that Such is

"...living out on a houseboat in Corpus Christi, Texas. Sold his house, his guitars...He's back with his wife that actually left him back on that first record".

SULTON, KASIM

The revered American bass player who is famous, in particular, for his collaborations with Todd Rundgren. Sulton is also known for his work with Meat Loaf and has been a member of Meat Loaf's band The Neverland Express for many years. He has also toured with Cheap Trick, Blue Öyster Cult, Hall and Oates, Patti Smith and Joan Jett. In 2005 he joined The New Cars, a new version of the band Cars. He has also released four solo albums.

As bassist, Sultan toured with Richie Sambora during his *Undiscovered Soul* world tour. Sulton says:

"I've known Richie and Jon for some years now and have a tremendous amount of respect for their talent and success. In 1998, I was attending the NAMM Trade Show in Los Angeles and happened to run into Richie. He had just finished his second solo record and was preparing to put some dates together for a tour. I mentioned that I had some time off and if he needed a bass player, I would jump at the chance to work with him.

A few phone calls later, I found myself in rehearsals for what would turn out to be a year on and off the road with his band visiting Australia, Japan, the UK and Germany. I can't remember having a better time with any artist I've ever worked with. Not only is Richie one of the best guitarists in music today, I can't say I've ever been treated better by anyone in the business before or since. His kindness and respect for me touched me so deeply that I felt compelled to write his mother a letter telling her what a wonderful person her son is".

Visit *kasimsulton.com*

SUMMERTIME

Written by Jon Bon Jovi, Richie Sambora and John Shanks, 'Summertime' is the second track on the band's tenth album, 2007's *Lost Highway*. Although it was not properly released as a single, it made it to Number 39 in the Canadian singles chart solely on airplay.

SUNRISE AVENUE

Formed in 2002 in Helsinki, Finland, Sunrise Avenue have had success in the native country with several singles as well as their 2006 album *On The Way To Wonderland* which peaked at Number 2 in the Finnish album charts. They supported Bon Jovi at the Magna Racino in Ebreichsdorf, Austria on June 4, 2008.

Visit *sunriseave.com*

SUPA, RICHIE

An American songwriter and musician who is especially known for his numerous collaborations with Aerosmith. He has also written for Pink, and he co-wrote much of Richie Sambora's *Undiscovered Soul* album. Supa joined Sambora's solo band (as a guitarist) in '98, playing to audiences in Japan, Australia and Europe. He co-wrote the following songs with Sambora:

'Made In America' *(Sambora/Supa)*
'Hard Times Come Easy' *(Sambora/Supa)*
'Fallen From Graceland' *(Sambora/Bryan/Supa)*
'If God Was A Woman' *(Sambora/Bryan/Supa)*
'All That Really Matters' *(Sambora/Supa)*
'In It For Love' *(Sambora/Supa)*
'Harlem Rain' *(Sambora/Supa)*
'Downside Of Love' *(Sambora/Bryan/Supa)*
'Undiscovered Soul' *(Sambora/Supa)*

Visit *myspace.com/richiesupa*

T

TALIEFERO, CRYSTAL

Undoubtedly one of the most re-spected percussionists in the busi-ness, Crystal Taliefero began play-ing rhythm and blues at the age of 11, having been inspired by the likes of Tina Turner and Aretha Franklin. During her professional career she has performed with the likes of Billy Joel, Bruce Springsteen, Elton John and John Mellencamp. She toured with Richie Sambora during his short US tour after the release of *Stranger In This Town,* and she also toured with him during the European leg of his 1998 tour in support of *Undiscov-ered Soul.*

Visit *crystaltaliefero.com*

TALK BOX

During the seventies the talk box became popular with many musi-cians, including Peter Frampton, Ste-vie Wonder, George Harrison and Jeff Beck. A talk box is essentially a musical device that allows a musician to modify the sound of their instru-ment by changing the shape of their mouth. Richie Sambora began using one in the early eighties, and famous-ly used it on 'Livin' On A Prayer.' He has since used it on the songs 'It's My Life', 'One Wild Night 2001', 'Bounce', 'Everyday', 'Complicated', 'Put The Boy Back In Cowboy', 'I Want To Be Loved' and 'We Got It Goin' On'.

In 2002, Sambora told rock journal-ist Joe Matera:

"I got the chance to use it a lot on this record [Bounce]. It's a crazy lit-tle instrument that not many people utilize. I grew up listening to it to the likes of Joe Walsh and Peter Framp-ton and then I brought it back into play as no-one was using it for years and years until I brought it back into vogue on 'Livin' On A Prayer'. Then I didn't use it for awhile myself until 'It's My Life'. Sometimes it can sound a little goofy, so you have to be care-ful what you do with it".

THANK YOU FOR LOVING ME

Released in the UK on December 9, 2000 'Thank You For Loving Me' was the third and final single taken from the hit album *Crush*; it peaked at Number 12 in the UK Top 40 sin-gles chart. The lyrics were written by Jon and Richie Sambora. The addi-tional tracks on the UK edition were live versions of 'Just Older' and 'Born To Be My Baby'. It only made it to Number 57 in the American *Billboard* Hot 100, proving that the Americans prefer Bon Jovi rock songs to Bon Jo-vi ballads.

THAT'S THE STORY OF LOVE

This is the final song on Ted Nu-gent's 1988 album *If You Can't Lick 'Em...Lick 'Em.*

It was written by Jon Bon Jovi and Richie Sambora, together with Nugent.

THESE DAYS (ALBUM)

Right after the release of their *Cross Road* collection, Bon Jovi began preparing material for their new album, which had the working title, *Open All Night*. This would be the first album *not* to feature original bassist Alec John Such; Hugh McDonald took his place in the studio and on stage, although all subsequent artwork would feature Bon Jovi as just a four piece act.

Commencing in November '94, *These Days* was recorded at various studios in the States: Bearsville Sound Studios in Woodstock, 16th Ave. Sound in Nashville, One On One Studios in Hollywood, Ocean Way Recording in Hollywood and A&M Studios in LA. It was produced by Peter Collins, Jon Bon Jovi and Richie Sambora, engineering was completed by David Thoener and Obie O'Brien, and mixing was done by Bob Clearmountain.

The songwriting was taken care of by Jon, Sambora and Desmond Child. The lyrics are certainly darker and more introspective than the band's previous work.

These Days was released in the UK on July 1, 1995 and hit Number 1 immediately, spending 50 weeks in the charts. It spawned five singles: 'This Ain't A Love Song', 'Something For The Pain', 'Lie To Me', 'These Days' and 'Hey God'. Elsewhere the album peaked at Number 1 in Germany and Australia but in the States it only

managed Number 9 in the *Billboard 200*.

Various editions were released worldwide: a French edition with a bonus CD, a Japanese edition with a bonus CD, an Australian tour edition and a global 'Special Edition 2 CD' package, featuring demos, cover versions and live tracks.

Track Listing:

1. 'Hey God'
2. 'Something For The Pain'
3. 'This Ain't A Love Song'
4. 'These Days'
5. 'Lie To Me'
6. 'Damned'
7. 'My Guitar Lies Bleeding In My Arms'
8. '(It's Hard) Letting You Go'
9. 'Hearts Breaking Even'
10. 'Something To Believe In'
11. 'If That's What It Takes'
12. 'Diamond Ring'
13. 'All I Want Is Everything'*
14. 'Bitter Wine'*
* *(Included on the UK version but not all releases in other territories)*

Special Edition Bonus Cd

1. 'Fields Of Fire' *(Demo)*
2. 'I Thank You'
3. 'Mrs. Robinson'
4. 'Let's Make It Baby' *(Demo)*
5. 'I Don't Like Mondays' *(Live at Wembley Stadium; feat. Bob Geldof)*
7. 'Crazy' *(Live, feat. Tico Torres on lead vocal)*
8. 'Tumblin' Dice' *(Live, feat. David Bryan on lead vocal)*
9. 'Heaven Help Us All' *(Live, feat. Richie Sambora on lead vocal)*

Author's Review:

It has been said many times that These Days is Bon Jovi's darkest album; many of the issues written about

in the lyrics include depression, despair, homelessness and poverty. Just listen to Jon screaming out the chorus during 'Hey God'; I don't think he has ever sounded so convincing. Bon Jovi had gone for a different style of music on Keep The Faith *but this album goes one step deeper. The standout songs include 'Hey God', the title track, and the surprisingly powerful 'Something To Believe In'. 'All I Want Is Everything' has a slight 'grungy' edge which adds a harder aspect to the album.*

The production is excellent and fully professional, and again, David Bryan has been given more room for his piano skills. But some of the slower tracks like 'Diamond Ring' are not that inspiring. In hindsight, we know that this album and its predecessor divided their fanbase, and that would be one of the reasons why they returned to a harder rock sound for their next album, Crush. *It's a nice try but the cynics would say that a bunch of millionaires talking about homelessness is a little patronising.*

*Rating ***

THESE DAYS (SINGLE)

The fourth single release taken from the album of the same name, written by Jon and Sambora. 'These

Days' was issued in the UK on March 9, 1996 and made it to Number 7, spending six weeks in the charts. The song tackles dark themes such as the struggles of everyday life, difficult relationships, homelessness and other social issues.

THESE DAYS TOUR (1995-1996)

To promote the album *These Days* Bon Jovi scheduled a road jaunt that would see them crossing the world from April 26, 1995 to July 19, 1996. They also had *Cross Road*, their 1994 greatest hits collection, to promote. It was the first tour with bassist Hugh McDonald, although Bon Jovi remains, officially, a four piece outfit.

For the second British leg of the tour in July, 1996 support on selected dates came from Gun (Milton Keynes and Glasgow), Skunk Anansie (Manchester and Glasgow) and Joan Osborne (Milton Keynes only.)

Steve Beebee reviewed the Milton Keynes Bowl show on July 6 in *Kerrang!* and enthused: *"In scenes reminiscent of the glory days of 1988, the group open with 'Lay Your Hands On Me', accompanied by blinding pyrotechnics and a gargantuan lighting rig".*

THESE DAYS TOUR

ASIAN DATES (& VENUES)

April 26, 1995 - Andheri Stadium, Bombay (India)
April 28, 1995 - Fottball Stadium, Taipei (Taiwan)
April 30, 1995 - Araneta Stadium Manila (Philippines)
May 2, 1995 - Army Stadium, Bangok (Thailand)
May 5, 1995 - Shahlaam Stadium, Kuala Lumpur (Malaysia)

May 6, 1995 - Ancol Stadium, Jakarta (Indonesia)
May 8, 1995 – Arena, Singapore (Singapore)
May 10, 1995 - Olympic Stadium, Seoul (South Korea)
May 13, 1995 - Fukuoka Dome, Fukuoka (Japan)
May 16, 1995 - Nishinomiya Stadium, Osaka (Japan)
May 19, 1995 - Tokyo Dome, Tokyo (Japan)

EUROPEAN DATES (& VENUES) PART I

May 23, 1995 – Acuatica, Milan (Italy)
May 26, 1995 – Weserstadium, Bremen (Germany)
May 27, 1995 – Weserstadium, Bremen (Germany)
May 28, 1995 - Goffert Park, Nijmegen (Netherlands)
May 30, 1995 - Georg Melches Stadium, Essen (Germany)
June 1, 1995 – Sportsforumpark, Chemnitz (Germany)
June 3, 1995 - Rock am Ring, Nürburgring (Germany)
June 4, 1995 - Rock Im Park, Munich (Germany)
June 6, 1995 – Waldbuhne, Berlin (Germany)
June 7, 1995 – Waldbuhne, Berlin (Germany)
June 10, 1995 - St. Jakob Stadium, Basel (Switzerland)
June 11, 1995 – A1 Ring, Zeltweg (Austria)
June 13, 1995 - Estadio Olímpico de Montjuïc, Barcelona (Spain)
June 15, 1995 - Alvalade Stadium, Lisbon (Portugal)
June 17, 1995 - Werchter Festival Site, Werchter (Belgium)
June 18, 1995 – Airfield, Lahr (Germany)

June 21, 1995 - Cardiff Arms Park, Cardiff (Wales)

June 23, 1995 - Wembley Stadium, London (England)

June 24, 1995 - Wembley Stadium, London (England)

June 25, 1995 - Wembley Stadium, London (England)

June 27, 1995 - Gateshead Stadium, Newcastle (England)

June 28, 1995 - Don Valley Stadium, Sheffield (England)

June 30, 1995 - Hippodrome de Longchamps, Paris (France)*

July 1, 1995 - Hippodrome de Longchamps, Paris (France)*

July 2, 1995 – RDS, Dublin (Ireland)

July 4, 1995 - Naval Arena, Stockholm (Sweden)

July 6, 1995 - Feyernoord Stadium, Rotterdam (Netherlands)

July 9, 1995 - Strahov Stadium, Prague (Czech Republic)

*Opened for the Rolling Stones during their *Voodoo Lounge* tour

NORTH AMERICAN DATES (& VENUES)

July 21, 1995 - Jones Beach, Long Island, NY (USA)

July 22, 1995 - Jones Beach, Long Island, NY (USA)

July 23, 1995 - Jones Beach, Long Island, NY (USA)

July 25, 1995 - Sony Entertainment Center, Camden, NJ (USA)

July 27, 1995 - Starlake Amphitheater, Pittsburgh, PA (USA)

July 30, 1995 - Great Woods, Mansfield, MA (USA)

August 1, 1995 – SPAC, Saratoga, NY (USA)

August 2, 1995 – Forum, Montreal (Canada)

August 4, 1995 - Avalon Music, St. John's (Canada)

August 5, 1995 - Sports Complex, Niagara Falls (Canada)

August 7, 1995 - Citadel Hills, Halifax (Canada)

August 9, 1995 - Merriweather Pavilion, British Columbia (Canada)

August 11, 1995 - Marcus Amphitheater, Milwaukee, WI (USA)

August 12, 1995 - World Music Arena, Chicago, IL (USA)

August 15, 1995 - Target Center, Minneapolis, MN (USA)

August 16, 1995 - Sandstone Center, Kansas City, KS (USA)

August 18, 1995 - Red Rocks Amphitheater, Denver, CO (USA)

August 20, 1995 - Wolf Mountain, Park City, UT (USA)

August 23, 1995 – Riverport, St. Louis, MO (USA)

August 24, 1995 - Deer Creek, Indianapolis, IN (USA)

August 26, 1995 - Pine Knob, Detroit, MI (USA)

August 27, 1995 - River Bend Arena, Cincinnati, OH (USA)

August 29, 1995 - Montage Mountain, Wilkes-Barre, PA (USA)

August 30, 1995 - Blossom Music Center, Cleveland, OH (USA)

September 9, 1995 - Miami Arena, Miami, FL (USA)

September 9, 1995 - Sun Dome, Tampa, FL (USA)

September 12, 1995 - UTC Arena, Charlotte, NC (USA)

September 13, 1995 - UTC Arena, Charlotte, NC (USA)

September 15, 1995 - Walnut Creek, Raleigh, NC (USA)

September 16, 1995 - Lakewood Amphitheater, Atlanta, GA (USA)

September 19, 1995 – Blockbuster, Chattanooga, TN (USA)

September 20, 1995 – Starwood, Nashville, TN (USA)

September 23, 1995 – Woodlands, Houston, TX (USA)

September 24, 1995 – Starplex, Dallas, TX (USA)
September 26, 1995 - Desert Sky, Phoenix, AZ (USA)
September 29, 1995 - Great Western Forum, Los Angeles, CA (USA)
September 30, 1995 - Concord Pavilion, Concord, CA (USA)
October 1, 1995 - Shoreline Amphitheater, Mountain View, CA (USA)
October 3, 1995 - General Motors Place, Vancouver (Canada)
October 4, 1995 – Northlands, Edmonton (Canada)
October 5, 1995 – Arena, Saskatoon (Canada)
October 7, 1995 – Arena, Winnipeg (Canada)

SOUTH AMERICAN DATES (& VENUES)

October 22, 1995 - Sports Palace, Mexico City (Mexico)
October 24, 1995 - Stadium Caracas, Venezuela (Mexico)
October 26, 1995 - Praca de Apoteose, Rio De Janeiro (Brazil)
October 27, 1995 - Pista de Atletismo Ibirabuera, Sao Paulo (Brazil)
October 28, 1995 - Pedreira Paulo Leminski, Curitiba (Brazil)
October 31, 1995 - Estadio Olympico, Quito (Ecuador)
November 2, 1995 - Estadio el Campin, Bogota (Colombia)
November 4, 1995 - River Plate Stadium, Buenos Aires (Argentina)

NEW ZEALAND & AUSTRALIAN DATES (& VENUES)

November 8, 1995 – Supertop, Auckland (New Zealand)
November 10, 1995 - Olympic Park, Melbourne (Australia)

November 11, 1995 - Olympic Park, Melbourne (Australia)
November 12, 1995 - Formula 1 Racetrack, Adelaide (Australia)
November 14, 1995 - Burswood Dome, Perth (Australia)
November 17, 1995 - ANZ Stadium, Brisbane (Australia)
November 18, 1995 - Eastern Creek, Sydney (Australia)

SOUTH AFRICAN DATES (& VENUES)

November 28, 1995 - Green Point Stadium, Cape Town (South Africa)
December 1, 1995 - Athletics Stadium, Johannesburg (South Africa)
December 3, 1995 – Kings Park Rugby Stadium, Durban (South Africa)

JAPANESE DATES (& VENUES)

May 14, 1996 - Fukuoka Dome, Fukuoka (Japan)
May 16, 1996 - Nishinomiya Stadium, Osaka (Japan)
May 18, 1996 - Yokohama Stadium, Yokohama (Japan)
May 19, 1996 - Yokohama Stadium, Yokohama (Japan)
May 20, 1996 - Yokohama Stadium, Yokohama (Japan)

EUROPEAN DATES (& VENUES) PART II

June 1, 1996 - Estadio Vicente Calderón, Madrid (Spain)
June 4, 1996 - El Molinón, Gijon (Spain)
June 5, 1996 - El Sadar, Pamplona (Spain)
June 8, 1996 – Megaland, Landgraaf (Netherlands)

June 9, 1996 - Het Rutbeek,
Enscheede (Netherlands)
June 11, 1996 – Pontaise, Lausanne
(Switzerland)
June 13, 1996 – Steigerwald
Stadium, Erfurth (Germany)
June 15, 1996 – Niedersachsen
Stadium, Hanover (Germany)
June 16, 1996 - Canstatter Wasen,
Stuttgart (Germany)
June 18, 1996 - Student Island,
Budapest (Hungary)
June 20, 1996 - Airport Field,
Vienna (Austria)
June 21, 1996 - Airport Field, Wels
(Austria)
June 23, 1996 - Letzigrund Stadium,
Zurich (Switzerland)
June 28, 1996 - Mungersdorfer
Stadium, Cologne (Germany)
June 29, 1996 - Mungersdorfer
Stadium, Cologne (Germany)
June 30, 1996 – Waldstadium,
Frankfurt (Germany)
July 2, 1996 - Hippodrome
Wellington, Ostend (Belgium)
July 3, 1996 - Le Bercy, Paris
(France)
July 6, 1996 - National Bowl, Milton
Keynes (England)
July 7, 1996 - National Bowl, Milton
Keynes (England)
July 9, 1996 - Maine Road Stadium,
Manchester (England)
July 11, 1996 - Ibrox Stadium,
Glasgow (Scotland)
July 14, 1996 - Volkswagen Plant
Site, Wolfsburg (Germany)
July 16, 1996 – Franken Stadium,
Nuremberg (Germany)
July 19, 1996 - Helsinki Olympic
Stadium, Helsinki (Finland)

THIN LIZZY

Formed in Dublin in '69, Thin Lizzy
are a much-loved band among classic
rock fans. Famed for their memorable
choruses, melodic riffs and the lovea-

ble nature and charisma of the band's
late front man Phil Lynott, Thin Lizzy never quite achieved the success
they deserved in the States, although
they notched up plenty of hits in the
UK. Their most famous singles include 'The Boys Are Back In Town',
'Whiskey In The Jar' and 'Jailbreak'.
A new incarnation of the band tours
the UK regularly.

A young Jon Bon Jovi bought the
album *Jailbreak* when it was initially released in 1976, and Thin Lizzy's
more melodic rock nature would influence him in his drive to become
a chart-topping rock star. Like Bon
Jovi, Thin Lizzy also had a pop-ori-
entated side which was occasionally
at odds with their rock fan base. Bon
Jovi covered 'The Boys Are Back In
Town' for the 1989 compilation *Stairway To Heaven/Highway To Hell,* for
Doc McGhee's Make A Difference
campaign.

Visit *thinlizzyonline.com*

.38 SPECIAL

Bon Jovi supported this Southern
American country-rock band around
the States in September, 1986, just after *Slippery When Wet* had been released. .38 Special has strong connections with the legendary Lynyrd
Skynryd; guitarist, singer and co-
founder Don Barnes was a childhood friend of Skynyrd's late singer
Ronnie Van Zant, who died in an air-
craft accident in 1977, and Ronnie's
younger brother Donnie is the singer

and other co-founder of .38 Special. Another sibling, Johnny Van Zant, is now the singer in Lynyrd Skynyrd. .38 Special are known for their eighties hit singles 'Caught Up In You', 'If I'd Been The One', 'Hold On Loosely', 'Second Chance' and 'Back Where You Belong'. The band is still together and headed by Van Zant and Barnes.

Visit *38special.com*

THIS AIN'T A LOVE SONG

The first single taken from *These Days*. The song was penned by Jon, Richie Sambora and Desmond Child. Issued in the UK on June 10, 1995, it peaked at Number 6. In the States it hit Number 14 in the *Billboard* 200, making it the only hit single from the album in the band's native country. It was also a big success in South America.

THIS LEFT FEELS RIGHT (ALBUM)

A controversial album for Bon Jovi fans, *This Left Feels Right* is a 12 track collection of the band's reworkings of their own greatest hits, hence the album's marketing line 'Greatest Hits...With A Twist'. The initial idea came about when the band were on tour in Japan in early '03: they wanted to make an acoustic live album but

they were not keen on what they had recorded. They made five new acoustic renditions at a studio in Amsterdam in June, on their days off during the *Bounce* tour, but again they were unhappy and those recordings were later scrapped. They consequently brought in Patrick Leonard, who had produced some of the MTV *Unplugged* albums.

This Left Feels Right was recorded at Jon's personal recording facility Sanctuary II Studio in New Jersey, with additional recording completed at Henson Recording Studios in Hollywood. Jon Bon Jovi and Richie Sambora were co-producers, and the whole thing was completed in 23 days, beginning on August 21, 2003 (the *Bounce* tour had finished in the States on August 8). Mixing was done by Obie O' Brien and the mastering completed by George Marino at Sterling Sound in New York City.

Two songs were put aside and not included on the album: the original versions of 'Last Man Standing' and 'Thief Of Hearts' were both included in the box-set *100,00,000 Bon Jovi Fans Can't Be Wrong*. 'Last Man Standing' was actually reworked and used on *Have A Nice Day*.

This Left Feels Right was released in the UK on November 15, 2003 and peaked at Number 4, spending eight weeks in the album charts. It made it to Number 14 on the *Billboard* 200 in America. The album was critically mauled on the grounds that there was really no need to rework songs that had already been hits and were memorable for being mostly good songs in the first place.

Track Listing:
1. 'Wanted Dead Or Alive'
2. 'Livin' On A Prayer'
3. 'Bad Medicine'

4. 'It's My Life'
5. 'Lay Your Hands On Me'
6. 'You Give Love A Bad Name'
7. 'Bed Of Roses'
8. 'Everyday'
9. 'Born To Be My Baby'
10. 'Keep The Faith'
11. 'I'll Be There For You'
12. 'Always'

13. 'The Distance' *(Live – Record-ed on January 19, 2003 in Yokohama, Japan) (Bonus track on the British, European and Japanese releases)*

14. 'Joey' *(Live – Recorded on January 19, 2003 in Yokohama, Japan) (Bonus track on the British, European and Japanese releases)*

15. 'Have A Little Faith In Me' *(Live - Recorded on January 19, 2003 in Yokohama, Japan) (Bonus track on the Japanese release)*

Author's Review:

This Left Feels Right *is an embar-rassing and frankly unmemorable album. What is the point? The worst song is 'Livin' On A Prayer', which is just dreadful, although 'Wanted Dead Or Alive' still has its famous western vibe. 'You Give Love A Bad Name' is annoyingly cheesy and Jon is almost whispering rather than singing. The whole concept just reeks of a com-mercially motivated endeavour. On this album they have completely ru-ined the main reason why they are so popular - that they know how to make a good melodic rock song for the masses. There are no trademark electric riffs, cool keyboard intros or soaring choruses on any of these songs. It was a silly idea and prob-ably the lowest point in their career*

from a creative viewpoint. The title is pretty naff too. Avoid.

Rating *

THIS LEFT FEELS RIGHT (DVD)

Directed by David Mallet and Brian Lockwood and released on DVD in 2004, *This Left Feels Right* is the third full concert release from Bon Jovi following on from *Live In London* (1995) and *The Crush Tour* (2001). It was recorded on November 14 and 15, 2003 at the Borgata Hotel Casino and Spa in Atlantic City, New Jersey. The concert features the re-recorded versions of the band's greatest hits from the album of the same name. Bonus material includes a 30 minute behind the scenes documentary. The limited edition DVD included six songs from the band's huge concert in Hyde Park, London, on June 23, 2003.

Track Listing:
1. 'Love For Sale'
2. 'You Give Love A Bad Name'
3. 'Wanted Dead Or Alive'
4. 'Livin' On A Prayer'
5. 'It's My Life'

6. 'Misunderstood'
7. 'Lay Your Hands On Me'
8. 'Someday I'll Be Saturday Night'
9. 'Last Man Standing'
10. 'Sylvia's Mother'
11. 'Everyday'
12. 'Bad Medicine'
13. 'Bed Of Roses'
14. 'Born To Be My Baby'
15. 'Keep The Faith'
16. 'Joey'
17. 'Thief Of Hearts'
18. 'I'll Be There For You'
19. 'Always'
20. 'Blood On Blood'

TILL WE AIN'T STRANGERS ANYMORE

Written by Jon, Richie Sambora and the country singer-songwriter Brett James, 'Till We Ain't Strangers Anymore' is collaboration with country pop singer LeAnne Rimes. The song was only released in America as a single and peaked at Number 123 in the *Billboard* Hot 100 and Number 47 in the *Billboard* Hot Country Songs.

TOKYO ROAD: BEST OF BON JOVI

A greatest hits set exclusive to Japan. Also known as *Bon Jovi Rocks*, it was released on March 28, 2001, and has sold in excess of 400,000 copies.

Track Listing:
1. 'One Wild Night 2001'
2. 'Bad Medicine'
3. 'Livin' On A Prayer'
4. 'You Give Love A Bad Name'
5. 'Keep The Faith'
6. 'It's My Life'
7. 'Blood On Blood'
8. 'Something For The Pain'
9. 'Born To Be My Baby'
10. 'Tokyo Road'
11. 'Hey God'
12. 'Just Older'

13. 'I'll Sleep When I'm Dead'
14. 'Runaway'
15. 'Wild In The Streets'
16. 'Next 100 Years'
17. 'Tokyo Road' *(Bonus track on selected copies - live version)*
18. 'Not Fade Away' *(Bonus track on selected copies – recorded live during Jon Bon Jovi's solo tour)*
19. 'Next 100 Years' *(Bonus track on selected copies - live version)*
20. 'Father Time' *(Bonus track on selected copies – recorded live during one of Richie Sambora's solo tours)*

TOMMY & GINA

A fictional couple who first appeared in 'Livin' On A Prayer'. They also appeared in '99 In The Shade' on *New Jersey* and 'It's My Life' on *Crush*. Their characters were inspired by people Jon went to high school with. It's the typical working class story of a high school sports stud meeting a good looking girl, getting her pregnant and having to find a job to support his new family and not following his dream.

Jon told *Classic Rock*'s Malcolm Dome:

"...they could've been me, if I hadn't learned to play guitar. Tommy and Gina aren't two specific people – they represent a lifestyle".

TOPLOADER

An English five piece alternative rock band, formed in 1997. They are famous for their cover of 'Dancing In The Moonlight,' originally sung by King Harvest.

Toploader supported Bon Jovi during the first (30 day) European leg of the mammoth *Crush* tour in 2000. In the British Isles they played shows in Stoke-On-Trent, Newcastle and Dublin, and on August 19/20 they performed at the newly rebuilt Wembley Stadium, the first British band to play there.

TORRES, TICO

Nicknamed "The Hitman", Tico Torres was born Hector Samuel Juan Torres on October 7, 1953 in New York. He was brought up Colonia, New Jersey, and attended John F. Kennedy Memorial High School. He met Alec John Such in the band Phantom's Opera, which also featured Dean Fasano of Message and

Prophet. As a longstanding friend, Such recommended Torres to Jon in mid-1983 just as Jon was putting a band together after getting his deal with PolyGram (Such and keyboardist David Bryan had already joined the fold). The timing was perfect, as Torres had just completed a tour with Franke and The Knockouts, and had been struggling to support his wife and child with the modest income he had been receiving from sporadic session work and occasional bouts of touring.

While Jon and Sambora inevitably take much of the limelight, Torres, McDonald and Bryan are happy to provide a tight and professional rhythm section. Tico has also provided the occasional backing vocals, mostly on the band's earlier work and co-wrote the track 'Sweet Dreams' with Jon, Sambora and Bill Gradowski. In 1988, it was alleged by an American gossip magazine that Jon was not happy with Torres and Such's

weight gain and ordered them both to undergo liposuction. This has been denied by the band.

During his career Torres has worked on stage and in the studio with a variety of artists, including Lou Christie, Pat Benatar, Chuck Berry, Cher, Alice Cooper and Stevie Nicks. He is credited as drummer on the 1991 CD release *Timespace - The Best of Stevie Nicks*. In 1991, he joined David Bryan as the pair showed their support for Richie Sambora's superlative debut solo album *Stranger In This Town*: Torres played drums on the album and in Sambora's touring band during their short tour of America.

Outside Bon Jovi, Torres, like Rolling Stones rhythm guitarist Ronnie Wood, is a painter. His art, which he has exhibited around the States and abroad since 1994, can be viewed at *walnutst.com*. By way of contrast owns *Rock Star Babies,* selling designer clothing and other accessories

for babies. This can be found at *rockstarbaby.com*.

Torres divorced his first wife prior to the formation of Bon Jovi. He married his second wife, the Czech-born model Eva Herzigova, in Sea Bright, New Jersey in 1996, but divorced followed just a couple of years later. Third time lucky? Torres married Maria Alejandra in September, 2001 and on January 9, 2004 she gave birth to their son, Hector Alexander.

Visit *tico-torres.com*

TRANSITION

While attending Herbert Hoover Junior High School in NJ, David Bryan played keyboards in this high school band along with cello player Steve Sileo. A popular outfit, they played at Herbert Hoover's teen dances.

TWENTY YEARS WITH AIDS

To raise awareness of AIDS, Bon Jovi took part in the 2001 benefit concert Twenty Years With Aids, which was organised by Elton John. Other performers included Matchbox Twenty, Sting, Rufus Wainwright, LeAnne Rimes, Craig David, Alicia Keys and Pete Yorn. The concert

lasted approximately three hours and raised $1 million.

Bon Jovi played John Lennon's 'Imagine' and two of their own songs, 'Livin' On A Prayer' and 'Wanted Dead Or Alive'. They also accompanied Elton John on two of his songs, 'Levon' and 'The Bitch Is Back'.

TWIN TOWERS RELIEF BENEFIT

A charity concert held at The Stone Pony in Asbury Park, New Jersey on September 28, 2001. Jon played an unexpected acoustic set, and the proceeds from the event were donated to the victims and the victims' families of the 9/11 terrorist attacks.

U

U-571

Released in the States in April of 2000, *U-571* was a commercially successful and critically acclaimed World War II submarine drama directed by Jonathan Mostow. The film stars Matthew McConaughey, Bill Paxton, Harvey Keitel and Jon Bon Jovi as Chief Engineer Lt. Pete Emmett. Filming was done mostly in Malta and Rome. *U-571* won an Os-

car for 'Best Sound Editing' and was also nominated for 'Best Sound'.

UK MUSIC HALL OF FAME

An awards ceremony that began in 2004 as a British equivalent of the USA's Rock and Roll Hall of Fame. Nominees and inductees can be of any nationality, with the artists being chosen by a team of 60 journalists and music business experts. Bon Jovi were inducted into the UK Music Hall of Fame in 2006 by Dave Stewart. At the ceremony the band performed the triumvirate of 'Livin' On A Prayer', 'Wanted Dead Or Alive' and 'It's My Life'. Fellow inductees on the evening included Led Zeppelin, Rod Stewart, James Brown, Brian Wilson, Dusty Springfield and Prince.

UNDISCOVERED SOUL

A lull in Bon Jovi's career enabled Richie Sambora to work on his second solo album, which was unleashed in 1998 through Mercury. Produced by the esteemed American producer and musician Don Was (bass, Wurlitzer and handclaps) and arranged by Sambora, *Undiscovered Soul* was recorded at Ocean Way Recording, The Record Plant, The Voodoo Lounge and Record One studios. As with his first album, Sambora managed to entice a number of esteemed musicians to collaborate with him, notably the revered Billy Preston (Hammond B-3 organ, background vocals).

Other personnel included Mark Goldenberg (guitar and handclaps), Chuck Leavell (piano and electric piano), Greg Phillinganes (piano and background vocals), David Paitch (electric piano and synthesizer), Rami Jaffee (Hammond B3 organ, accordion and hand claps), Robbie Buchanan (synthesizer), Jamie Muhoberac (synthesizer programming), Pino Paladino (fretless bass), Kenny Aronoff (drums, percussion and handclaps), Paulinho da Costa (percussion), James "Hutch" Hutchinson (background vocals, bass and handclaps), Myrna Smith, Portia Griffin, Sweet Pea Atkinson, Harry Bowens, Hook (background vocals) and Richie Supa (acoustic duet on 'Harlem Rain').

On the songwriting side, Sambora collaborated with some old pals, notably Richie Supa on 'Made In America', 'Hard Times Come Easy', 'All That Really Matters', 'In It For Love', 'Harlem Rain' and 'Undiscovered Soul'. Bon Jovi keyboardist David Bryan even chipped in, co-writing the following songs with Sambora and Supa: 'Fallen From Graceland', 'If God Was A Woman' and 'Downside Of Love'. 'You're Not Alone' was written with his old pal Tommy Marolda as was 'Chained' (also with guitarist Ernie White), and 'Who I Am' was written with Marti Frederiksen, who is known for his collaborations with Aerosmith and Mötley Crüe.

Sambora told journalist Dave Reynolds at *Hard Roxx* magazine:

"Sure, the writing process involved my own life experiences and memories to an extent, although 'Harlem Rain' takes a more journalistic outlook. I think I was looking to find my-

self too, hence the title. I enjoyed the search and I felt privileged to work with the people that became involved in the project".

Undiscovered Soul was released in the States on March 3 and in the UK on March 14, 1998. Reaching Number 24 in the UK and spending just two weeks in the charts, it was not a major commercial success, although it received good reviews. A special edition version of the album was issued with 'We All Sleep Alone' as a bonus track. It produced two singles: 'Hard Times Come Easy' was released on March 7 in the UK and just made it into the UK Top 40 at Number 37, and 'In It For Love' was released as a single on August 1 in the UK, reaching number 58.

Track Listing:

1. 'Made In America'
2. 'Hard Times Come Easy'
3. 'Fallen From Graceland'
4. 'If God Was A Woman'
5. 'All That Really Matters'
6. 'You're Not Alone'
7. 'In It For Love'
8. 'Chained'
9. 'Harlem Rain'
10. 'Who I Am'
11. 'Downside Of Love'
12. 'Undiscovered Soul'
13. 'We All Sleep Alone' *(Bonus track on the Special Edition)*

Author's Review:

Undiscovered Soul *is a mixed bag with less consistency than* Stranger In This Town *and with varying influences, but there's still a hell of a lot of passion here. What both albums have in common is the introspective nature of the lyrics and the music; they also show Sambora's eagerness to illus-*

trate his musical influences. It's not all about rock. Maybe this is Sambora having a go at emulating New Jersey hero Bruce Springsteen? Undiscovered Soul *is not an upbeat album; in fact many of the songs are acoustic based, laidback and soulful. You can't really argue against Sambora's vocals or guitar playing, which are first rate.*

The first track 'Made In America' is a nifty anthem that's a lot of fun. 'Hard Times Come By' is notable for the use of keys and a great melody based around acoustic and electric guitars; Sambora is vocally at his best here. 'Fallen From Graceland' is a slow number that is just a bit too slow. 'If God Was A Woman' is a blues tinged mid-tempo track with some great harmonica play-

ing. 'All That Really Matters' slows things down somewhat; as these sorts of ballads go, it's okay, just a bit too slushy although the short guitar solo is worth hearing. 'You're Not Alone' picks up speed and is a well-performed song while 'In It For Love' is another unwanted slow acoustic track, although Sambora's voice is impressive. 'Chained' is a catchy track with a bit of soul and 'Harlem Rain' is actually a very tender and moving song. 'Who I Am' begins with some heavier thumping that lasts literally seconds; it has one of those slows down-speeds up melodies. The guitar work is excellent. 'Downside Of Love' is a Southern American type ballad with soulful backing vocals that give it a gospel feel. The final track is 'Undiscovered Soul' which is *a mid-tempo track that makes an instant impression.*

Undiscovered Soul *is good in parts but the problem is there are too many ballads and not nearly enough memorable guitars. There's no question about it, the musicianship is superlative and Sambora proves again that he has plenty to offer, but the album lacks excitement.*

Rating ***½

UNDISCOVERED SOUL TOUR (1998)

In the summer of 1998 Richie Sambora committed himself to a tour of Europe, UK, Australia and Japan to promote his second solo album *Undiscovered Soul*. The UK dates included two shows in London at the Shepherds Bush Empire (July 22 and 23) and one at the Manchester Apollo (July 24).

His solo band consisted of guitarist Richie Supa, drummer Ron Wikso, bassist Kasim Sulton and keyboardist Tommy Mandel. Percussionist Everett Bradley joined the band for the Japanese leg of the tour, while Gioia Bruno performed with them in Australia and Crystal Taliefero in Europe and the UK.

Rob Evans reviewed the Manchester Apollo show in the magazine *Hard Roxx*:

"...I can safely say that without Sambora Bon Jovi would not be the band they are today, as he is the ultimate professional whether it's his stunning vocals or breathtaking guitar playing, he never ceases to entertain".

VAN HALEN

VAMPIRES: LOS MUERTOS

A loose sequel to the disastrous 1998 film *John Carpenter's Vampires*. Written and directed by Tommy Lee Wallace and produced by Mr. Carpenter, *Vampires: Los Muertos* stars Jon Bon Jovi as a vampire slayer and Cristián de la Fuente as a priest doing battle against the undead in Mexico. The film also stars Natasha Gregson Wagner, Arly Jover and Diego Luna; it was released in Britain on VHS in November, 2002 and had gone straight to cable TV in the States months before.

Jon told *Classic Rock* in February, 2001, before filming commenced:

"I hope it's a much better movie than the first one...It's a very intelligent script, Carpenter's producing and one of his prodigies is directing".

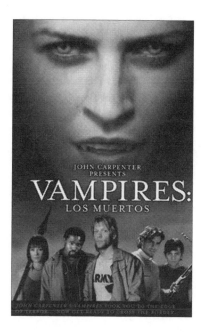

One of America's most successful hard rock bands, Van Halen was formed in 1974 in Pasadena, California by brothers Eddie (guitarist) and Alex (drummer) Van Halen, with singer David Lee Roth and bassist Michael Anthony. With Roth they released six albums, including the mammoth hit *1984*. Roth was replaced by Sammy Hagar in 1985, and the first album they released together was 1986's *5150*. After four studio albums, Hagar was replaced by Mitch Malloy who was in turn replaced by ex-Extreme singer Gary Cherone, with whom the band they released the critically mauled and commercially unsuccessful *Van Halen III*. A reunion tour with Hagar took place during 2004, but the band temporally folded until a tour with Roth (with Wolfgang Van Halen, Eddie's son, replacing Anthony on bass) which kicked off in 2007.

Van Halen, who were actually on the road themselves to promote *Balance*, the last studio album featuring Sammy Hagar, supported Bon Jovi on two European dates during the *These Days* tour.

Visit *van-halen.com*

VAN VELZEN, ROEL

Popularly known in his native Netherlands as VanVelzen, Roel is a singer-songwriter-pianist. He has released a handful of singles, cover versions of songs that were not originally hits in the Netherlands. He supported Bon Jovi on June 13, 2008 at the Amsterdam Arena.

Visit *vanvelzenmusic.com*

VAN ZANDT, STEVE

Born in Boston, Steve Van Zandt grew up in New Jersey and soaked up the local sounds of the times, becoming a well-known figure in the Jersey Shore scene. He was a member of Bruce Springsteen's E-Street Band, playing guitar and mandolin, and was an integral collaborator on the albums *Darkness On The Edge Of Town*, *The River* and *Born In The U.S.A.* The Boss was best man at his wedding. Steve was also a founding member of Southside Johnny and The Asbury Jukes, co-writing 'I Don't Wanna Go Home' and co-producing 1978's *Hearts Of Stone* for the band. As a solo artist, under the name Lit-

tle Steven, his debut solo album was 1982's *Men Without Women,* and his latest was 1999's *Born Again Savage*, followed by a *Greatest Hits* compilation. In addition to his work as a musician, Van Zandt is also a successful actor and radio DJ - he has a radio show in New York called *Little Steve's Underground Garage*, on which Jon and Richie Sambora have both appeared.

Steve was an early inspiration to Jon Bon Jovi, and they remain good friends to this day.

Visit *littlesteven.com*

VERY SPECIAL CHRISTMAS 2, A

Released in 1992 by A&M Records, this 19 track compilation album, put together in aid of the Special Olympics, features Bon Jovi's cover version of 'Please Come Home For Christmas'.

VIEW FROM THE TOP

A 2003 romantic comedy, starring Christina Applegate, about a woman whose ambition is to become a flight attendant. Bon Jovi's classic eighties rocker 'Livin' On A Prayer' is part of the soundtrack.

X

X-FACTOR, THE

A British TV show akin to *American Idol*. The basic premise of the show is that wannabe pop stars audition in front of a panel of judges (usually former pop stars and producers) in the hope of winning a million pound contract with the record label of the show's creator Simon Cowell.

In the closing weeks of the 2008 series, the Spanish singer Ruth Lorenzo sang a powerhouse version of the Bon Jovi ballad 'Always' but it wasn't quite good enough to prevent her being voted out by the public.

Y

YES

Formed in 1968 in London, progressive rock band Yes have had a long and complicated history. Founding members Jon Anderson and Chris Squire still run the band, which also features Steve Howe and Alan White. Lineup changes over the years have seen many band members come and go, including Bill Bruford, Tony Kaye, Peter Banks, Patrick Moraz, Trevor Rabin, Trevor Horn, Geoff Downes, Billy Sherwood, Igor Khoroshev and Rick Wakeman. Their best-known albums include *Fragile* and *Close To The Edge* from the early seventies,

and *90125* from *1983*. A 2008 40th Anniversary tour, entitled *Close To The Edge And Back,* was cancelled due to concerns for Anderson's health.

Classically trained keyboardist David Bryan became entranced with popular music as a teenager after watching a Yes gig, a formative moment in his career.

Visit *yesworld.com*

YOU GIVE LOVE A BAD NAME

The first single release from Bon Jovi's classic *Slippery When Wet* album. Issued in the UK on August 9, 1986, it only peaked at Number 14, although it did spend 10 weeks in the singles chart. On the other hand, it hit the top spot in the American *Billboard* Hot 100 on November 29, giving Bon Jovi their first Number 1 single. The song was written with Desmond Child, and is said to have been inspired by Jon's brief relationship with actress Diane Lane. The promotional music video was filmed at Mayo Civic Center in Rochester, Minnesota. The single went on to sell well over one million copies.

(YOU WANT TO) MAKE A MEMORY

This, the first single taken from *Lost Highway*, was issued in the UK on June 25, 2007 but only peaked at Number 33, the band's lowest singles position since 'Living In Sin' in 1989. The B-side on the UK version was 'Put The Boy Back In Cowboy.' Two versions of the song were released: a country version was issued in America, but elsewhere a pop version was released. The song made it to Number 27 in the American *Billboard* Hot 100, and peaked at Number 35 in the *Billboard* Hot Country Songs.

YOUNG, JAMES

From Chicago, James Young is a member of the melodic rock band Styx. He wrote their popular tracks

'Miss America' and 'Snowblind', and has released the solo albums *City Slicker, Out On A Day Pass* and *Raised By Wolves*. In 1998, along with former Bon Jovi bassist Alec John Such, Young managed the Chicago band 7th Heaven.

YOUNG GUNS II

Directed by Geoff Murphy, *Young Guns II* is a sequel to the hit 1988 comedy western *Young Guns*. As well as composing the soundtrack, Jon Bon Jovi made his debut onscreen appearance as actor in a brief (uncredited) cameo. The acting bug would not be long in resurfacing.

The film essentially follows the life of the outlaw Billy The Kid, played by Emilio Estevez, and stars William Peterson, Christian Slater, Kiefer Sutherland, James Coburn and Viggo Mortensen. Its initial release received mixed reviews and modest success at the box office.

Z

ZZ TOP

A Texas based blues rock trio, consisting of bearded frontmen Billy Gibbons and Dusty Hill and drummer Frank Beard, who is, ironically, the one without a beard. They achieved a period of enormous commercial success in the eighties with the multi-platinum album *Eliminator*. Their videos for 'Gimme All Your Lovin'', 'Sharp Dressed Man' and 'Legs' gave the band huge exposure on MTV. They were inducted into the Rock and Roll Hall of Fame in 2005. Their fourteenth album, *Mescalero*, was released in 2003 and in 2008 they signed a deal with uber-producer Rick Rubin with plans for their fifteenth opus. Their debut, *ZZ Top's First Album*, was released in 1971.

Bon Jovi supported ZZ Top at Madison Square Garden in New York City in 1984. Manager Doc McGhee was in the audience and he was so impressed he took the band under his wing and signed them to his management company.

Both bands played at the Monsters Of Rock festival at Donington, England, on August 17, 1985. ZZ Top headlined, with Marillion, Bon Jovi, Metallica, Ratt and Magnum running behind. Bon Jovi's set list was:

1. 'Tokyo Road'
2. 'Breakout'
3. 'Only Lonely'
4. 'Runaway'
5. 'In And Out Of Love'
6. 'I Don't Wanna Go Home'
7. 'Get Ready'

As quoted in *Metal Hammer* (No. 20, Vol. 3) David Bryan reflects:

"We were BRIGHT green, and ZZ Top were the greatest. We walked out in front of 22,000 people, Richie started his guitar and the amp blew. The audience started chanting ' Zee Zee Top, Zee Zee Top, ZEE ZEE TOP.' It probably only last 30 seconds but it felt like 15 years. The amp was replaced and we came back to kill 'em...we were the underdogs but we came back and gave 'em hell".

Visit *zztop.com*

APPENDIX I

BACKSTAGE AREA

Performers, musicians and writers were invited 'backstage' to discuss their experiences of meeting the band...

Steve Blaze
(Lillian Axe)

"I met Jon once when Lillian Axe played Houston right when his first album came out. I hung out with the first bassist [Alec John Such] at a guitar show in Florida when I was there as a featured artist... I highly respect the band and what they have accomplished. They have mastered the art of writing songs that appeal to a large cross section of the public. Very talented group. Their music is honest and passionate."

Andreas Carlsson
(Songwriter)

"I saw Bon Jovi in the '80s opening for KISS in Sweden; I was always a big fan. Slippery When Wet *is probably one of the best rock albums ever made, and Jon is the ultimate front man. Watching him closely onstage is a treat."*

Holly Knight
(Musician/Songwriter)

"I saw Bon Jovi live at Irvine [California.] I flew there in a helicopter with Don Johnson, who was the 'Man Of The Moment' on Miami Vice*. I remember it was kind of surrealistic for me; I brought Don backstage*

to meet Jon and there I was, sandwiched in-between the two of them, wearing this tight long black dress, and they're both commenting on how they loved working with me! And all I could think is: this [song] writing gig is cool! Who would've thought Beethoven could lead to moments like this. Pretty crazy..."

Mónica Castedo-López
(Fireworks Melodic
Rock Magazine)

"I started listening to rock music when I was about 12; and one of the first bands that caught my eye and my ear due to the ample mass media coverage was Bon Jovi. Their music was fresh, powerful, rocking and moving. I would take the big cassette player that my granddad bought me to the park and listen to their tapes over and over again with some friends. This was the time of the Slippery When Wet *album. Years went by and when I was 22, in 1996, they announced a gig in el Molinón football stadium in Gijón, Spain. By then I was a bit more affluent and I could afford the trip; I drove four odd hours with some friends and my boyfriend at the time to see the gig. This was one of the first big shows I'd ever been to and the expectations were high even though I wasn't sure what to expect. When I walked in I remember I was shocked by the high proportion of women – or girls, rather - compared to men. Girls were chanting the band's name, cheering hysterically and almost fainted when the band turned up onstage. I had only read about this sort of behaviour in magazines or seen it on TV, but my naive brain never wanted to accept it as reality that women could behave*

in such manner. It's been many years since that show and my memory is not the greatest of them all, but this is one of the two main facts that I remember of that June 4, gig. The other was my amazement at seeing the band immaculately perform anthems such as 'Keep The Faith,' 'You Give Love A Bad Name' and 'Bad Medicine.' I was awed by the charisma and self-confidence of each member, particularly of Richie Sambora and Jon. How could just five guys draw the attention of such a big crowd and keep it going for the two hours that the show lasted? That was genius... Great musicians, fantastic performance and an awesome show. May they continue for many more years."

Jason McMaster
(Dangerous Toys)

"The day that we shot the back cover of the first Dangerous Toys release (somewhere around November/December, 1988) Bon Jovi - with a new band called Skid Row - were playing in Austin, Texas where I live. The photographer was the infamous Mark Weiss, who is also from New Jersey where Jovi as well as Skid Row are from; they just happened to all be friends. Mark got all of us into the show, backstage and the like...We did photos with Skid Row, and Jon Bon Jovi was kind enough to take a quick candid shot with yours truly and the only known print of that was in an issue of Metal Edge *magazine (USA) during that summer of 1989. He was very nice, but I gotta say, even though I am not a fan of his music; he is a great songwriter and all his band mates were super cool to us..."*

Kas Mercer
(Mercenary PR)

"Once, at the Milton Keynes Bowl, they had a bar on stage and the label ran a competition so fans could go behind the bar and serve the band drinks as they played. I had to look after the comp winners, so I was on stage for over half the set. Another one was when they busked in Covent Garden; we weren't allowed to let anyone know until an hour before, but it was still mobbed. It was funny watching the reactions of people just passing by when they realised it really WAS Bon Jovi."

Jason Ritchie
(Get Ready To Rock.com)

"I saw them in 1987 at the Victoria Hall, Hanley on the Slippery When Wet *tour (hands up who remembers the t-shirts with the scantily clad lady on them?) and it was a good turnout. Again, the band were on fire and they were certainly more confident on stage, with Jon Bon Jovi and Richie Sambora both running all over the stage and working the crowd. 'Livin' On A Prayer' brought the house down and the good thing about a Bon Jovi gig back then was that they attracted a healthy quota of females. This was the last hall-sized tour of the UK as next time they came back they were into the arenas. I am always glad I saw them in a smaller venue like the Victoria Hall as the band really thrived off the closeness of the audience and their response to the music."*

Marc Storace
(Krokus)

"I once shook hands and exchanged greetings with Jon Bon Jo-

vi at the celebrity launching party for the then brand new US magazine SPIN, in New York City, somewhere back in the mid-eighties. It was a meet and greet event for the US Press, where I also remember meeting the late great John Entwistle, bass player of The Who. Bon Jovi had the hit single 'Runaway' in the charts shortly before that."

Mike Tramp
(White Lion)

"I have been lucky enough to have been on stage with Jon and the band twice. Once was on my birthday in 1989, when Bon Jovi played in Hawaii. Jon invited me up to sing with him and we performed Thin Lizzy's 'The Boys Are Back In Town.' The second time was in San Diego and I joined him again for Free's 'All Right Now.'"

Joe Lynn Turner
(ex-Deep Purple & Rainbow)

"Yeah, they are a great rock band and still going strong. It was very different in our hair band days. It was less corporate, more gritty rock and roll as far as the scene goes. Desmond Child and I even wrote a song with him [called] 'Rage Of Angels' which was vowed not to be released and that's too bad. Desmond did take the middle section and put it into... [an] Aerosmith song so he obviously used it later; it was also very reminiscent of 'Livin' On A Prayer' but that is only natural and it happens when people collaborate."

Jonathan Valen
(ex-Legs Diamond)

"When I was on the Andy Taylor tour we were playing at the NHK Hall in Tokyo, Japan. After our show, we decided to go to a club called the Lexington Queen in Roppongi; our guitar player, Paul Hansen, brought an amp and a guitar and was playing his mayhem to everyone in the club. And much to my surprise there was Tico Torres, sitting in the back of the club with a few girls having a drink. We spent the whole night rallying with him...lots of fun!"

Jeb Wright
(ClassicRockRevisited.com)

"I was pumped to see the Scorpions on the **Love At First Sting** tour in Wichita, Kansas. After all, they are one of my favourite bands. Opening up for the Scorps were a band I had never heard of...Bon Jovi. I didn't even know what a Bon Jovi was and must admit that I was more interested in drinking beer and looking at girls then seeing the opening act. When the lights went down, however, a few facts became clear. First off, the guitar player was a bad ass. He could flat out jam. The other thing that caught my eye was the fact that the lead singer had big eighties hair and looked a lot better than most of the girls I had been scoping out. The music was more pop metal than I was used to but at the end of each song every girl in the audience screamed like they were watching The Beatles. I turned and looked to my friend and said: 'Dude, hard rock is changing.' Boy was I right. Bon Jovi went on to be one of the biggest bands of all time. The only song I recognized when they played that night was 'Runaway.' But I could tell I was witnessing the start of something special."

APPENDIX II

BON JOVI
DISCOGRAPHY

BON JOVI:
STUDIO ALBUMS

BON JOVI
(Mercury, 1984)

Track Listing:
Runaway/Roulette/She Don't Know
Me/Shot Through The Heart/Love
Lies/Breakout/Burning For Love/
Come Back/Get Ready

7800° FAHRENHEIT
(Mercury, 1985)

Track Listing:
In And Out Of Love/The Price
Of Love/Only Lonely/King Of
The Mountain/Silent Night/Tokyo

Road/The Hardest Part Is The Night/
Always Run To You/(I Don't Wanna
Fall) To The Fire/Secret Dreams/In
And Out Of Love*

*Live CD video on the remastered
version*

SLIPPERY WHEN WET
(Mercury, 1986)
Track Listing:
Let It Rock/ You Give Love A Bad
Name/Livin' On A Prayer/Social
Disease/Wanted Dead Or Alive/
Raise Your Hands/Without Love/I'd
Die For You/Never Say Goodbye/
Wild In The Streets/Wanted Dead
Or Alive*

**Live CD video on the remastered
version*

NEW JERSEY
(Mercury, 1988)
Track Listing:
Lay Your Hands On Me/Bad
Medicine/Born To Be My Baby/
Living In Sin/Blood On Blood/
Homebound Train/Wild Is The
Wind/Ride Cowboy Ride/Stick To
Your Guns/I'll Be There For You/99
In The Shade/Love For Sale/Lay
Your Hands On Me*

**Live CD video on the remastered
version*

KEEP THE FAITH
(Mercury, 1992)

Track Listing:
I Believe/Keep The Faith/I'll Sleep
When I'm Dead/In These Arms/Bed
Of Roses/If I Was Your Mother/Dry
County/Woman In Love/Fear/I Want
You/Blame It On The Love Of Rock
& Roll/Little Bit Of Soul/Keep The
Faith*

**Live CD video on the remastered
version*

THESE DAYS
(Mercury, 1995)

Track Listing:
Hey God/Something For The Pain/
This Ain't A Love Song/These Days/
Lie To Me/Damned/My Guitar Lies
Bleeding In My Arms/(It's Hard)
Letting You Go/Hearts Breaking
Even/Something To Believe In/If
That's What It Takes/Diamond
Ring/All I Want Is Everything/Bitter
Wine

CRUSH
(Island, 2000)

Track Listing:
It's My Life/Say It Isn't So/Thank
You For Loving Me/Two Story
Town/Next 100 Years/Just Older/
Mystery Train/Save The World/
Captain Crash & The Beauty Queen
From Mars/She's A Mystery/I Got
The Girl/One Wild Night/I Could
Make A Living Out Of Lovin' You*/
It's My Life+/Say It Isn't So

*Demo bonus track
+ Remix bonus track

BOUNCE
(Island, 2002)

Track Listing:
Undivided/Everyday/The Distance/
Joey/Misunderstood/All About
Lovin' You/Hook Me Up/Right Side
Of Wrong/Love Me Back To Life/
You Had Me From Hello/Bounce/
Open All Night

*(NB: This release includes
EXCLUSIVE BONUS VIDEO
FOOTAGE)*

HAVE A NICE DAY
(Island, 2005)

Track Listing:
Have A Nice Day/I Want To Be
Loved/Welcome To Wherever
You Are/Who Says You Can't Go
Home/Last Man Standing/Bells Of
Freedom/Wildflower/Last Cigarette/
I Am/Complicated/Novocaine/
Story Of My Life/Dirty Little
Secret*/Unbreakable*

*Bonus tracks

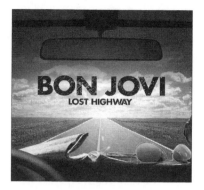

LOST HIGHWAY
(Mercury Nashville, 2007)

Track Listing:
Lost Highway/Summertime/(You
Want To) Make A Memory/Whole
Lot Of Leavin'/We Got It Going On/
Any Other Day/
Seat Next To You/Everybody's
Broken/Till We Ain't Strangers
Anymore *(featuring LeAnn Rimes)*/
The Last Night/One Step Closer/I
Love This Town/Lonely

BON JOVI:
COMPILATIONS

CROSS ROAD: THE GREATEST HITS
(Mercury, 1994)

Track Listing:
Livin' On A Prayer/Keep The Faith/
Someday I'll Be Saturday Night/
Always/Wanted Dead Or Alive/Lay
Your Hands On Me/You Give Love
A Bad Name/Bed Of Roses/Blaze
Of Glory/In These Arms/ Bad

Medicine/I'll Be There For You/In
And Out Of Love/Runaway/Never
Say Goodbye

THIS LEFT FEELS RIGHT
(Island, 2003)

Track Listing:
Wanted Dead Or Alive/Livin' On A
Prayer/Bad Medicine/It's My Life/
Lay Your Hands On Me/You Give
Love A Bad Name/Bed Of Roses/
Everyday/Born To Be My Baby/
Keep The Faith/I'll Be There For
You/Always/The Distance*/Joey*

*Bonus live tracks

**100,000,000 BON JOVI FANS
CAN'T BE WRONG**
(Island, 2004)

Track listing:

(Disc 1)
Why Aren't You Dead?/The Radio
Saved My Life Tonight/Taking It
Back/Someday I'll Be Saturday
Night*/Miss Fourth Of July/Open
All Night/These Arms Are Open All
Night/I Get A Rush/Someday Just
Might Be Tonight/Thief Of Hearts/
Last Man Standing/I Just Want to Be
Your Man
*Demo

(Disc 2) Garageland/Starting All
Over Again/Maybe Someday/Last
Chance Train/The Fire Inside/Every
Beat Of My Heart/Rich Man Living

In A Poor Man's House/The One
That Got Away/You Can Sleep
While I Dream/Outlaws Of Love/
Good Guys Don't Always Wear
White/We Rule The Night

(Disc 3)
Edge Of A Broken Heart/Sympathy/
Only In My Dreams*/Shut Up And
Kiss Me/Crazy Love/Lonely At The
Top/Ordinary People/Flesh And
Bone/Satellite/If I Can't Have Your
Love+/Real Life/Memphis Lives In
Me*/Too Much Of A Good Thing
* *Feat. Tico Torres on vocals*
+ *Feat. Richie Sambora on vocals*
* *Feat. David Bryan on vocals from
the musical* Memphis

(Disc 4)
Love Ain't Nothing But A Four
Letter Word/Love Ain't Nothing But
A Four Letter Word*/River Runs
Dry/Always*/Kidnap An Angel/
Breathe/Out Of Bounds/Letter To
A Friend/Temptation/Gotta Have
A Reason/All I Wanna Do Is You/
Billy/Nobody's Hero*/Livin' On A
Prayer+

* *Demo*
+ Previously unreleased, hidden track
(NB: Discs 1-3 are collections of
previously unreleased tracks, B-
sides, demos, soundtrack compositions and obscurities. The forth disc
is a DVD of interviews and archive
footage.)

BON JOVI:
LIVE ALBUMS

ONE WILD NIGHT LIVE:
1985-2001
(Island, 2001)

Track Listing:
It's My Life *(Recorded: November 27, 2000 in Toronto, Ontario, Canada)*/Livin' On A Prayer *(Recorded: August 30, 2000 in Zurich, Switzerland)* /You Give Love A Bad Name *(Recorded: August 30, 2000 in Zurich, Switzerland)*/Keep The Faith *(Recorded: September 20, 2000 in New York City, USA)*/ Someday I'll Be Saturday Night *(Recorded: November 10, 1995 in Melbourne, Australia)*/Rockin' In The Free World *(Recorded: December 1, 1995 in Johannesburg, South Africa)*/Something To Believe In *(Recorded: May 19, 1996 in Yokohama, Japan)*/ Wanted Dead Or Alive *(Recorded: September 20, 2000 in New York City, USA)*/ Runaway*(Recorded: April 28, 1985 in Tokyo, Japan)*/In And Out Of Love*(Recorded: April 28, 1985 in Tokyo, Japan)*/I Don't Like Mondays* *(Recorded: June 25, 1995 at Wembley Stadium, London, England)*/Just Older*(Recorded: November 27, 2000 in Toronto, Ontario, Canada)* /Something For The Pain*(Recorded: November 10, 1995 in Melbourne, Australia)*/Bad Medicine*(Recorded: August 30, 2000 in Zurich, Switzerland)*/One Wild Night 2001+ *(Recorded: November 27, 2000 in Toronto, Ontario, Canada)*

*With Bob Geldof
+Remix

BON JOVI:
SINGLES

'The Hardest Part Is The Night'
(1985)
'You Give Love A Bad Name'
(1986)
'Livin' On A Prayer'
(1986)
'Wanted Dead Or Alive'
(1987)
'Never Say Goodbye'
(1987)
'Bad Medicine'
(1988)
'Born To Be My Baby'
(1988)
'I'll Be There For You'
(1989)
'Lay Your Hands On Me'
(1989)

'Living In Sin'
(1989)
'Keep The Faith'
(1992)
'Bed Of Roses'
(1993)
'In These Arms'
(1993)
'I'll Sleep When I'm Dead'
(1993)
'I Believe'
(1993)
'Dry County'
(1994)
'Always'
(1994)
'Please Come Home For Christmas'
(1994)
'Someday I'll Be Saturday Night'
(1995)
'This Ain't A Love Song'
(1995)
'Something For The Pain'
(1995)
'Lie To Me'
(1995)
'These Days'
(1996)
'Hey God'
(1996)
'Real Life'
(1999)
'It's My Life'
(2000)
'Say It Isn't So'
(2000)
'Thank You For Loving Me'
(2000)
'One Wild Night'
(2001)

'Everyday'
(2002)
'Misunderstood'
(2002)
'All About Lovin' You'
(2003)
'Have A Nice Day'
(2005)
'Who Says You Can't Go Home'
(2006)
'Welcome To Wherever You Are'
(2006)
'(You Want To) Make A Memory'
(2007)
'Lost Highway'
(2007)

BON JOVI: VIDEOGRAPHY

VHS
Breakout: Video Singles
(1985)
Slippery When Wet: The Videos
(1987)
New Jersey: The Videos
(1989)
Access All Areas: A Rock & Roll Odyssey
(1990)
Keep The Faith: A Evening With Bon Jovi
(1993)
Keep The Faith: The Videos
(1993)
Cross Road
(1994)

DVD
Live From London

(1995 – VHS & DVD)
The Crush Tour
(2000 – VHS & DVD)
This Left Feels Right
(2003)
Live From Atlantic City
(2004)
Lost Highway: The Concert
(2007)

SOLO WORK

JON BON JOVI: STUDIO ALBUMS

BLAZE OF GLORY
(Vertigo, 1990)

Track Listing:
Billy Get Your Guns/Miracle/Blaze
Of Glory/Blood Money/Santa Fe/
Justice In The Barrel/Never Say
Die/You Really Got Me Now/Bang
A Drum/Dyin' Ain't Much Of A
Livin'/Guano City

DESTINATION ANYWHERE
(Polygram, 1997)

Track Listing:
Queen Of New Orleans/Janie, Don't
Take Your Love To Town/Midnight
In Chelsea/Ugly/Staring At Your
Window With A Suitcase In My
Hand/Every Word Was A Piece Of
My Heart/It's Just Me/Destination
Anywhere/Learning How To Fall/
Naked/Little City/August 7/Cold
Hard Heart*

*Demo version

THE POWER STATION YEARS: 1980-1983
(Masquerade Music, 1997)

Track Listing:
Who Said It Would Last Forever/
Open Your Heart/Stringin' A
Line/Don't Leave Me Tonight/More
Than We Bargained For/For You/
Hollywood Dreams/All Talk, No
Action/Don't Keep Me Wondering/
Head Over Heels/No One Does It
Like You/What You Want/Don't You
Believe Him/Talkin' In Your Sleep

*(NB: This was not authorised by the
Bon Jovi management)*

JON BON JOVI:
SINGLES

'Blaze Of Glory'
(1990)
'Miracle'
(1990)

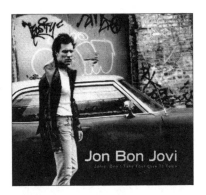

'Midnight In Chelsea'
(1997)
'Queen Of New Orleans'
(1997)
'Jamie, Don't Take Your Love To
Town'
(1997)

JON BON JOVI:
VIDEOGRAPHY

Destination Anywhere: The Film
(1997 – VHS & DVD)

RICHIE SAMBORA:
STUDIO ALBUMS - SHARK FRENZY

SHARK FRENZY - VOLUME 1: 1978

(Castle/Sanctuary, 2004)
Track Listing:
Come Saturday Night/Live Fast, Love Hard, Die Young/Law Of The

Come Down/Any Woman Like You/I Need Your Love/Crusing Liner/I Haven't Changed/Out In The Heat/Good Life/Man With A Dragon/Confessions Of A Teenage Lycanthrope

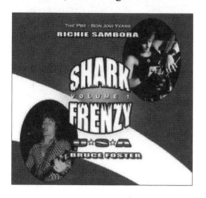

Jungle/Nobody/The Ones With Angel's Eye's/The Power/I'll Play The Fool/Laura's Birthday/Southern Belle/Don't Stop Loving Me Now

SHARK FRENZY - VOLUME 2: 1980-1981

(Cherry Red/Lemon Recordings, 2004)

Track Listing:
Goodbye To Me/Crashing Kites/ Devil On The Run/Til The Walls

RICHIE SAMBORA: STUDIO ALBUMS - SOLO

STRANGER IN THIS TOWN
(Mercury, 1991)

Track Listing:
Rest In Peace/Church Of Desire/ Stranger In This Town/Ballad Of Youth/One Light Burning/Mr. Bluesman/Rosie/River Of Love/

Father Time/The Answer/The Wind Cries Mary*

*Not available on every release

UNDISCOVERED SOUL
(Mercury, 1998)

Track Listing:

Made In America/Hard Times Come
Easy/Fallen From
Graceland/If God Was A Woman/
All That Really Matters/You're
Not Alone/In It For Love/Chained/
Harlem Rain/Who I Am/Downside
Of Love/Undiscovered Soul

RICHIE SAMBORA:
SINGLES

'Ballad Of Youth'
(1991)
'Hard Times Come Easy'
(1998)
'In It For Love'
(1998)

DAVID BRYAN:
STUDIO ALBUMS

ON A FULL MOON
(Ignition, 1995)

Track Listing:
Awakening/In These Arms/It's A
Long Road/April/Kissed By An

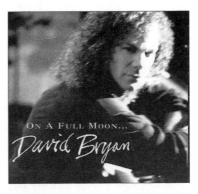

Angel/Endless Horizon/Lullaby
For Two Moons/Interlude/Midnight
Voodoo/Room Full Of Blues/Hear
Our Prayer/Summer Of Dreams/Up
The River/Netherworld Waltz

LUNAR ECLIPSE
*(Rounder/Moon Junction Music,
2000)*

Track Listing:
Second Chance/I Can Love/It's
A Long Road/On A Full Moon/
April/Kissed By An Angel/Endless
Horizon/Lullaby For Two Moons/
Interlude/Room Full Of Blues/Hear
Our Prayer/Summer Of Dreams/Up
The River/Netherworld Waltz/In
These Arms

More **BON JOVI** from Chrome Dreams

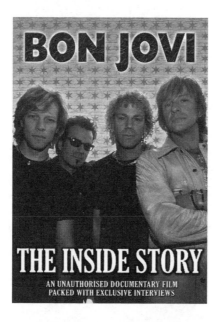

Bon Jovi - Inside Story

With more than 20 years in the music business and numerous best-selling albums under their collective belt, Bon Jovi are undoubtedly the kings of stadium rock. Despite the trappings of the Rock n' Roll lifestyle, these New Jersey boys continue to provide their own unique, anthemic brand of American rock metal. On 'Bon Jovi: The Inside Story' we go behind the music to discover what it took for one working class boy with a passion for music to put together a band that would change the face of modern Rock. Packed with interviews, this documentary film takes you where the cameras never previously pried to achieve a no holds barred look at this seminal band.

More **BON JOVI** from Chrome Dreams

Maximum Bon Jovi

Maximum Bon Jovi is a spoken word audio-biography CD that tells the full story of this incredible group. The biography benefits from freshly re-searched information throughout, and includes exclusive interviews with the artists themselves, to give the listener a stunning level of insight into the subject. The package is completed with the collector in mind, boasting deluxe full-colour slipcase, fold-out poster and an 8-page booklet featuring rarely seen photographs.

Bon Jovi X-Posed

Maximum Bon Jovi is a spoken word audio-biography CD that tells the full story of this incredible group. The biography benefits from freshly re-searched information throughout, and includes exclusive interviews with the artists themselves, to give the listener a stunning level of insight into the subject. The package is completed with the collector in mind, boasting deluxe full-colour slipcase, fold-out poster and an 8-page booklet featuring rarely seen photographs.

More **BON JOVI** from Chrome Dreams

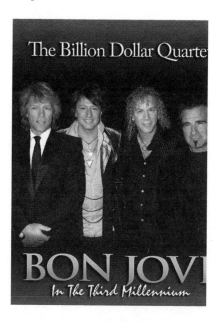

The Billion Dollar Quartet: Bon Jovi In The Third Millenium

This film concentrates on the band's startling rejuvenation during the past decade – their contribution to the music of the third millennium. It was during this time the band released records as powerful and diverse as Crush, Bounce, Have A Nice Day and Lost Highway. All of the above and much more are covered in this programme which in completion provides a fascinating document of their work across this incredible period.
This DVD features:
• Live and studio recordings of the band's finest tracks from this period
• Rare footage, archive interviews with the groupand seldom seen photographs
• Exclusive contributions from; Jovi producers Brian Scheuble and Ryan Freeland; JBJ's close friend, journalist Lonn French; the man who put them on the radio, DJ Jeff Duran; legendary rock journalist and author of the band's official biography, Malcolm Dome, and many other friends, colleagues and experts.
• Location shoots, newsclips, bonus material and lots more besides
• Features Jovi classics such as; It's My Life, One Wild Night, Misunderstood, All About Lovin' You, Have A Nice Day, Who Says You Can't Go Home, Lost Highway, Seat Next To You and many, many more.

THANK YOU AND GOOD NIGHT!